Morning
by
Morning

meditations for daily living

C. H. SPURGEON

MORNING BY MORNING

ISBN: 0-88368-156-0
Printed in the United States of America
Copyright © 1984 by Whitaker House

Whitaker House
580 Pittsburgh Street
Springdale, PA 15144

7 8 9 10 11 12 13 14 15 16 / 99 98 97 96 95

January 1

"They did eat of the fruit of the land of Canaan that year" (Joshua 5:11).

Israel's weary wanderings were all over, and the promised rest was attained. No more moving tents, fiery serpents, fierce Amalekites, and howling wilderness. They came to the land which flowed with milk and honey, and they ate the old corn of the land. Perhaps this year, beloved Christian reader, this may be your case or mine. Rest assured that we have already experienced more ills than death at its worst can cause us. Let us banish every fearful thought and rejoice with exceeding great joy in the prospect that this year we will begin to be forever with the Lord. A part of the host will tarry on earth to do service for their Lord. If this is our lot, the New Year's text is still true. "We who have believed do enter into rest" (Hebrews 4:3). The Holy Spirit is the foretaste of our inheritance. Those who are in heaven are secure, and so are we preserved in Christ Jesus; there they triumph over their enemies, and we have victories too. Celestial spirits enjoy communion with their Lord, and this is not denied to us either; they rest in His love, and we have perfect peace in Him; they sing His praise, and it is our privilege to bless Him too. We will this year gather celestial fruits on earthly ground, where faith and hope have made the desert like the garden of the Lord. Man ate angel's food of old, and why not now? Oh for grace to feed on Jesus and to eat of the fruit of the land of Canaan this year.

January 2

"Continue in prayer" (Colossians 4:2).

It is interesting to notice how large a portion of the Word is occupied with the subject of prayer. We scarcely open the Bible before we read, "Then began men to call upon the name of the Lord" (Genesis 4:26); and just as we are about to close the volume, the "Amen" of an earnest supplication meets our ear. Instances are plentiful. Here we find a wrestling Jacob—there a Daniel who prayed three times a day—and a David who with all his heart called on his God. On the mountain we see Elias; in the dungeon Paul and Silas. We have multitudes of commands and myriads of promises. What does this teach us, but the sacred importance and necessity of prayer? We may be certain that whatever God has made prominent in His Word, He intended to be conspicuous in our lives. If He has said much about prayer, it is because He knows we have much need of it. So deep are our necessities that until we are in heaven we must not cease to pray. A prayerless soul is a Christless soul. If you are a child of God, you will seek your Father's face and live in your Father's love. Pray that this year you may be holy, humble, zealous, and patient. Pray for a closer communion with Christ. Enter into His banqueting-house of love more often. Pray that you may be an example and a blessing to others and that you may live more to the glory of your Master.

January 3

"I will give thee for a covenant of the people" (Isaiah 49:8).

Jesus Christ is Himself the sum and substance of the covenant. As one of its gifts, He is the property of every believer. Believer, can you estimate what you have received in Christ? "In him dwelleth all the fulness of the Godhead bodily" (Colossians 2:9). Consider that word "God" and its infinity, and then meditate upon "perfect man" and all his beauty; for all that Christ, as God and man, ever had is yours. Our blessed Jesus, as God, is omniscient, omnipresent, omnipotent. Has He power? That power is yours to support and strengthen you, to overcome your enemies, and to preserve you even to the end. Has He love? There is not a drop of love in His heart which is not yours. Has He justice? It may seem a stern attribute, but even that is yours; for He will, by His justice, see to it that all which is promised to you in the covenant of grace will be secured to you. And all that He has as perfect man is yours. As a perfect man the Father's delight was upon Him. He stood accepted by the Most High. O believer, God's acceptance of Christ is your acceptance. Do you know that the love which the Father set on a perfect Christ, He sets on you *now?* That perfect righteousness which Jesus carefully formed through His stainless life is yours and is imputed to you. Christ is in the covenant.

"Grow in grace, and in the knowledge of our Lord and Saviour Jesus Christ" (2 Peter 3:18).

Grow in grace. Grow in that root-grace, *faith*. Believe the promises more firmly than you have done. Let faith increase in fullness, constancy, and simplicity. Grow also in *love*. Ask that your love become extended, more intense, more practical, influencing every thought, word, and deed. Grow likewise in *humility*. As you grow in humility, seek also to grow nearer to God in prayer and experience more intimate fellowship with Jesus. May God the Holy Spirit enable you to *"grow in the knowledge of our Lord and Saviour."* He who does not grow in the knowledge of Jesus, refuses to be blessed. To know Him is "life eternal," and to advance in the knowledge of Him is to increase in happiness. Absence from Christ is hell; but the presence of Jesus is heaven. Seek to know more of Him in His divine nature, in His human relationship, in His finished work, in His death, in His resurrection, in His present glorious intercession, and in His future royal advent. An increase of love for Jesus and a more perfect understanding of His love for us is one of the best tests of growth in grace.

January 5

"And God saw the light, that it was good: and God divided the light from the darkness" (Genesis 1:4).

Light might well be good, since it sprang from that command of goodness, "Let there be light." *Physical* light is said by Solomon to be sweet, but *gospel* light is infinitely more precious because it reveals eternal things. It also ministers to our immortal natures. When the Holy Spirit gives us *spiritual* light and opens our eyes to behold the glory of God in the face of Jesus Christ, we behold sin in its true colors and ourselves in our real position. We see the Most Holy God as He reveals Himself, the plan of mercy as He proposed it, and the world to come as the Word describes it. Spiritual light has many beams and prismatic colors. Whether they are knowledge, joy, holiness, or life, they are all divinely good. O Lord, give us more of Yourself, the true light. No sooner is there a good thing in the world, than a division is necessary. Light and darkness have no communion. God has divided them; let us not change them. Sons of light must not have fellowship with deeds, doctrines, or deceits of darkness. The children of the day must be sober, honest, and bold in their Lord's work, leaving the works of darkness to those who will dwell in it forever. Our churches should, by discipline, divide the light from the darkness. We, by our distinct separation from the world, should do the same. O Lord Jesus, be our light throughout this day, for Your light is the light of men.

January 6

"Casting all your cares upon him; for he careth for you" (1 Peter 5:7).

It is a happy way of soothing sorrow when we can feel—"He careth for *me*." Christian, do not dishonor your Savior by always wearing a brow of care. Cast your burden upon your Lord. You are staggering beneath a weight which your Father would not feel. What seems to you a crushing burden would be to Him as the small dust of the balance. Oh, child of suffering, be patient. God has not passed you over in His providence. He who is the feeder of sparrows will also furnish you with what you need. Take up the arms of faith against a sea of trouble. There is One who cares for you. His eye is fixed on you, His heart beats with pity for your woe, and His omnipotent hand will bring you the needed help. The darkest cloud will scatter itself in showers of mercy. The blackest gloom will give place to the morning. He, if you are one of His family, will bind up your wounds and heal your broken heart. Do not doubt His grace because of your tribulation, but believe that He loves you as much in seasons of trouble as in times of happiness. What a serene and quiet life you might lead if you would leave providing to the God of Providence! With a little oil in the cruse and a handful of meal in the barrel, Elijah outlived the famine, and you will do the same. If God cares for you, why must you care too? Can you trust Him for your soul, and not for your body? He has never refused to bear your burdens, He has never fainted under their weight. Precious child, leave all your concerns in the hand of a gracious God.

January 7

"For me to live is Christ, and to die is gain" (Philippians 1:21).

The believer did not always live for Christ. He only began to after the Holy Spirit convinced him of sin and when, by grace, he was brought to see the dying Savior making a propitiation for his guilt. From the moment of the new and celestial birth, the man began to live for Christ. Jesus is to believers the one pearl of great price for whom we are willing to part with all that we have. He has subsequently won our heart, and it beats alone for Him. To His glory, we would live. In defense of His gospel, we would die. He is the pattern of our life and the model after which we would sculpture our character. Paul's words mean more than most men think. They imply that the aim and end of his life was Christ. In the words of an ancient saint, he did eat, drink, and sleep eternal life. Jesus was his very breath, the soul of his soul, the heart of his heart, the life of his life. Can you say, as a professing Christian, that you live up to this idea? Can you honestly say that for you to live is Christ? Are you, in your business, living for Christ? If a Christian professes to live for Christ, how can he live for another object without committing spiritual adultery? Who would dare say that he has lived wholly for Christ as the apostle did? Yet, this alone is the true life of a Christian. Lord, accept me; I present myself, praying to live only in You and for You.

"The iniquity of the holy things" (Exodus 28:38).

What a veil is lifted up by these words, and what a disclosure is made! It will be humbling and profitable for us to pause a while and see this sad sight. The iniquities of our public worship, its formality, lukewarmness, and wandering of heart! Our work for the Lord, its selfishness, carelessness, and slackness! Our private devotions, their laxity, coldness, neglect, sleepiness, and vanity! Dr. Payson, writing to his brother, says, "My parish, as well as my heart, resembles the garden of the sluggard; and what is worse, I find that many of my desires for the improvement of both, proceed either from pride, vanity, or laziness. I look at the weeds which overrun my garden and breathe out an earnest wish that they were uprooted. But why? What prompts the wish? It may be that I may walk out and say to myself, 'In what fine order my garden is kept!' This is *pride*. Or it may be that my neigbors may look over the wall and say, 'My, how your garden flourishes!' This is *vanity*. Or I may wish for the destruction of the weeds, because I am weary of pulling them up. This is *indolence*." Even our desire after holiness may be polluted by ill motives. How cheering is the thought that, when the High Priest bore the iniquity of the holy things, he wore upon his brow the words, "Holiness to the Lord." Even while Jesus bears our sin, He presents before His Father's face not our unholiness, but His own holiness.

January 9

"I will be their God" (Jeremiah 31:33).

Christian, here is all you can require. If you can pour this promise into your cup, you can say, "My cup runneth over; I have more than anyone's heart can wish." When this is fulfilled, "I am thy God," are you not a possessor of all things? Desire is insatiable as death, but He who fills all in all can fill it. Who can measure the capacity of our wishes? But the immeasurable wealth of God can more than overflow it. But you want more than quiet satisfaction; you desire rapturous delight. Here is music fit for heaven in this your portion, for God is the maker of heaven. Not all the music blown from sweet instruments or drawn from living strings can yield such melody as this sweet promise, "I will be their God" (Genesis 17:8). Here is a deep sea of bliss, a shoreless ocean of delight. Bathe your spirit in it. Swim forever and you will find no shore. Dive throughout eternity and you will find no bottom. If this does not make your eyes sparkle and your heart beat high with bliss, then your soul is not in a healthy state. This is the masterpiece of all the promises. Its enjoyment makes a heaven below and will make a heaven above. Dwell in the light of your Lord, and let your soul be saturated with His love. Get out the marrow and fatness which this portion yields you. Live up to your privileges and rejoice with unspeakable joy.

January 10

"There is laid up for me a crown of righteousness" (2 Timothy 4:8).

Doubting one, you have often said, "I fear I will never enter heaven." Fear not! all the people of God will enter there. I love the quaint saying of a dying man who exclaimed, "I have no fear of going home; I have sent all before; God's finger is on the latch of my door, and I am ready for Him to enter." "But," said one, "are you not afraid lest you miss your inheritance?" "No," said he, "There is one crown in heaven which the angel Gabriel could not wear. It will fit no head but mine. There is one throne in heaven which Paul the apostle could not fill. It was made for me, and I will have it." Oh Christian, what a joyous thought! *Your* portion is secure. "But can I forfeit it?" No, it is assigned. If I am a child of God, I will not lose it. It is mine as securely as if I were there. Come with me, believer, and let us sit on the top of Nebo and view the goodly land, even Canaan. See that little river of death glistening in the sunlight, and across it do you see the pinnacles of the eternal city? Do you mark the pleasant country and all its joyous inhabitants? Know then that if you could fly across you would see written on one of its many mansions, "This remaineth for such a one, preserved for him only. He will be caught up to dwell forever with God." Poor doubting one, see the fair inheritance. It is *yours.* If you believe in the Lord Jesus, if you have repented of sin, if you have been renewed in heart, you are one of the Lord's people. There is a place reserved for you, a crown laid up for you. There will be no vacant thrones in glory when all the chosen are gathered in.

January 11

"These have no root" (Luke 8:13).

My soul, examine yourself this morning by the light of this text. You have received the Word with joy. Your feelings have been stirred, and a lively impression has been made. Remember that to receive the Word in the ear is one thing, but to receive Jesus into your soul is quite another. In the parable, the seed in one case fell on ground having a rocky bottom covered over with a thin layer of earth. When the seed began to take root, its downward growth was hindered by the hard stone. Therefore, it used its strength in pushing its green shoot up as high as it could. But having no inward moisture derived from root nourishment, it withered away. Is this my case? Have I been making a fair show in the flesh without having a corresponding inner life? Good growth takes place upward and downward at the same time. Am I rooted in sincere allegiance and love to Jesus? If my heart remains unsoftened and unfertilized by grace, the good seed may germinate for a season; but it must ultimately whither, for it cannot flourish on a rocky, unbroken, unsanctified heart. Let me dread a godliness as rapid in growth and as lacking in endurance as Jonah's gourd. Let me count the cost of being a follower of Jesus. Let me feel the energy of His Holy Spirit, and then I will possess an abiding and enduring seed in my soul.

January 12

"Ye are Christ's; and Christ is God's" (1 Corinthians 3:23).

Ye are Christ's. You are His by donation, for the Father gave you to the Son. You were purchased by His blood for He counted the price for your redemption. You are His by dedication, for you have consecrated yourself to Him; His by relation, for you are named by His name, and made one of His brethren and joint-heirs. When tempted to sin, reply, "I cannot do this great wickedness, for I am Christ's." When wealth is before you to be won by sin, say that you are Christ's, and do not touch it. Are you exposed to difficulties and dangers? Stand fast in the evil day, remembering that you are Christ's. Are you placed where others are sitting down idly, doing nothing? Rise to the works with all your powers. When the sweat stands upon your brow, and you are tempted to loiter, cry, "No, I cannot stop, for I am Christ's." When the cause of God invites you, give yourself to it. When the poor need you, give yourself and your goods away, for you are Christ's. Always be one of those whose manners are Christian, whose speech is like the Nazarene, whose conduct and conversation is so suggestive of heaven that all who see you will know that you are the Savior's. Let your argument for holiness be, "I am Christ's."

January 13

"Jehoshaphat made ships of Tharshish to go to Ophir for gold but they went not; for the ships were broken at Ezion-geber" (1 Kings 22:48).

Solomon's ships had returned in safety, but Jehoshaphat's vessels never reached the land of gold. Providence prospers one and frustrates the desires of another in the same business and at the same time. Yet, the great ruler is as good and wise at one time as another. May we have grace today, in the remembrance of this text, to bless the Lord for ships broken at Ezion-geber, as well as for vessels loaded with earthly blessings. Let us not envy the more successful or murmur at our losses as though we were singularly and specially tried. The secret cause of Jehoshaphat's loss is worthy of notice, for it is the root of much of the suffering of the Lord's people. It was his alliance with a sinful family, his fellowship with sinners that caused the disaster. In 2 Chronicles 20:37, we are told that the Lord sent a prophet to declare, "Because thou hast joined thyself with Ahaziah, the Lord hath broken thy works." This was a fatherly chastisement, which appears to have been blessed to him. Let Jehoshaphat's experience be a warning to the rest of the Lord's people to avoid being unequally yoked together with unbelievers! Oh, for such love for Jesus that, like Him, we may be holy, harmless, undefiled, and separate from sinners.

"Mighty to save" (Isaiah 63:1).

By the words "to save," we understand the whole of the great work of salvation, from the first holy desire onward to complete sanctification. Christ is not only "mighty to save" those who repent, but He is able to make men repent. He will carry those to heaven who believe; but He is, moreover, mighty to give men new hearts and to work faith in them. He is mighty to make the man who hates holiness love it and to constrain the despiser of His name to bend the knee before Him. The life of a believer is a series of miracles formed by the Mighty God. The bush burns, but it is not consumed. He is mighty enough to keep His people holy after He has made them so and to preserve them in His fear and love until He consummates their spiritual existence in heaven. Christ's power does not lie in making a believer and then leaving him to shift for himself. He who begins the good work carries it on. Believer, here is encouragement. Are you praying for some beloved one? Don't stop praying, for Christ is "mighty to save." You are powerless to reclaim the rebel, but your Lord is all powerful. Lay hold on that mighty arm, and rouse it to put forth its strength. Does your own case trouble you? Fear not, for His strength is sufficient for you. Whether to begin with others or to carry on the work in you, Jesus is "mighty to save;" the best proof of which lies in the fact that He saved you.

"Do as thou hast said" (2 Samuel 7:25).

God's promises were never meant to be thrown aside as waste paper. He intended that they should be used. He loves to see His children bring them up to Him and say, "Lord, do as thou hast said." We glorify God when we plead His promises. Do you think that God will be any poorer for giving you the riches He has promised? He has said, "Come, now, and let us reason together, saith the Lord: though your sins be as scarlet, they shall be as white as snow; though they be red like crimson, they shall be as wool" (Isaiah 1:18). Faith goes straight to the throne and pleads, "Lord, here is the promise. Do as thou hast said." Our Lord replies, "Be it unto thee even as thou wilt." Our heavenly banker delights to cash His own notes. Never let the promise rust. Do not think that God will be troubled by your persistence in reminding Him of His promises. It is His delight to grant favors. He is more ready to hear than you are to ask. The sun is not weary of shining, nor the fountain of flowing. It is God's nature to keep His promises; therefore, go at once to the throne with "Do as thou hast said."

January 16

"I will help thee, sayeth the Lord" (Isaiah 41:14).

This morning let us hear the Lord Jesus speak to each one of us. "It is but a small thing for Me, your God, to help you. Consider what I have done already. What! not help you? Why, I bought you with My blood. I have died for you; and if I have done the greater, will I not do the less? It is the least thing I will ever do for you. I have done more and will do more. Before the world began I chose you. I made the covenant for you. I laid aside My glory and became a man for you. I gave My life for you. If I did all this, I will surely help you now. In helping you, I am giving you what I have bought for you already. If you had need of a thousand times as much help, I would give it to you. You require little compared with what I am ready to give. It is much for you to need, but it is nothing for Me to bestow. Help you? Fear not! If there were an ant at the door of your granary asking for help, it would not ruin you to give him a handful of your wheat. You are nothing but a tiny insect at the door of My all-sufficiency. I will help you." Oh, my soul, is this not enough? Do you need more strength than the omnipotence of the united Trinity? Do you want more wisdom than exists in the Father, more love than displays itself in the Son, or more power than is manifest in the influences of the Spirit? Behold, this river of God is full for your supply. What can you desire beside?

"And I looked, and, lo, a Lamb stood on the Mount Zion" (Revelation 14:1).

The apostle John was privileged to look within the gates of heaven. In describing what he saw, he begins by saying, "I looked, and lo, a Lamb!" This teaches us that the chief object of contemplation in the heavenly state is "the Lamb of God, which takes away the sins of the world." Nothing else attracted the apostle's attention so much as the person of that divine being, who has redeemed us by His blood. He is the theme of the songs of all glorified spirits and holy angels. In a little while, when tears have been wiped from your eyes, you will see *the same Lamb exalted on His throne*. It is the joy of your heart to hold daily fellowship with Jesus. You will have the same joy to a higher degree in heaven. You will enjoy the constant vision of His presence. You will dwell with Him forever. "I looked, and, lo, a Lamb!" Why, that Lamb is heaven itself. As good Rutherford says, "Heaven and Christ are the same thing." To be with Christ is to be in heaven, and to be in heaven is to be with Christ. That prisoner of the Lord very sweetly writes in one of his glowing letters—"O my Lord Christ, if I could be in heaven without You, it would be a hell; and if I could be in hell, and have You still, it would be a heaven to me, for You are all the heaven I want." It is true, Christian. All you need to make you blessed is "to be with Christ."

"There remaineth therefore a rest to the people of God" (Hebrews 4:9).

How different the state of the believer will be in heaven from what it is here! Here he is born to toil and suffer weariness. In the land of the immortal, fatigue is never known. Anxious to serve his Master, he finds his strength unequal to his zeal. If he is completely active, he will have much labor; not too much for his will, but more than enough for his power, so that he will cry out, "I am not wearied of the labor, but I am wearied in it." Christian, the hot day of weariness will not last forever. The sun is nearing the horizon. It will rise again with a brighter day than you have ever seen, on a land where they serve God day and night, and yet rest from their labors. *Here,* rest is but partial; *there,* it is perfect. Toil-worn laborer, only think when you will rest forever! Can you conceive it? It is a rest *eternal.* There, everything is immortal. The harp abides unrusted, the crown unwithered, the eye undimmed, the voice unfaltering, the heart unwavering, and the immortal being is wholly absorbed in infinite delight. It will be a happy day when mortality will be swallowed up!

"I sought him, but I found him not" (Song of Solomon 3:1).

Tell me where you lost the company of Christ, and I will tell you the most likely place to find Him. Have you lost Christ in the closet by restraining prayer? Then it is there you must seek and find Him. Did you lose Christ by sin? You will find Christ in no other way but by the giving up of the sin and seeking by the Holy Spirit to mortify the member in which the lust dwells. Did you lose Christ by neglecting the Scriptures? You must find Christ in the Scriptures. The saying is true, "Look for a thing where you dropped it; it is there." Look for Christ where you lost Him. He has not gone away. It is hard work to go back for Christ. Bunyan tells us that the pilgrim found the piece of the road back to the Arbor of Ease, where he lost his roll, the hardest he had ever traveled. Twenty miles onward is easier than to go one mile back for the lost evidence. Take care, when you find your Master, to cling close to Him. But how is it you have lost Him? One would have thought you would never have parted with such a precious Friend, whose presence is sweet, whose words are comforting. How is it that you did not watch Him every moment for fear of losing sight of Him? Yet, since you have let Him go, what a mercy that you are seeking Him. Go on seeking, for it is dangerous to be without your Lord.

"Abel was a keeper of sheep" (Genesis 4:2).

As a shepherd, Abel sanctified his work to the glory of God and offered a sacrifice of blood on his altar. The Lord had respect unto Abel and his offering. This early type of our Lord is exceedingly clear and distinct. Like the first streak of light which tinges the east at sunrise, it does not reveal everything, but it clearly manifests the great fact that the sun is coming. As we see Abel, a shepherd and yet a priest, offering a sacrifice of sweet smell unto God, we recognize our Lord, who brings before His Father a sacrifice which Jehovah respects. Abel was hated by his brother—hated without a cause; and the Savior experienced the same hatred. The natural and carnal man hated the accepted man in whom the Spirit of grace was found and rested not until his blood had been shed. Abel fell and sprinkled his altar and sacrifice with his own blood. Likewise, the Lord Jesus was slain by the enmity of man while serving as a priest before the Lord. The good Shepherd layeth down His life for the sheep. Abel's blood spoke. The Lord said unto Cain, "The voice of thy brother's blood crieth unto me from the ground" (Genesis 4:10). The blood of Jesus has a mighty tongue, and its prevailing cry is not vengeance, but mercy. Abel is the first shepherd in order of time, but our hearts will always place Jesus first in order of excellence. Great keeper of the sheep, we the people of Your pasture bless You with our whole hearts when we see You slain for us.

"And so all Israel shall be saved" (Romans 11:26).

When Moses sang at the Red Sea, it was his joy to know that all Israel was safe. Part of that song was, "Thou in thy mercy hast led forth the people which thou hast redeemed" (Exodus 15:13). In the last time, when the elect will sing the song of Moses, the servant of God, and of the Lamb, it will be the boast of Jesus, "Of all whom thou hast given me, I have lost none" (John 18:9). In heaven there will not be a vacant throne. As many as God has chosen, as many as Christ has redeemed, as many as the Spirit has called, as many as believe in Jesus, will safely cross the dividing sea. The front line of the army has already reached the shore. We are marching through the depths; we are at this day following hard after our Leader into the heart of the sea. Let us be of good cheer. The rearguard will soon be where the vanguard already is. The last of the chosen ones will soon have crossed the sea, and then will be heard the song of triumph, when all are secure. But oh, if one were absent. If one of His chosen family should be cast away, it would make an everlasting discord in the song of the redeemed.

"Son of man, What is the vine tree more than any tree, or than a branch which is among the trees of the forest?" (Ezekiel 15:2).

These words are for the humbling of God's people. They are called God's vine. They, by God's goodness, have become fruitful, having been planted in a good soil. The Lord has trained them on the walls of the sanctuary, and they bring forth fruit to His glory. But what are they without their God? What are they without the continual influence of the Spirit? Oh, believer, learn to reject pride, seeing that you have no ground for it. Whatever you are, you have nothing to make you proud. The more you have, the more you are in debt to God. Consider your origin! Look back to what you were. Consider what you would have been but for divine grace. Look upon yourself as you are now. Does your conscience reproach you? And if He has made you anything, are you not taught that it is grace which has made you to differ? You would have been a great sinner if God had not changed you. Therefore, do not be proud, though you have a large estate—a wide domain of grace; once you did not have a single thing to call your own except your sin and misery.

"I have exalted one chosen out of the people" (Psalm 89:19).

Why was Christ chosen out of the people? Was it not that He might be able to be our brother in the blest tie of kindred blood? Oh, what relationship there is between Christ and the believer! The believer can say, "I have a brother in heaven. I may be poor, but I have a brother who is rich and is a King. Will He allow me to be in need while He is on His throne? Oh, no! He loves me; He is my brother." Believer, cherish this blessed thought. He is a brother, born for adversity; treat Him as such. Christ was also chosen out of the people that He might know our wants and sympathize with us. "He was tempted in all points like as we are, yet without sin" (Hebrews 4:15). In all our sorrows, we have His sympathy. Temptation, pain, disappointment, weakness, weariness, poverty—He knows them all, for He has felt all. Remember this, Christian, and let it comfort you. However difficult and painful your road, it is marked by the footsteps of your Savior. Even when you reach the dark valley of the shadow of death and the deep waters of the swelling Jordan, you will find His footprints there. Take courage! Royal feet have left a blood-red track on the road and consecrated the thorny path forever.

"Surely he shall deliver thee from the snare of the fowler" (Psalm 91:3).

God delivers His people from the snare of the fowler in two senses: from and out of. First, He delivers them *from* the snare—does not let them enter it. Secondly, if they are caught, He delivers them *out of* it. "He shall deliver thee from the snare" (Psalm 91:3). How? Trouble is often the means whereby God delivers us. God knows that our backsliding will soon end in our destruction, and He, in mercy, sends the rod. At other times, God keeps His people from the snare of the fowler by giving them great spiritual strength, so that when they are tempted to do evil, they say, "How can I do this great wickedness, and sin against God?" But what a blessed thing it is that if the believer does, in an evil hour, come into the net, yet God will bring him out of it! Oh, backslider, be cast down, but do not depair. Hear what your Redeemer says—"Return, backsliding children; I will have mercy upon you" (Jeremiah 3:22). But you say you cannot return, for you are a captive. You will yet be brought out of all the evil into which you have fallen. Repent of your ways. He that has loved you will not cast you away. He will receive you and give you joy and gladness.

"I will mention the lovingkindnesses of the Lord, and the praises of the Lord, according to all that the Lord hath bestowed on us" (Isaiah 63:7).

Can you do this? Are there mercies which you have experienced? There must surely be some precious milestone along the road of life not quite grown over with moss, on which you can read a happy memorial of His mercy toward you. Have you ever been sick and did He not restore you? Were you ever poor before, and did He not supply your needs? Were you never in trouble before, and did He not deliver you? Do not forget what your God has done for you. Turn over the book of your remembrance and consider the days of old. Have you ever been helped in time of need? I know you have. Go back to the choice mercies of yesterday. Although today's circumstances look dark, light up the lamps of the past. They will glitter through the darkness, and you will trust in the Lord until day breaks and the shadows flee away. "Remember, O Lord, your tender mercies and your lovingkindness, for they have been ever of old."

January 26

"Your heavenly Father" (Matthew 6:26).

God's people are doubly His children. They are His offspring by creation, and they are His sons by adoption in Christ. Hence they are privileged to call Him, "Our Father which art in heaven" (Matthew 6:9). Father! Oh, what a precious word! Here is *authority*. "If I be a Father, where is mine honor?" If you are sons, where is your obedience? Here is *affection* mingled with authority; an authority which does not provoke rebellion; an obedience demanded which is most cheerfully rendered. The obedience which God's children yield to Him must be *loving* obedience. Do not go about the service of God as slaves to their taskmaster's toil, but run in the way of His commands because it is your Father's way. Yield your bodies as instruments of righteousness, because righteousness is your Father's will. His will should be the will of His child. Father! Here is honor and love. How great is a father's love for his children! That which friendship cannot do and mere benevolence will not attempt, a father's heart and hand must do for his sons. They are his offspring, he must bless them. They are his children, he must show himself strong in their defense. If an earthly father watches over his children with unceasing love and care, how much more does our heavenly Father! Abba, Father! He who can say this has uttered better music than cherubim or seraphim can reach. There is heaven in the depth of that word—Father!

January 27

"And of his fulness have all we received" (John 1:16).

These words tell us that there is a fullness in Christ. There is a fullness of essential Deity, for in Him dwelleth all the fullness of the Godhead. There is a fullness of perfect manhood, for in Him, bodily, that Godhead was revealed. There is a fullness of atoning efficacy in His blood for "the blood of Jesus Christ, his Son, cleanseth us from all sin" (1 John 1:7). There is a fullness of justifying righteousness in His life for "there is therefore now no condemnation to them that are in Christ Jesus" (Romans 8:1). "He is able to save to the uttermost them that come unto God by him; seeing He ever liveth to make intercession for them" (Hebrews 7:25). There is a fullness of victory in His death, for through death He destroyed him that had the power of death, that is, the devil. There is a fullness of efficacy in His resurrection from the dead, for by it, "we are begotten again unto a lively hope" (1 Peter 1:3). There is a fullness of triumph in His ascension for "when he ascended up on high, he led captivity captive, and gave gifts unto men" (Ephesians 4:8). There is a fullness of grace to pardon, of grace to regenerate, of grace to sanctify, of grace to preserve, and of grace to perfect. There is a fullness at all times, a fullness of comfort in affliction, and a fullness of guidance in prosperity. A fullness of every divine attribute, of wisdom, of power, of love; a fullness which is impossible to survey, much less to explore. Come, believer, and get all your need supplied.

"Perfect in Christ Jesus" (Colossians 1:28).

Do you feel in your own soul that perfection is not in you? Every tear which trickles from your eye weeps imperfection; every sigh which bursts from your heart cries imperfection; every harsh word which proceeds from your lip mutters imperfection. You have too frequently had a view of your own heart to dream for a moment of any perfection in yourself. But amid this sad consciousness of imperfection, here is comfort for you—you are "perfect *in Christ Jesus.*" In God's sight, you are "complete in Him." Even now, you are "accepted in the beloved." But there is a second perfection, yet to be realized, which is promised to all the seed. Is it not delightful to look forward to the time when every stain of sin will be removed from the believer, and he shall be presented faultless before the throne, without spot, or wrinkle, or any such thing? The Church then will be so pure, that not even the eye of omniscience will see a spot or blemish in her. Then we will know and feel the happiness of this vast but short sentence, "Complete in Christ." Not until then will we fully comprehend the heights and depths of the salvation of Jesus. Christ takes a black and deformed thing and makes it clean and matchless in His glory, peerless in His beauty, and fit to be the companion of angels. Oh my soul, stand and admire this blessed truth of perfection in Christ.

January 29

"The things which are not seen" (2 Corinthians 4:18).

In our Christian pilgrimage, it is well, for the most part, to be looking forward. Forward lies the crown, and onward is the goal. Whether it is for hope, for joy, for consolation, or for inspiring of our love, the future must, after all, be the grand object of the eye of faith. Looking into the future, we see sin cast out, the body of sin and death destroyed, the soul made perfect and fit to be a partaker of the inheritance of the saints in light. Looking further yet, the believer's enlightened eye can see death's river passed, the gloomy stream forded, and the hills of light attained. He sees himself enter within the pearly gates, hailed as more than conqueror, crowned by the hand of Christ, embraced in the arms of Jesus, glorified with Him. He is made to sit together with Jesus on His throne, even as He has overcome and has sat down with the Father on His throne. The thought of this future may well relieve the darkness of the past and the gloom of the present. The joys of heaven will surely compensate for the sorrows of earth. This world is but a narrow span, and you will soon have passed it. Time, how short—eternity, how long! Death, how brief—immortality, how endless!

January 30

"When thou hearest the sound of a going in the tops of the mulberry trees, then thou shalt bestir thyself" (2 Samuel 5:24).

The members of Christ's Church should be very prayerful, always seeking the anointing of the Holy One to rest upon their hearts, that the Kingdom of Christ may come, and that His "will be done on earth, even as it is in heaven" (Matthew 6:10). There are times when God seems especially to favor Zion. Such seasons ought to be to them like "the sound of a going in the tops of mulberry trees." We should be doubly prayerful, doubly earnest, wrestling more at the throne than has been our habit. Oh, for Pentecostal outpourings and Pentecostal labors! Christian, in yourself there are times "when thou hearest the sound of a going in the tops of the mulberry trees." You have a peculiar power in prayer. The Spirit of God gives you joy and gladness. The Scripture is open to you. The promises are applied. You walk in the light of God's face. You have a peculiar freedom and liberty in devotion and a closer communion with Christ. Now, at such joyous periods, is the time to rouse yourself. Now is the time to get rid of any evil habit, while God the Spirit helps your infirmities.

"The Lord our righteousness" (Jeremiah 23:6).

It will always give a Christian the greatest calm, quiet, ease, and peace, to think of the perfect righteousness of Christ. There are some who are always talking about corruption and the innate evil of the soul. This is quite true, but why not go a little further and remember that we are "perfect in Christ Jesus?" Surely, if we call to mind that Christ is made unto us righteousness, we will be of good cheer. Even though distresses afflict me, Satan assaults me, and there may be many things to be experienced before I get to heaven, those are done for me in the covenant of divine grace. There is nothing wanting in my Lord. Christ has done it all. On the cross, He said, "It is finished" (John 19:30). If it is finished, then I am complete in Him. I can rejoice with unspeakable joy and full of glory, "not having mine own righteousness, which is of the law, but that which is through the faith of Christ, the righteousness which is of God by faith" (Philippians 3:9). When the believer says, "I live on Christ alone; I rest on Him completely for salvation; and I believe that, however unworthy, I am still saved in Jesus," then there rises up as a motive of gratitude this thought—"Will I not live for Christ? Will I not love Him and serve Him, seeing that I am saved by *His* merits?" "The love of Christ constraineth us" (2 Corinthians 5:14).

"They shall sing in the ways of the Lord" (Psalm 138:5).

The time when Christians begin to sing in the ways of the Lord is when they first lose their burden at the foot of the cross. Not even the songs of the angels seem so sweet as the first song of rapture which gushes from the soul of the forgiven child of God. Believer, do you remember the day when your chains fell off? Do you remember the place where Jesus met you and said, "I have loved thee with an everlasting love; I have blotted out as a cloud thy transgressions, and as a thick cloud thy sins; they shall not be mentioned against thee any more forever" (Jeremiah 31:3). How wonderful it is when Jesus takes away the pain of sin! It is not only at the beginning of the Christian life that believers have reason for song. As long as they live, they discover cause to sing in the ways of the Lord. Their experience of His constant lovingkindness leads them to say, "I will bless the Lord at all times: His praise shall continually be in my mouth" (Psalm 34:1).

February 2

"Without shedding of blood is no remission" (Hebrews 9:22).

In none of the Jewish ceremonies were sins, even typically, removed without blood-shedding. By no means can sin be pardoned without atonement. It is clear that there is no hope for me out of Christ. There is no other blood-shedding which is worth a thought as an atonement for sin. Is the blood of His atonement truly applied to my soul? All men are on a level as to their need of Him. What a blessing that there is the one way of pardon! Persons of merely formal religion cannot understand how we can rejoice that all our sins are forgiven us for Christ's sake. Their works, prayers, and ceremonies give them very poor comfort. They are neglecting the one great salvation and endeavoring to get remission without blood. It is in vain, when conscience is aroused, to fly to feelings and evidences for comfort. This is a habit we learned in the past. The only remedy for a guilty conscience is a sight of Jesus suffering on the cross. "The blood is the life thereof," says the Levitical law. Let us rest assured that it is the life of faith and joy and every other holy grace.

"Therefore, brethren, we are debtors" (Romans 8:12).

As God's creatures, we are all debtors to Him. Having broken His commandments, as we all have, we are debtors to His justice. We owe Him a vast amount which we are not able to pay. It can be said of the Christian that he does not owe God's justice anything, for Christ has paid the debt His people owed. For this reason the believer owes the more to love. I am a debtor to God's grace and forgiving mercy; but I am no debtor to His justice, for He will never accuse me of a debt already paid. Christ said, "It is finished!" By that He meant that whatever His people owed was wiped away forever from the book of remembrance. Christ, to the uttermost, has satisfied divine justice. The account is settled. The handwriting is nailed to the cross, the receipt is given, and we are debtors to God's justice no longer. Christian, pause for a moment. What a debtor you are to divine sovereignty! How much you owe to His love! He gave His own Son that He might die for you. Consider how much you owe to His forgiving grace. After ten thousand affronts, He loves you as infinitely as ever. Consider what you owe to His power. He has raised you from your death in sin and preserved your spiritual life. Though you have changed a thousand times, He has not changed once. To God you owe yourself and all you have.

February 4

"The love of the Lord" (Hosea 3:1).

Believer, look back through all your experiences and think of the way the Lord your God led you in the wilderness, and how He has fed and clothed you every day. He has put up with all your murmurings and all your longings after the flesh-pots of Egypt. He has opened the rock to supply you and fed you with manna that came down from heaven. Think of how His grace has been sufficient for you in all your troubles—how His blood has been a pardon to you in all your sins—how His rod and His staff have comforted you. When you have looked back on the love of the Lord, then let faith survey His love *in the future.* Remember that Christ's covenant and blood have something more in them than the *past.* He who has loved you and pardoned you, will never cease to love and pardon. He is the Alpha, and He will be the Omega also. Therefore, when you pass through the valley of the shadow of death, you need fear no evil, for He is with you. When you stand in the cold floods of Jordan, you need not fear, for death cannot separate you from His love. When you come into the mysteries of eternity, you need not tremble, "for I am persuaded, that neither death, nor life, nor angels, nor principalities, nor powers, nor things present, nor things to come, nor height, nor depth, nor any other creature, shall be able to separate us from the love of God, which is in Christ Jesus our Lord" (Romans 8:38-39). Surely as we meditate on "the love of the Lord," our hearts burn within us, and we long to love Him more.

February 5

"The Father sent the Son to be the Saviour of the world" (1 John 4:14).

There is peace in knowing that Jesus Christ did not come without His Father's permission, authority, consent, and assistance. He was sent by the Father to be the Savior of men. While there are distinctions as to the *persons* in the Trinity, there are no distinctions of honor. We too frequently ascribe the honor of our salvation more to Jesus Christ than we do to the Father. This is a mistake. Did not His Father send Him? If He spoke wondrously, did not His Father pour grace into His lips that He might be an able minister of the new covenant? He who knows the Father, and the Son, and the Holy Spirit as he should know them, never sets one before another in his love. Since to the Man Christ Jesus you are brother and hold close fellowship, you are also linked with God the Eternal. Did you ever consider the depth of love in the heart of Jehovah, when God the Father equipped His Son for the great enterprise of mercy? The Father sent Him! Contemplate that subject. Think how Jesus works what the Father wills. In the wounds of the dying Savior, see the love of the great I AM. Let every thought of Jesus be also connected with the Eternal, ever-blessed God, for "it pleased the Lord to bruise him; he hath put him to grief" (Isaiah 53:10).

February 6

"Praying always" (Ephesians 6:18).

We have all spoken a large number of prayers since the moment we learned to pray! Our first prayer was a prayer for ourselves. We asked God to have mercy upon us and blot out our sin. He heard us. But when He had blotted out our sins, we had more prayers for ourselves. We have had to pray for sanctifying grace, for constraining and restraining grace; we have been led to crave for a fresh assurance of faith, for deliverance in the hour of temptation, for help in the time of duty, and for relief in the day of trial. We have been compelled to go to God for our souls. Bear witness, children of God, you have never been able to get anything for your souls elsewhere. All the bread your soul has eaten has come down from heaven. All the water of which it drank flowed from the living Rock—Christ Jesus the Lord. Your wants were innumerable, and, therefore, the supplies have been infinitely great. Your prayers have been as varied as the mercies have been countless. You can say, "I love the Lord, because He heard the voice of my supplication." He has heard you in the day of trouble, has strengthened you, and helped you, even when you dishonored Him by trembling and doubting at the mercy seat. Remember this, and let it fill your heart with gratitude to God. "Bless the Lord, O my soul, and forget not all his benefits" (Psalm 103:2).

"Arise ye, and depart" (Micah 2:10).

The hour is approaching when the message will come to us, as it comes to all—"Arise, and go forth from the home in which you have dwelt, from the city in which you have done your business, from your family, from your friends. Arise, and take your last journey." We have read a little and some has been revealed to us by the Spirit, but how little we know of the realms of the future! We know that there is a black and stormy river called "Death." God bids us cross it, promising to be with us. And, after death, what comes? What scene of glory will be unfolded to our view? We know enough of the heavenly land to make us welcome our summons there with joy and gladness. The journey of death may be dark, but we may go forth on it fearlessly, knowing that God is with us as we walk through the gloomy valley, and therefore we need fear no evil. We will be departing from all we have known and loved here, but we will be going to our Father's house—where Jesus is—to that royal "city which hath foundations, whose builder and maker is God" (Hebrews 11:10). This will be our last removal, to dwell forever with Him we love, in the midst of His people, in the presence of God. Christian, meditate much on heaven. It will help you to press on and to forget the toil of the way. This vale of tears is but the pathway to the better country. This world of woe is but the stepping-stone to a world of bliss.

February 8

"Thou shalt call his name Jesus" (Matthew 1:21).

When a person is dear, everything connected with him becomes dear. Likewise is the person of the Lord Jesus in the estimation of all true believers. They consider everything about Him to be beyond all price. "All thy garments smell of myrrh, and aloes, and cassia," said David, as if the very vestments of the Savior were so sweetened by His person that he could not but love them. There is not a spot where that hallowed foot walked, a word those blessed lips uttered, or a thought which His loving Word revealed that is not priceless to us. This is true of the names of Christ—they are all sweet in the believer's ear. But if there is one name sweeter than another in the believer's ear, it is the name of *Jesus*. Jesus! it is the name which moves the harps of heaven to melody. Jesus! the life of all our joys. If there is one name more charming, more precious than another, it is this name. Many of our hymns begin with it, and scarcely any, that are good for anything, end without it. It is the sum total of all delights. It is the music with which the bells of heaven ring; a song in a word; an ocean for comprehension, although a drop for brevity; a matchless oratorio in two syllables; a gathering up of the hallelujahs of eternity in five letters.

"And David inquired of the Lord" (2 Samuel 5:23).

The Philistines came in great number, but, with the help of God, David easily put them to flight. Notice that when they came a second time, David did not go up to fight them without inquiring of the Lord. Once he had been victorious, he might have said, as many have in other cases, "I shall be victorious again; I may rest quite sure that if I have conquered once, I shall triumph yet again. Why should I tarry to seek at the Lord's hands?" Not so David. He had gained one battle by the strength of the Lord. He would not venture on another until he insured the same. He inquired, "Shall I go up against them?" He waited until God's sign was given. Learn from David to take no step without God. A Puritan said, "If a Christian carves for himself, he'll cut his own fingers." This is a great truth. A believer once said, "He that goes before the cloud of God's providence goes on a fool's errand;" and so he does. We must have God's providence leading us. If providence tarries, tarry until providence comes. He who goes before providence will be very glad to run back again. "I will instruct thee and teach thee in the way which thou shalt go" (Psalm 32:8). This is God's promise to His people. Let us, then, take all our perplexities to Him and say, "Lord, what will you have me to do?" Do not leave your home this morning without inquiring of the Lord.

"I know how to abound" (Philippians 4:12).

There are many who know "how to be abased," who have not learned "how to abound." When they are set on the top of a pinnacle, their heads grow dizzy, and they are ready to fall. The Christian far more often disgraces his profession in prosperity than in adversity. It is a dangerous thing to be prosperous. The crucible of adversity is a less severe trial to the Christian than the refining-pot of prosperity. Oh, what leanness of soul and neglect of spiritual things have been brought on through the very mercies and bounties of God! Yet, this is not a matter of necessity, for the apostle tells us that he knew how to abound. When he had much, he knew how to use it. Abundant grace enabled him to bear abundant prosperity. It takes more than human skill to carry the brimming cup of mortal joy with a steady hand. Yet, Paul had learned that skill, for he declares, "In all things I am instructed both to be full and to be hungry." It is a divine lesson to know how to be full, for the Israelites were full once. But while the flesh was yet in their mouth, the wrath of God came upon them. Many have asked for mercies that they might satisfy their own hearts' lust. Fullness of bread has often made fullness of blood, and that has brought on wantonness of spirit. We are full, and we forget God. Satisfied with earth, we are content to do without heaven. Take care that you ask in your prayers that God would teach you "how to be full."

February 11

"And they took knowledge of them, that they had been with Jesus" (Acts 4:13).

A Christian should be a striking likeness of Jesus Christ. If we were what we profess to be and what we should be, we would be pictures of Christ. We are to imitate Him so closely that the world will have no doubt we have been with Jesus. A Christian should be like Christ in his *boldness*. Be like Jesus—very valiant for your God. Imitate Him in your *loving* spirit. Think kindly, speak kindly, and do kindly, that men may say of you, "He has been with Jesus." Imitate Jesus in His *holiness*. Was He zealous for His Master? So should you be always going about doing good. Do not waste time. It is too precious. Was He self-denying, never looking to His own interest? Be the same. Was He devout? Then you should be. Did He defer to His Father's will? So submit yourselves to Him. Was He patient? Then learn to endure. And best of all, as the highest portraiture of Jesus, try to forgive your enemies, as He did. Let those sublime words of your Master, "Father, forgive them; for they know not what they do" (Luke 23:34) always ring in your ears. Forgive, as you have been forgiven. Heap coals of fire on the head of your foe by your kindness to him. Good for evil, remember, is godlike.

February 12

"For as the sufferings of Christ abound in us, so our consolation also aboundeth by Christ" (2 Corinthians 1:5).

Here is a blessed proportion. The Ruler of providence bears a pair of scales—in this side He puts His people's trials, and in that He puts their consolations. When the scale of trial is nearly empty, you will always find the scale of consolation in nearly the same condition. When the scale of trial is full, you will find the scale of consolation just as heavy. When the black clouds gather most, the light is more brightly revealed to us. It is a blessed thing, that when we are most cast down, then it is that we are most lifted up by the consolations of the Spirit. One reason is, because trials make more room for consolation. Great hearts can only be made by great troubles. The humbler a man lies, the more comfort he will always have. Another reason why we are often most happy in our troubles, is this—then we have the closest dealings with God. When the barn is full, man can live without God. When the purse is bursting with gold, we try to do without so much prayer. But take our food away, and we want our God. Cleanse the idols out of our house, and we are compelled to honor Jehovah. "Out of the depths have I cried unto thee, O Lord" (Psalm 130:1). There is no cry as good as that which comes from the bottom of the mountains; no prayer half as hearty as that which comes up from the depths of the soul, through deep trials and afflictions. They bring us to God, and we are happier; for nearness to God is happiness. Troubled believer, do not fret over your heavy troubles, for they are the heralds of weighty mercies.

"Behold, what manner of love the Father hath bestowed upon us, that we should be called the sons of God: therefore the world knoweth us not, because it knew him not. Beloved, now are we the sons of God" (1 John 3:1-2).

Consider who we were and what we feel ourselves to be even now when corruption is powerful in us, and you will wonder at our adoption. Yet, we are called "the sons of God." What a high relationship is that of a son, and what privileges it brings! What care and tenderness the son expects from his father, and what love the father feels toward the son! But all that, and more than that, we now have through Christ. As for the temporary drawback of suffering with the elder brother, this we accept as an honor: "Therefore the world knoweth us not, because it knew him not" (1 John 3:1). We are content to be unknown with Him in His humiliation, for we are to be exalted with Him. "Beloved, now are we the sons of God." That is easy to read, but it is not so easy to feel. How is it with your heart this morning? Are you in the lowest depths of sorrow? Does corruption rise within your spirit, and grace seem like a poor spark trampled underfoot? Does your faith almost fail you? Fear not, it is neither your graces nor feelings on which you are to live. You must live simply by faith in Christ. "Ah, but," you say, "see how I am arrayed! my graces are not bright; my righteousness does not shine with apparent glory." But read verse two: *"It doth not yet appear what we shall be: but we know that, when he shall appear, we shall be like him."* The Holy Spirit will purify our minds, and divine power will refine our bodies; then will we see Him as He is.

February 14

"And his allowance was a continual allowance given him of the king, a daily rate for every day, all the days of his life" (2 Kings 25:30).

Jehoiachim was not sent away from the king's palace with a store to last him for months, but his provision was given him as a daily pension. He well pictures the happy position of all the Lord's people. A daily portion is all that a man really needs. Sufficient for the day is all that we can enjoy. We cannot eat or drink or wear more than the day's supply of food and raiment. The surplus gives us the care of storing it and the anxiety of watching against a thief. Enough is not only as good as a feast, but is all that even a glutton can truly enjoy. This is all that we should expect. A craving for more than this in ungrateful. When our Father does not give us more, we should be content with his daily allowance. Jehoiachim's case is ours. We have a sure portion, a portion given us by the King, a gracious portion, and a perpetual portion. Here is surely ground for thankfulness. Beloved Christian reader, in matters of grace, you need a daily supply. You have no store of strength. Day by day you must seek help from above. It is a sweet assurance that a daily portion is provided for you. In the Word, through the ministry, by meditation, in prayer, and waiting on God you will receive renewed strength. In Jesus all needful things are laid up for you. Then enjoy your continual allowance.

"To him be glory both now and forever" (2 Peter 3:18).

Heaven will be full of the ceaseless praises of Jesus. To Him be glory. Is He not a "Priest forever, after the order of Melchizedek?" To Him be glory. Is He not King forever? King of kings and Lord of lords, the everlasting Father? To Him be glory forever. His praises will never cease. That which was bought with blood deserves to last while immortality endures. The glory of the Cross must never be eclipsed. The luster of the grave and of the resurrection must never be dimmed. O Jesus, You will be praised forever! Believer, you are anticipating the time when you will join the saints above in ascribing all glory to Jesus; but are you glorifying Him *now?* The apostle's words are, "To Him be glory both *now* and forever." Will you make it your prayer today? "Lord, help me to glorify You. I have talents; help me to extol You by using them for You. I have time; Lord, help me to redeem it, that I may serve You. I have a head to think; Lord, help me to think of You. You have put me in this world for something. Lord, show me what that is and help me to work out my life-purpose. I cannot do much; but as the widow put in her two mites, which were all her living, I cast my time and eternity, too, into Your treasury. I am all Yours. Take me and enable me to glorify You now, in all that I say, in all that I do, and with all that I have."

"I have <u>learned,</u> in whatsoever state I am, therewith to be content" (Philippians 4:11).

Philippians 4:11 shows us that contentment is not a natural inclination of man. Covetousness, discontent, and murmuring are as natural to man as thorns are to the soil. The precious things of the earth must be cultivated. If we would have wheat, we must plow and sow. If we want flowers, there must be the garden and all the gardener's care. Contentment is one of the flowers of heaven. If we want it, it must be cultivated. It will not grow in us by nature. It is the new nature alone that can produce it, and even then we must be especially careful and watchful that we maintain and cultivate the grace which God has sown in us. Paul says, "I have learned. . .to be content;" as much as to say, he did not know how at one time. It cost him some pains to attain to the mystery of that great truth. No doubt he sometimes thought he had learned, and then broke down. And when at last he had attained it and could say, "I have learned, in whatsoever state I am, therewith to be content," he was an old, gray-headed man, upon the borders of the grave—a poor prisoner shut up in Nero's dungeon at Rome. Do not indulge the notion that you can be contented without learning, or learn without discipline. It is not a power that may be exercised naturally, but a science to be acquired gradually. We know this from experience. Hush that murmur, natural though it be, and continue as a diligent pupil in the Word.

"Isaac dwelt by the well Lahai-roi" (Genesis 25:11).

Hagar had once found deliverance there, and Ishmael drank from the water so graciously revealed by the God who lives and sees the sons of men. But this was merely a casual visit, such as worldlings pay to the Lord in times of need, when it serves their turn. They cry to Him in trouble, but forsake Him in prosperity. Isaac *dwelt* there, and made the well of the living and all-seeing God his constant source of supply. The usual tenor of a man's life, the dwelling of his soul, is the true test of his state. Perhaps the providential visitation experienced by Hagar struck Isaac's mind and led him to revere the place. Its mystical name endeared it to him. His frequent musings by its brim made him familiar with the well. His meeting Rebecca there had made his spirit feel at home near the spot. Best of all, the fact that he enjoyed fellowship with the living God there made him select that hallowed ground for his dwelling. Let us learn to live in the presence of the living God. The well of the Creator never fails. Happy is he who dwells at the well. The Lord has been a sure helper to others: His name is Shaddai, God All-Sufficient. Through Him our soul has found her glorious Husband, the Lord Jesus. In Him we live, move, and have our being. Let us dwell in close fellowship with Him. Glorious Lord, constrain us that we may never leave You but dwell by the well of the living God.

"Show me wherefore thou contendest with me" (Job 10:2).

There are some of your graces which would never be discovered if it were not for your trials. Love is too often like a glow-worm showing little light except in the midst of surrounding darkness. Hope itself is like a star—not to be seen in the sunshine of prosperity and only to be discovered in the night of adversity. Afflictions are often the black foils in which God sets the jewels of His children's graces to make them shine the better. How can you know that you have faith until your faith is exercised? God often allows our trials that our graces may be discovered. Besides, it is not merely discovery; real growth in grace is the result of sanctified trials. God often removes our comforts and our privileges in order to make us better Christians. He trains His soldiers, not in tents of ease and luxury, but by turning them out and using them to forced marches and hard service. He has them ford through streams, swim through rivers, climb mountains, and walk many a long mile with heavy knapsacks on their backs. Could this account for the troubles which you are experiencing? Is the Lord bringing out your graces and making them grow? Is this the reason He is contending with you?

"Thus saith the Lord God: I will yet for this be inquired of by the house of Israel, to do it for them" (Ezekiel 36:37).

Prayer precedes mercy. Turn to sacred history, and you will find that scarcely ever did a great mercy come to this world unheralded by supplication. You have found this true in your own personal experience. God has given you many an unsolicited favor, but still great prayer has always been the prelude of great mercy with you. When you have had rapturous joys, you have been obliged to look on them as answers to your prayers. When you had great deliverances out of trouble and mighty help in danger, you have been able to say, "I sought the Lord, and he heard me, and delivered me from all my fears" (Psalm 34:4). Prayer is always the preface to blessing. When the sunlight of God's mercies rises on our necessities, it cast the shadow of prayer far down on the plain. Prayer is connected with the blessing to show us the value of it. If we had the blessings without asking for them, we would think them common things. Prayer makes our mercies more precious than diamonds. The things we ask for are precious, but we do not realize their preciousness until we have sought for them earnestly.

"God, that comforteth those that are cast down" (2 Corinthians 7:6).

Who comforts like Him? Go to some poor, melancholy, distressed child of God. Tell him sweet promises, and whisper in his ear choice words of comfort; he is like the deaf adder; he does not listen. He is in despair, and comfort him as you may, it will be only a sigh of resignation that you get from him. You will bring forth no psalms of praise, no hallelujahs, no joyful sonnets. But let *God* come to His child, let Him lift up His countenance, and the mourner's eyes glisten with hope. You could not have cheered him, but the Lord has done it. "He is the God of all comfort" (2 Corinthians 1:3). There is no balm in Gilead, but there is balm in God. There is no physician among the creatures, but the Creator is Jehovah-rophi. It is marvelous how one sweet word of God will make whole songs for Christians. One word of God is like a piece of gold. The Christian is the goldbeater, and he can hammer that promise out for weeks. Christian, you need not sit down in despair. Go to the Comforter and ask Him to give you consolation. You have heard it said that when a pump is dry, you must pour water down it first of all, and then you will get water. Christian, when you are dry, go to God, ask Him to shed abroad His joy in your heart, and then your joy will be full. Do not go to acquaintances, for you will find them Job's comforters after all. Go first and foremost to your "God, that comforteth those that are cast down" (2 Corinthians 7:6). You will soon say, "In the multitude of my thoughts within me thy comforts delight my soul" (Psalm 94:19).

"He hath said" (Hebrews 13:5).

If we can only grasp these words by faith, we have an all-conquering weapon in our hand. What fear is there which will not fall smitten with a deadly wound before this arrow from the bow of God's covenant? Yes, whether for delight in our quietude or for strength in our conflict, "He hath said" must be our daily resort. This may teach us the extreme value of searching the Scriptures. There may be a promise in the Word which would exactly fit your case, but you may not know of it, and therefore you miss its comfort. There may be a potent medicine in the Scripture, and you may continue being sick unless you will examine and search the Scriptures to discover what "He hath said." Should you not, besides reading the Bible, store your memories richly with the promises of God? You memorize the sayings of great men; you treasure the verses of renowned poets; should you not be profound in your knowledge of the words of God so that you may be able to quote them readily when you would solve a difficulty or over-throw a doubt? Since "He hath said" is the source of all wisdom and the fountain of all comfort, let it dwell in you richly as "a well of water, springing up into everlasting life" (John 2:14). So you will grow healthy, strong, and happy in the divine life.

"His bow abode in strength, and the arms of his hands were made strong by the hands of the mighty God of Jacob" (Genesis 49:24).

The strength God gives to His Josephs is *divine strength*. How did Joseph stand against temptation? God gave him aid. There is nothing we can do without the power of God. All true strength comes from "the mighty God of Jacob." Notice in what a blessedly familiar way God gave this strength to Joseph—"The arms of his hands were made strong by the hands of the mighty God of Jacob." Thus God is represented as putting His hands on Joseph's hands, placing His arms on Joseph's arms. Like a father teaches his children, so the Lord teaches them that fear Him. He puts His arms upon them. God Almighty, Eternal, Omnipotent, stoops from His throne and lays His hand upon the child's hand, stretching His arm upon the arm of Joseph, that he may be made strong! This strength was also covenant strength for it is ascribed to "the mighty God of Jacob." Now, whenever you read of the God of Jacob in the Bible, you should remember the covenant with Jacob. All the power, all the grace, all the blessings, all the mercies, all the comforts, all the things we have, flow to us from the well-head, through the covenant. If there were no covenant, then we would fail indeed, for all grace proceeds from it, as light and heat from the sun.

"I will never leave thee" (Hebrews 13:5).

No promise is of private interpretation. Whatever God has said to any one saint, He has said to all. When He opens a well for one, it is that all may drink. When He opens a granary-door to give out food, there may be one starving man who is the reason its being opened, but all hungry saints may come and feed, too. Whether He gave the Word to Abraham or to Moses, matters not. He has given it to you as one of the covenanted seed. There is not a brook of living water of which you may not drink. If the land flows with milk and honey, eat the honey and drink the milk, for both are yours. Be bold to believe, for He said, "I will never leave thee, nor forsake thee." In this promise, God gives everything to His people. Then no attribute of God can cease to be engaged for us. He will show Himself strong on the behalf of them that trust Him. With loving kindness He will have mercy on us. To summarize, there is nothing you can want, ask for, or need in time or in eternity, which is not contained in this text—"I will never leave thee, nor forsake thee."

"I will cause the shower to come down in his season: there shall be showers of blessing" (Ezekiel 34:26).

Here is sovereign mercy. There is only one voice which can speak to the clouds and bid them beget the rain. Who sends down the rain upon the earth? Who scatters the showers on the green herb? Do not I, the Lord? So grace is the gift of God and is not to be created by man. It is also needed grace. What would the ground do without showers? As absolutely needful is the divine blessing. In vain you labor, until God the plenteous shower bestows, and sends salvation down. Then, it is plenteous grace. "I will send them showers." It does not say, "I will send them drops," but "showers." So it is with grace. If God gives a blessing, He usually gives it in such a measure that there is not room enough to receive it. Plenteous grace! We cannot do without saturating showers of grace. Again, it is *seasonable grace*. "I will cause the shower to come down *in his season."* What is your season this morning? Is it the season of drought? Then that is the season for showers. Is it a season of great heaviness and depression? Then that is the season for showers. "As thy day, so shall thy strength be." And here is a varied blessing. "I will give thee showers of blessing." The word is in the plural. God will send all kinds of blessings. All God's blessings go together, like links in a golden chain. If He gives converting grace, He will also give comforting grace. He will send "showers of blessing." Look up today, parched plant, and open your leaves and flowers for a heavenly watering.

February 25

"The wrath to come" (Matthew 3:7).

It is pleasant to pass over a country after a rain and to smell the freshness of the herbs. That is the position of a Christian. He is going through a land where the storm has spent itself upon his Savior's head. If there are a few drops of sorrow falling, they distill from clouds of mercy. Jesus cheers him by the assurance that they are not for his destruction. But how terrible to witness the approach of a tempest, to see the forewarnings of the storm. How terrible to await the dread advance of a hurricane—such as occurs, sometimes, in the tropics—to wait in terrible apprehension. And yet, sinner, this is your present position. No hot drops have as yet fallen, but a shower of fire is coming. No terrible winds howl around you, but God's tempest is gathering its dread artillery. As yet the water-floods are dammed up by mercy, but the flood-gates will soon be opened. The thunderbolts of God are yet in His storehouse, but the tempest hastens and how awful will that moment be when God, robed in vengeance, will march forth in fury! Where, Oh sinner, will you hide your head, or where will you flee? Oh, that the hand of mercy may now lead you to Christ! He is freely set before you in the gospel. You know your need of Him. Believe in Him, and then the fury will pass over forever.

February 26

"Salvation is of the Lord" (Jonah 2:9).

Salvation is the work of God. It is He alone who quickens the soul "dead in trespasses and sins," and it is He also who maintains the soul in its spiritual life. He is both "Alpha and Omega." If I am prayerful, God makes me prayerful. If I have graces, they are God's gift to me. If I hold on in a consistent life, it is because He upholds me with His hand. I do nothing toward my own preservation, except what God Himself first does in me. If I sin, that is my own doing; but if I act rightly, that is of God, wholly and completely. Do I live before men a consecrated life? It is not I, but Christ who lives in me. Am I sanctified? I did not cleanse myself—God's Holy Spirit sanctifies me. Am I weaned from the world? I am weaned by God's chastisement sanctified to my good. Do I grow in knowledge? The great Instructor teaches me. He only is my rock and my salvation. Do I feed on the Word? That Word would be no food for me unless the Lord made it food for my soul and helped me to feed on it. Am I continually receiving fresh increase of strength? Where do I gather my might? My help comes from heaven's hills. Without Jesus I can do nothing. As a branch cannot bring forth fruit except it abide in the vine, no more can I, except I abide in Him. What Jonah learned in the great deep, let me learn this morning in my prayer closet. Salvation is of the Lord.

"Thou hast made the Lord, which is my refuge, even the Most High, thy habitation" (Psalm 91:9).

In the wilderness the Israelites were continually exposed to change. When the pillar stopped, the tents were pitched; but tomorrow, before the morning sun had risen, the trumpet sounded, the ark was in motion, and the fiery, cloudy pillar was leading the way through the narrow trails of the mountain, up the hillside, or along the arid waste of the wilderness. They had scarcely time to rest a little before they heard the sound of "Away! this is not your rest; you must still be onward journeying toward Canaan!" Even wells and palm trees could not detain them. Yet they had an abiding home in their God. His cloudy pillar was their roof, and its flame by night their household fire. They must go onward from place to place, continually changing. "Yet," says Moses, "though we are always changing, Lord, thou hast been our dwelling place throughout all generations." The Christian knows no change with regard to God. He may be rich today and poor tomorrow; he may be sickly today and well tomorrow; he may be in happiness today, tomorrow he may be distressed—but there is no change with regard to his relationship to God. If He loved me yesterday, He loves me today. He is my strong habitation whereunto I can continually resort (See Psalm 71:3). I am a pilgrim in the world, but I am at home in my God.

"My expectation is from him" (Psalm 63:5).

If the believer is looking for anything from the world, it is a poor expectation indeed. But if he looks to God for the supply of his wants, whether in temporal or spiritual blessings, his expectation will not be a vain one. Constantly he may draw from the bank of faith and get his need supplied out of the riches of God's lovingkindness. My Lord never fails to honor His promises. When we bring them to His throne, He never sends them back unanswered. Therefore, I will wait only at His door, for He ever opens it with the hand of grace. But we have expectations beyond this life. We will die soon, and then our expectation is from Him. Do we not expect that when death approaches, He will send angels to carry us to His bosom? We believe that when the pulse is faint, and the heart heaves heavily, some angelic messenger will stand and look with loving eyes on us and whisper, "Sister spirit, come away!" We are longing for the time when we will be like our glorious Lord—for "we shall see him as he is" (1 John 3:2). Oh, my soul, live for God; live with the desire to glorify Him from whom comes all your supplies.

"With lovingkindness have I drawn thee" (Jeremiah 31:3).

The law and judgment are used to bring us to Christ, but the final victory is affected by lovingkindness. The prodigal set out for his father's house from a sense of need. His father saw him a great way off and ran to meet him. The last steps that he took toward his father's house were with the kiss still warm upon his cheek and the welcome still musical in his ears. The Master came to the door and knocked with the iron hand of the law; the door shook and trembled on its hinges; but the man piled every piece of furniture which he could find against the door, for he said, "I will not admit the Man." The Master turned away, but He came back, and with His own soft hand, he knocked again softly and tenderly. This time the door did not shake, but strange to say, it opened, and there on his knees the once unwilling host was found rejoicing to receive his guest. "Come in, come in; You have so knocked that my heart is drawn to You. I could not think of Your pierced hand leaving its blood-mark on my door, and of You going away homeless. I yield, I yield. Your love has won my heart." So in every case; lovingkindness wins the day. What Moses with the tablets of stone could never do, Christ does with His pierced hand.

"Awake, O north wind; and come, thou south; blow upon my garden, that the spices thereof may flow out" (Song of Solomon 4:16).

Anything is better than the dead calm of indifference. Did not the spouse in this verse humbly submit herself to the reproofs of her Beloved? She entreated Him to send forth His grace in some form, making no stipulation as to the peculiar manner in which it should come. Did not she, like ourselves, become so utterly weary of deadness that she sighed for any visitation which would brace her to action? Yet, she desires comfort, too, the smiles of divine love, the joy of the Redeemer's presence; these are often mightily effectual to arouse our sluggish life. She desires either one or the other, or both, so that she may be able to delight her Beloved with the spices of her garden. She cannot endure to be unprofitable, nor can we. How cheering a thought that Jesus can find comfort in our poor feeble graces! It seems far too good to be true. The wisdom of the great Husbandman overrules diverse and opposite causes to produce the one desired result. It makes both affliction and consolation draw forth faith, love, patience, hope, resignation, joy, and the other fair flowers of the garden. May we know by sweet experience what this means!

"But all the Israelites went down to the Philistines, to sharpen every man his share, and his colter, and his axe, and his mattock" (1 Samuel 13:20).

We are engaged in a great war with the Philistines of evil. Every weapon within our reach must be used. Preaching, teaching, praying, giving, all must be brought into action, and talents which have been thought too useless for service must now be employed. Each moment of time, each fragment of ability, educated or untutored, each opportunity, favorable or unfavorable, must be used, for our foes are many, and our force is slender. Most of our tools need sharpening. We need quickness of perception, tact, energy, promptness—complete adaptation for the Lord's work. Practical common sense is a very scarce thing among the conductors of Christian enterprises. We might learn from our enemies and make the Philistines sharpen our weapons. This morning let us note enough to sharpen our zeal during this day by the aid of the Holy Spirit. Mark the heathen devotees, what tortures they endure in the service of their idols! Are they alone to exhibit patience and self-sacrifice? Observe the prince of darkness, how persevering in his endeavors, how unabashed in his attempts, how daring in his plans, how energetic in all! The devils are united as one man in their infamous rebellion, while we believers in Jesus are divided in our service of God and scarcely ever work with unanimity. Oh, that from Satan's infernal industry we may learn to go about like good Samaritans, seeking whom we may bless!

March 3

"I have chosen thee in the furnace of affliction" (Isaiah 48:10).

Comfort yourself, tried believer, with this thought: God saith, "I have chosen thee in the furnace of affliction." Does not the word come like a soft shower, assuaging the fury of the flame? Is it not an asbestos armor, against which the heat has no power? Whatever happens to me in this vale of tears, I know that He has chosen me. If, believer, you require still greater comfort, remember *that you have the Son of Man with you in the furnace.* In that silent room of yours, there sits by your side One whom you have not seen, but whom you love; and when you know it not, He makes all your bed in your affliction and smooths your pillow for you. Your friend sticks closely to you. You cannot see Him, but you may feel the pressure of His hands. Do you not hear His voice? Even in the valley of the shadow of death, He says, "Fear not, I am with thee." He will never leave one whom He has chosen for His own. "Fear not, for I am with thee" (Isaiah 43:5). This is His sure word of promise to His chosen ones in the furnace of affliction.

"My grace is sufficient for thee" (2 Corinthians 12:9).

If none of God's saints were poor and tried, we would not know half so well the consolation of divine grace. We may find a wanderer who has no place to lay his head, but who can say, "Still will I trust in the Lord." We may see a pauper starving on bread and water, but he still glories in Jesus. We may see a bereaved widow overwhelmed in affliction yet still believing in Christ. What honor they reflect on the gospel! God's grace is illustrated and magnified in the poverty and trials of believers. Saints bear up under every discouragement, believing that all things work together for their good. They believe that out of apparent evils a real blessing will ultimately spring—that their God will either work a deliverance for them speedily or most assuredly support them in the trouble. This patience of the saints proves the power of divine grace. The master-works of God are those men who stand, in the midst of difficulties, steadfast and unmovable. He who would glorify his God must set his account on meeting with many trials. No man can be illustrious before the Lord unless his conflicts are many. If, then, yours is a much-tried path, rejoice in it, because you will better show forth the all-sufficient grace of God. Never dream of His failing you. The God who has been sufficient until now can be trusted to the end.

"Let us not sleep, as do others" (1 Thessalonians 5:6).

There are many ways of promoting Christian wakefulness. Let me strongly advise Christians to converse together concerning the ways of the Lord. Christians who isolate themselves and walk alone are very liable to grow drowsy. Keep Christian company, and you will be kept wakeful by it and refreshed and encouraged to make quicker progress in the road to heaven. But as you thus take "sweet counsel" with others in the ways of God, take care that the theme of your conversation is your Lord Jesus. Let the eye of faith be constantly looking unto Him. Let your heart be full of Him. Let your lips speak of His worth. Friend live near to the cross, and you will not sleep. Labor to impress yourself with a deep sense of the value of the place to which you are going. If you think that hell is behind you, and the devil is pursuing you, you will not loiter. Christian, will you sleep while the pearly gates are open—the songs of angels waiting for you to join them—a crown of gold ready for your brow? Ah, no, in holy fellowship continue to watch and pray that you enter not into temptation!

"Ye must be born again" (John 3:7).

Regeneration is a subject which lies at the very basis of salvation. We should be very diligent to take heed that we really are "born again," for there are many who fancy they are, who are not. Being born in a Christian land and being recognized as professing the Christian religion is of no avail whatever, unless there is something more added to it—the being "born again" by the power of the Holy Spirit. To be "born again" is a matter so mysterious, the human words cannot describe it. "The wind bloweth where it listeth, and thou hearest the sound thereof, but canst not tell whence it cometh, and whither it goeth; so is every one that is born of the Spirit" (John 3:8). Nevertheless, it is a change which is known and felt. This great work is *supernatural*. It is not an operation which a man performs for himself. It is not a change of my name, but a renewal of my nature so that I am not the man I used to be, but a new man in Christ Jesus. If you have been "born again," your acknowledgment will be, "O Lord Jesus, the everlasting Father, You are my spiritual Parent; unless Your Spirit had breathed into me the breath of a new, holy, and spiritual life, I would have been to this day 'dead in trespasses and sins.' My heavenly life is wholly derived from You, to You I ascribe it. My life is hid with Christ in God. It is no longer I who live, but Christ who liveth in me." May the Lord enable us to be well assured on this vital point, for to be unregenerate is to be unsaved, unpardoned, without God, and without hope.

"Have faith in God" (Mark 11:22).

Love can make the feet move more swiftly, but faith is the foot which carries the soul. Faith is the oil enabling the wheels of holy devotion and of earnest piety to move well. Without faith the wheels are taken from the chariot, and we drag heavily. With faith I can do all things. Without faith I will neither have the inclination nor the power to do anything in the service of God. If you would find the men who serve God the best, you must look for the men of the most faith. Little faith will save a man, but little faith cannot do great things for God. Little faith stands desponding, mingling her tears with the flood; but great faith sings, "When you pass through the waters, I will be with you; and through the rivers, they will not overflow you," and she fords the streams at once. Would you be comfortable and happy? Would you have the religion of cheerfulness and not that of gloom? Then have faith in God. If you love darkness and are satisfied to dwell in gloom and misery, then be content with little faith; but if you love the sunshine and would sing songs of rejoicing, covet earnestly this best gift—"great faith."

"We must through much tribulation enter into the kingdom of God" (Acts 14:22).

God's people have their trials. It was never designed by God, when He chose His people, that they should be an untried people. Trials are a part of our lot. They were predestined for us in God's solemn decree and bequeathed us in Christ's last legacy. So surely as the stars are fashioned by His hands, and their orbits fixed by Him, so surely are our trials allotted to us. He has ordained their season and their place, their intensity, and the effect they will have on us. Good men must never expect to escape troubles; if they do, they will be disappointed, for none of their predecessors have been without them. Mark the patience of Job; remember Abraham, for he had his trials, and by his faith under them, he became the "Father of the faithful." Note well the biographies of all the patriarchs, prophets, apostles, and martyrs, and you will discover none of those whom God made vessels of mercy, who were not made to pass through the fire of affliction. It is ordained of old, that the cross of trouble should be engraved on every vessel of mercy, as the royal mark whereby the King's vessels of honor are distinguished. But although tribulation is thus the path of God's children, they have the comfort of knowing that their Master has traversed it before them. They have His presence and sympathy to cheer them, His grace to support them, and His example to teach them how to endure. When they reach the Kingdom, it will more than make amends for the much tribulation through which they passed to enter it.

"Yea, he is altogether lovely" (Song of Solomon 5:16).

The superlative beauty of Jesus is all-attracting. It is not so much to be admired, as it is to be loved. He is more than pleasant and fair, He is *lovely*. Surely the people of God can fully justify the use of this golden word, for He is the object of their warmest love. Look, disciples of Jesus, to your Master's lips and say, are they not most sweet? Do not His words cause your heart to burn within you as He talks with you by the way? Look up to His head of much fine gold and tell me, are not His thoughts precious to you? Is not your adoration sweetened with affection as you humbly bow before that countenance which is as Lebanon, excellent as the cedars? Is there not a charm in His every feature, and is not His whole person fragrant with such a savor of His good ointments? Our love is not a seal set on His heart of love alone. It is fastened on His arm of power also. There is not a single part of Him on which it does not fix itself. We anoint His whole person with the sweet spikenard of our fervent love. His whole life we would imitate. His whole character we would transcribe. In all other beings we see some lack, but in Him there is all perfection. The best even of His favored saints have had blots upon their garments and wrinkles upon their brows. He is nothing but loveliness. Christ Jesus is gold without alloy— light without darkness—glory without cloud— "Yea, He is altogether lovely."

"In my prosperity I said, I shall never be moved" (Psalm 30:6).

Give a man wealth and let his ships bring home continually rich freights. Let his lands yield abundantly and the weather be favorable to his crops. Let uninterrupted success attend him. Let him enjoy continued health, and give him a happy heart. Let his eyes be ever sparkling with joy, and the natural consequence of such an easy state, even if he is the best Christian who ever breathed, will be *presumption*. Even David said, "I shall never be moved," and we are not better than David or half as good. Beware of the smooth places of the way, if you are treading them. If the way is rough, thank God for it. If God would always rock us in the cradle of prosperity; if there were always few clouds in the sky; if we always had sweet drops in the wine of this life, we would become intoxicated with pleasure. Like the man asleep upon the mast, each moment we would be in jeopardy. We bless God in our afflictions; we thank Him for our changes; we extol His name during loss of property; for we feel that had He not chastened us thus, we might have become too secure. Continual worldly prosperity is a fiery trial.

"Sin. . .exceeding sinful" (Romans 7:13).

Beware of light thoughts of sin. At the time of conversion, the conscience is so tender that we are afraid of the slightest sin. Young converts have a holy timidity, a godly fear, lest they should offend God. But very soon the fine bloom on these first ripe fruits is removed by the rough handling of the surrounding world. It is sadly true that even a Christian may grow so callous that the sin which once startled him does not alarm him in the least. Men get familiar with sin by degrees. The ear in which the cannon has been booming will not notice slight sounds. At first a little sin startles us, but soon we say, "Is it not a little one?" Then there comes another, larger, and then another, until by degrees we begin to regard sin as simply a little slip up. Then follows an unholy presumption: "We have not fallen into open sin. True, we tripped a little, but we stood upright in the main. We may have uttered one unholy word, but as for the most of our conversation, it has been consistent." So we excuse sin; we throw a cloak over it; we call it by dainty names. Take heed lest you fall little by little. Sin, a *little* thing? Is it not a poison? Do not little strokes fell lofty oaks? Will not continual droppings wear away stones? Sin, a *little* thing? It girded the Redeemer's head with thorns and pierced His heart! If you could weigh the least sin in the scales of eternity, you would fly from it as from a serpent and abhor the least appearance of evil. Look on all sin as that which crucified the Savior, and you will see it to be "exceeding sinful."

"Thou shalt love thy neighbor" (Matthew 5:43).

Love your neighbor. Perhaps he rolls in riches, and you are poor and living in your little cottage beside his stately mansion. You see his estates, his fine linen, and his sumptuous banquets every day. God has given him these gifts; do not covet his wealth and think no hard thoughts concerning him. Be content with your own lot, if you cannot better it. But do not look on your neighbor and wish that he were as yourself. Love him, and then you will not envy him. On the other hand, perhaps you are rich, and you reside near the poor. Do not be too proud to call them neighbors. The world calls them your inferiors. In what way are they inferior? They are far more your equals than your inferiors, for God has made of one blood all people that dwell on the face of the earth. It is your coat which is better than theirs, but you are by no means better than they. They are men, and what are you more than that? Take heed that you love your neighbor even though he is in rags. But, perhaps, you say, "I cannot love my neighbors, because for all I do they return ingratitude and contempt." So much the more room for the heroism of love. Would you be a feather-bed warrior, instead of bearing the rough fight of love? He who dares the most will win the most. If rough is your path of love, tread it boldly. Heap coals of fire on their heads. If they are hard to please, seek not to please *them* but to please *your Master*. Love your neighbor, for in so doing you are following in the footsteps of Christ.

"Why sit we here until we die" (2 Kings 7:3).

Dear reader, this little book was mainly intended for the edification of believers; but if you are yet unsaved, our heart yearns over you. Open your Bible and read the story of the lepers. Mark their position, which was much the same as yours. If you remain where you are, you will perish. If you go to Jesus, you can only die. If you sit still in despair, no one can pity you when your ruin comes. None will escape who refuse to look to Jesus. To perish is so awful, that if there were but a straw to catch at, the instinct of self-preservation should lead you to stretch out your hand. We have been talking to you on your own unbelieving ground. We assure you, as from the Lord, that if you seek Him, He will be found. Jesus casts out none who come unto Him. You will not perish if you trust Him. On the contrary, you will find treasure far richer than the poor lepers gathered in Syria's deserted camp. May the Holy Spirit encourage you to go at once, and you will not believe in vain. When you are saved yourself, tell the good news to others. Don't keep it to yourself. Tell the Church first and unite with them in fellowship. Let the minister be informed of your discovery, and then proclaim the good news in every place. May the Lord save you before the sun goes down today.

"Let him that thinketh he standeth take heed lest he fall" (1 Corinthians 10:12).

It is a curious fact that there is such a thing as being proud of grace. A man says, "I have great faith; I shall not fall." "I have fervent love," says another, "I can stand; there is no danger of my going astray." He who boasts of grace has little grace to boast of. Some who do this imagine that their graces can keep them. If a continuous stream of oil does not come to the lamp, though it burn brightly today, it will smoke tomorrow, and its scent will be harmful. Take heed that you do not boast of your graces. Let all your confidence be in Christ and His strength. That is the only way you can be kept from falling. Spend more time in prayer. Spend more time in worship. Read the Scriptures more earnestly and constantly. Watch your life more carefully. Live nearer to God. Take the best example for your pattern. Let your conversation be holy. Show genuine compassion for men's souls. When that happy day comes, when Jesus says, "Come up higher," may it be your happiness to hear Him say, "You have fought a good fight, you have finished your course, and there is laid up for you a crown of righteousness which will not fade away." He alone is able "to keep you from falling and to present you faultless before the presence of his glory with exceeding joy" (Jude 24).

March 15

"Be strong in the grace that is in Christ Jesus" (2 Timothy 2:1).

Christ has grace without measure in Himself, but He has not retained it for Himself. As the reservoir empties itself into the pipes, so has Christ emptied out His grace for His people. "Of his fullness have all we received, and grace for grace" (John 1:16). He seems only to have in order to dispense to us. Like a tree, He bears sweet fruit to be gathered by those who need. Grace is always available from Him without price. As the blood of the body, though flowing from the heart, belongs equally to every member, so the influences of grace are the inheritance of every saint united to the Lamb. In this there is a sweet communion between Christ and His Church, inasmuch as they both receive the same grace. This is true communion: when the sap of grace flows from the stem to the branch and when it is perceived that the stem itself is sustained by the very nourishment which feeds the branch. As we receive grace from Jesus and more constantly recognize it as coming from Him, we will behold Him in communion with us and enjoy the happiness of communion with Him. Let us make daily use of our riches, taking from Him the supply of all we need with as much boldness as men take money from their own purse.

March 16

"I am a stranger with thee" (Psalm 39:12).

All my natural alienation from You Lord, your grace has effectually removed. Now, in fellowship with You, I walk through this sinful world as a pilgrim in a foreign country. You are a stranger in Your own world. Man forgets You, dishonors You, sets up new laws and alien customs, and knows You not. When Your dear Son came to His own, His own received Him not. He was in the world, and the world was made by Him, and the world knew Him not. It is no wonder, then, if I, who live the life of Jesus, should be unknown and a stranger here below. Lord, I would not be a citizen where Jesus was an alien. His pierced hand has loosened the cords which once bound my soul to earth, and now I find myself a stranger in the land. My speech seems to these Babylonians, among whom I dwell, an outlandish tongue, and my actions are strange. But here is the sweetness of my lot; I am a stranger with You. You are my fellow-sufferer, my fellow-pilgrim. Oh, what joy to wander in such blessed society! My heart burns within me when You speak to me.

March 17

"Remember the poor" (Galatians 2:10).

Why does God allow so many of His children to be poor? He could make them all rich if He pleased. He could lay bags of gold at their doors. He could send them a large annual income. He could scatter around their house an abundance of provisions, as He made the quails lie in heaps around the camp of Israel and rained bread out of heaven to feed them. "The cattle upon a thousand hills are his" (Psalm 50:10). He could make the richest and the mightiest bring all their power and riches to the feet of His children, for the hearts of all men are in His control. But He does not choose to do so. Why is this? There are many reasons: one is to give us, who are favored with enough, an opportunity to show our love for Jesus. We show our love for Christ when we sing of Him and pray to Him. But if there were no needy people in the world, we would lose the sweet privilege of evidencing our love by ministering in sacrificial giving to His poorer brethren. He has ordained that thus we should prove that our love stands not in word only, but in deed and in truth. If we truly love Christ, we will care for those who are loved by Him. Those who are dear to Him will be dear to us. Let us then look on it not as a duty, but as a privilege, to relieve the poor of the Lord's flock—remembering the words of the Lord Jesus, "Inasmuch as ye have done it unto one of the least of these my brethren, ye have done it unto me" (Matthew 25:40).

"Ye are all the children of God by faith in Christ Jesus" (Galatians 3:26).

The fatherhood of God is common to all His children. Ah, Little-faith, you have often said, "O that I had the courage of Great-heart, that I could wield His sword and be as valiant as He! But, alas, I stumble at every straw, and a shadow makes me afraid." Listen, Little-faith, Great-heart is God's child, and you are God's child, too. Great-heart is not one bit more God's child than you are. Peter and Paul, the highly favored aspostles, were of the family of the Most High. So are you also. The weak Christian is as much a child of God as the strong one. All the names are in the same family register. One may have more grace than another, but God, our heavenly Father, has the same tender heart toward all. One may do more mighty works and may bring more glory to his Father, but he whose name is the least in the Kingdom of heaven is as much the child of God as he who stands among the King's mighty men. Let this cheer and comfort us when we draw near to God and say, "Our Father." Yet, while we are comforted by knowing this, let us not rest contented with weak faith, but ask, like the apostles, to have it increased. However feeble our faith may be, if it is real faith in Christ, we will reach heaven at last. If, then, you would live to Christ's glory and be happy in His service, seek to be filled with the spirit of adoption more completely, until perfect love casts out fear.

"Strong in faith" (Romans 4:20).

Remember, *faith is the only way you can obtain blessings.* Prayer cannot draw down answers from God's throne except it be the earnest prayer of the man who believes. Faith is the angelic messenger between the soul and the Lord Jesus in glory. If faith is withdrawn, we can neither send up prayer nor receive the answers. Faith is the telegraphic wire which links earth and heaven—on which God's messages of love fly so fast that before we call, He hears us. But if that telegraphic wire of faith is snapped, how can we receive the promise? Am I in trouble? I can obtain help for trouble by faith. Am I beaten about by the enemy? My soul leans by faith on her dear refuge in God. But take faith away—in vain I call to God. There is no road between by soul and heaven. Faith links me with divinity. Faith clothes me with the power of God. Faith engages on my side the omnipotence of Jehovah. Faith insures every attribute of God in my defense. It helps me defy the hosts of hell. It makes me march triumphant over the necks of my enemies. But without faith how can I receive anything of the Lord? Let not him that wavereth expect that he will receive anything of God!" "If thou canst believe, all things are possible to him that believeth" (Mark 9:23).

"My beloved" (Song of Solomon 2:8).

This was a golden name which the ancient Church gave to the Anointed of the Lord. She sang, "My beloved is mine, and I am his: he feedeth among the lilies" (Song of Solomon 2:16). Ever in her song of songs does she call Him by that delightful name, "My beloved!" Even in the long winter, when idolatry had withered the garden of the Lord, her prophets found space to lay aside the burden of the Lord for a little season and to say, as Isaiah did, "Now will I sing to my well-beloved a song of my beloved touching His vineyard" (Isaiah 5:1). Though the saints never saw His face, though as yet He was not made flesh or had dwelt among us or had man beheld His glory, yet He was the consolation of Israel, the hope and joy of all the chosen, the "beloved" of all those who were upright before the Most High. We, in the summer days of the Church, desire to speak of Christ as the Beloved of our soul and to feel that He is very precious, the chiefest among ten thousand, and the altogether lovely. So true is it that the Church loves Jesus and claims Him as her Beloved, that the apostle dares to defy the whole universe to separate her fom the love of Christ and declares that neither persecution, distress, affliction, perils, or the sword have been able to do it. He joyously boasts, "In all these things we are more than conquerors through him that loved us" (Romans 8:37). Oh, that we knew more of the ever precious One!

Ye shall be scattered, every man to his own, and shall leave me alone" (John 16:32).

Few were involved with the sorrows of Gethsemane. The majority of the disciples were not sufficiently advanced in grace to be admitted to behold the mysteries of "the agony." Occupied with the passover feast at their own houses, they represent the many who live according to the letter, but are mere babes as to the spirit of the gospel. To eleven men only was the privilege given to enter Gethsemane and see "this great sight." Out of the eleven, eight were left at a distance. Only three highly favored ones could approach the veil of our Lord's mysterious sorrow. Within that veil even these must not intrude. A stone's-cast distance must be left between. He must tread the wine-press alone. To some selected spirits it is given, for the good of others and to strengthen them for future conflict, to enter the inner circle and hear the pleadings of the suffering High Priest. They have fellowship with Him in His sufferings and are made conformable unto His death. Yet, even these cannot penetrate the secret places of our Saviour's woe. There was an inner chamber in our Master's grief, shut out from human knowledge and fellowship. There Jesus is "left alone." Here Jesus was more than ever an "unspeakable gift."

March 22

"And he went a little farther, and fell on his face, and prayed." (Matthew 26:39).

There are several instructive features in our Savior's prayer in His hour of trial. It was *lonely prayer*. He withdrew even from His three favored disciples. Believer, be much in solitary prayer, especially in times of trial. Family prayer, social prayer, or prayer in the church will not suffice. These are very precious, but the best devotions are held where no ear hears but God's. It was *humble prayer*. Luke says He knelt, but another evangelist says, "He. . .fell on His face." Humility gives us good foot-hold in prayer. There is no hope of prevalence with God unless we humble ourselves so that He may exalt us in due time. It was the prayer of a Son. "Abba, Father." You will find it a stronghold in the day of trial to plead your adoption. Do not be afraid to say, "My Father, hear my cry." Observe that it was *persevering prayer*. He prayed three times. Cease not until you prevail. Be as the persistent widow whose continual coming earned what her first supplication could not win. Continue in prayer and watch with thanksgiving. Lastly, *it was the prayer of resignation.* "Nevertheless, not as I will, but as thou wilt" (Luke 22:42). Yield, and God yields. Let it be as God wills, and God will determine the best. Be content to leave your prayer in His hands, who knows when to give, how to give, what to give, and what to withhold. So pleading, earnestly, yet with humility and resignation, you will surely prevail.

"His sweat was as it were great drops of blood falling down to the ground" (Luke 22:44).

The mental pressure on our Lord forced His frame to an unnatural excitement. His pores sent forth great drops of blood which fell down to the ground. This demonstrates the mighty power of His love. If men suffer great pain of mind, apparently, the blood rushes to the heart. The cheeks are pale; fainting may occur; the blood has gone inward, as if to nourish the inner man while passing through its trial. But see our Savior in His agony. He is so utterly oblivious of self that instead of His agony driving His blood to the heart to nourish Himself, it drives it outward. The agony of Christ, inasmuch as it pours Him out on the ground, pictures the fullness of the offering which He made for men. Do we not perceive how intense the wrestling must have been through which He passed, and will we not hear its voice to us? "Ye have not yet resisted unto blood, striving against sin" (Hebrews 12:4) Behold the great High Priest of our profession sweat blood rather than yield to the great tempter of your souls.

"He was heard in that he feared" (Hebrews 5:7).

Did this fear arise from the infernal suggestion that Jesus was utterly forsaken? There may be sterner trials than this, but surely it is one of the worst to be utterly forsaken. "See," said Satan, "You have a friend nowhere! Your Father has shut up the bowels of His compassion against You. Not an angel in His courts will stretch out his hand to help You. All heaven is alienated from You. Son of Mary, see Your brother James, see Your loved disciple John, and Your bold apostle Peter: how the cowards sleep when You are in your sufferings! You have no friend left in heaven or in earth. All hell is against You. I have stirred up my infernal den. I have sent my letters throughout all regions, summoning every prince of darkness to come against You this night. We will spare no arrows. We will use all our infernal might to overwhelm You. What will You do?" He was heard in that He feared. He was no more alone, but heaven was with Him. Jesus was heard in His deepest woe. My soul, you will be heard also.

"Betrayest thou the Son of man with a kiss" (Luke 22:48).

Be on guard when the world puts on a loving face, for it will betray you, as it did your Master, with a kiss. Whenever a man is about to stab religion, he usually professes very great reverence for it. Beware of the sleek-faced hypocrisy which is armor-bearer to heresy and infidelity. Knowing the deceivableness of unrighteousness, be wise as a serpent to detect and avoid the designs of the enemy. The young man, void of understanding, was led astray by the kiss of the strange woman. May your soul be so graciously instructed all this day that "the much fair speech" of the world may have no effect upon you! But what if you should be guilty of the same accursed sin as Judas, that son of perdition? You have been baptized into the name of the Lord Jesus. You are a member of His visible Church; you sit at His communion table. All these are so many kisses of my lips. Are you sincere in them? Do you live in the world as carelessly as others do, and yet make a profession of being a follower of Jesus? Surely you act inconsistently. You are a Judas. It would be better for you if you had never been born. O Lord, make us sincere and true. Preserve us from every false way. Never let us betray our Savior. We do love you, Jesus; and although we often grieve You, yet we desire to abide faithful even to death.

"Jesus said unto them, If ye seek me, let these go their way" (John 18:8).

Mark, my soul, the care Jesus manifested, even in His hour of trial, toward the sheep of His hand! The ruling passion is strong in death. He resigns Himself to the enemy, but He interposes a word of power to set His disciples free. As to Himself, like a sheep before her shearers, He is dumb and opens not His mouth. Yet, for His disciples' sake, He speaks with Almighty energy. This is love—constant, unselfish, faithful love. But is there more here than is to be found on the surface? Have we not the very soul and spirit of the atonement in these words? The Good Shepherd lays down His life for the sheep and pleads that they must therefore go free. The Surety is bound, and justice demands that those for whom He stands a substitute should go their way. In the midst of Egypt's bondage, that voice rings as a word of power, "Let these go their way." The redeemed must come out of the slavery of sin and Satan. In every cell of the dungeons of despair the sound is echoed, "Let these go their way." Satan hears the well-known voice and lifts his foot from the neck of the fallen. Death hears it, and the grave opens her gates to let the dead arise. Their way is one of progress, holiness, triumph, and glory, and none will dare to stop them in it. "The hind of the morning" has drawn the cruel hunters on himself, and now the most timid roes and hinds of the field may graze at perfect peace among the lilies of his loves. The thundercloud has burst over the Cross of Calvary, and the pilgrims of Zion will never be smitten by the bolts of vengeance. Come, rejoice in the immunity your Redeemer has secured for you, and bless His name all the day and every day.

"Then all the disciples forsook him and fled" (Matthew 26:56).

He never deserted them, but they, in cowardly fear of their lives, fled from Him in the very beginning of His sufferings. This is but one instance of the frailty of all believers if left to themselves. They are but sheep at best, and they flee when the wolf comes. They had all been warned of the danger and had promised to die rather than leave their Master. Yet, they were seized with sudden panic and took to their heels. It may be that I, at the opening of this day, have braced my mind to bear a trial for the Lord's sake, and I imagine myself to be certain to exhibit perfect fidelity. But let me be very jealous of myself, lest, having the same evil heart of unbelief, I should depart from my Lord as the apostles did. It is one thing to promise, and quite another to perform. It would have been to their eternal honor to have stood at Jesus' side. They fled from honor. May I be kept from imitating them! Where else could they have been so safe as near their Master who could easily call for twelve legions of angels? They fled from their true safety. O God, do not let me play the fool also. Divine grace can make the coward brave. These very apostles, who were timid as hares, grew to be bold as lions after the Spirit had descended on them. Even so, the Holy Spirit can make my spirit brave to confess my Lord and witness for His truth. What anguish must have filled the Savior as He saw His friends so faithless! This was one bitter ingredient in His cup, but that cup is drained dry. Let me not put another drop in it. If I forsake my Lord, I will crucify Him afresh and put Him to an open shame. Keep me, O blessed Spirit, from an end so shameful!

"The love of Christ, which passeth knowledge" (Ephesians 3:19).

The love of Christ passes all human comprehension. Words cannot describe His matchless love toward men. It is so vast and boundless that, as the swallow skims the water and dives not into its depths, so all descriptive words only touch the surface, while depths immeasurable lie beneath. Before we can have any right idea of the love of Jesus, we must understand His previous glory. But who can tell us the majesty of Christ? When He was enthroned in the highest heavens, He was very God of very God. By Him were the heavens made and all the hosts thereof. His own almighty arm upheld the spheres. The praises of cherubim and seraphim perpetually surrounded Him. The full chorus of the hallelujahs of the universe unceasingly flowed to the foot of His throne. He reigned supreme above all His creatures. God over all, blessed forever. And who, on the other hand, can tell how low He descended? To be a man was something, but to be a man of sorrows was far more. To bleed, to die, and to suffer were much for Him who was the Son of God. But to suffer such unparalleled agony and to endure a death of shame and desertion by His Father, this is a depth of condescending love which the most inspired mind must utterly fail to fathom.

"Though he were a Son, yet learned he obedience by the things which he suffered" (Hebrews 5:8).

The Captain of our salvation was made perfect through suffering. Therefore, we who are sinful and far from being perfect must not wonder if we are called to pass through suffering too. Will the head be crowned with thorns, and will the other members of the body be rocked on the dainty lap of ease? Must Christ pass through seas of His own blood to win the crown, and are we to walk to heaven in silver slippers? No, our Master's experience teaches us that suffering is necessary. But there is one very comforting thought in the fact of Christ's "being made perfect through suffering." It is that He can have complete sympathy with us. He is not a high priest who cannot be touched with the feelings of our infirmities. In this sympathy of Christ, we find a sustaining power. Believer, lay hold of this thought in all times of agony. Let the thought of Jesus strengthen you as you follow in His steps. Find a sweet support in His sympathy. Remember that to suffer is an honorable thing. To suffer for Christ is glory. The apostles rejoiced that they were counted worthy to do this. The Lord will give us grace to suffer *for* and *with* Christ. The jewels of a Christian are his afflictions. The regalia of the kings whom God has anointed are their troubles, their sorrows, and their griefs. "If we suffer, we shall also reign with him" (2 Timothy 2:12).

March 30

"He was numbered with the transgressors" (Isaiah 53:12).

This wonderful condescension was justified by many powerful reasons. In such a character He could better become their advocate. In some trials there is an identification of the counselor with the client. Now, when the sinner is brought to the court, Jesus appears there Himself. He stands to answer the accusation. He points to His side, His hands, His feet and challenges Justice to bring anything against the sinners whom He represents. He pleads His blood so triumphantly that the Judge proclaims, "Let them go their way; deliver them from going down into the pit, for He hath found a ransom." Our Lord Jesus was numbered with the transgressors in order that they might feel their hearts drawn toward Him. Who can be afraid of one who is written in the same list with us? Surely we may come boldly to Him and confess our guilt. He who is numbered with us cannot condemn us. He was holy, while we were guilty. He transfers His name from the list of the holy to this black indictment, and our names are taken from the indictment and written in the roll of acceptance. There is a complete transfer made between Jesus and His people. All our estate of misery and sin Jesus has taken, and all that Jesus has comes to us. Rejoice, believer, in your union to Him who was numbered among the transgressors. Prove that you are truly saved by being manifestly numbered with those who are new creatures in Him.

"With his stripes we are healed" (Isaiah 53:5).

Pilate delivered our Lord to the Roman officers to be scourged. The Roman scourge was a most dreadful instrument of torture. It was made of the sinews of oxen, and sharp bones were intertwined among the sinews so that every time the lash came down these pieces of bone inflicted terrible lacerations and tore off the flesh from the bone. The Savior was, no doubt, bound to the column and thus beaten. He had been beaten before, but this beating by the Roman officers was probably the most severe of His flagellations. My soul, stand here and weep over His poor stricken body. Believer in Jesus, can you gaze on Him without tears as He stands before you in the mirror of agonizing love? He is at once fair as the lily for innocence and red as the rose with the crimson of His own blood. As we feel the sure and blessed healing which His stripes have wrought in us, does not our heart melt at once with love and grief? If ever we have loved our Lord Jesus, surely we must feel that affection glowing now within our bosoms. Beloved, print the image of Your bleeding self on the tablets of our hearts all day, and at nightfall we will return to commune with You and feel sorrow that our sins have cost You so much.

April 1

"Let him kiss me with the kisses of his mouth" (Song of Solomon 1:2).

In beginning a new month, let us seek the same desires after our Lord as those which glowed in the heart of the elect spouse. See how she leaps at once to Him. She does not even mention His name. How bold is her love! It was much condescension which permitted the weeping woman to anoint His feet with spikenard. It was rich love which allowed the gentle Mary to sit at His feet and learn of Him. Esther trembled in the presence of Ahasuerus, but the spouse in joyful liberty of perfect love knows no fear. If we have received the same free spirit, we may ask the same question. By kisses, we mean those varied manifestations of affection by which the believer is made to enjoy the love of Jesus. The kiss of *reconciliation* we enjoyed at our conversion. The kiss of *acceptance* is still warm on our brow, as we know that He has accepted us and our works through rich grace. The kiss of daily *communion* is desired day after day, until it is changed into the kiss of *reception,* which removes the soul from earth, and the kiss of *consummation,* which fills it with the joy of heaven. Faith is our walk, but fellowship sensibly felt is our rest. Faith is the road, but communion with Jesus is the well from which the pilgrim drinks.

April 2

"He answered him to never a word" (Matthew 27:14).

He had never been slow of speech when He could bless the sons of men, but He would not say a single word for Himself. Never did a man speak like this man, and never was a man silent like Him. Was this singular silence the index of His perfect self-sacrifice? Did it show that He would not utter a word to stay the slaughter of His sacred person which He had dedicated as an offering for us? Had He so entirely surrendered Himself that He would not interfere in His own behalf, even in the minutest degree, but be bound and slain an unstruggling, uncomplaining victim? Nothing can be said to excuse human guilt; and, therefore, He who bore its whole weight stood speechless before His judge. Is not patient silence the best reply to a gainsaying world? Calm endurance answers some questions infinitely more conclusively than the loftiest eloquence. Did not the silent Lamb of God furnish us with a grand example of wisdom? Evidently our Lord, by His silence, furnished a remarkable fulfillment of prophecy. A long defense of Himself would have been contrary to Isaiah's prediction: "He is brought as a lamb to the slaughter, and as a sheep before her shearers is dumb, so he openeth not his mouth" (Isaiah 53:7). By His silence, He conclusively proved Himself to be the true Lamb of God. As such we salute Him this morning. Be with us, Jesus, and in the silence of our heart let us hear the voice of Your love.

April 3

"They took Jesus, and led him away" (John 19:16).

He had been in agony all night. He spent the early morning at the hall of Caiaphas. He had been hurried from Caiaphas to Pilate, from Pilate to Herod, and from Herod back again to Pilate. He had, therefore, little strength left, and neither refreshment nor rest was permitted Him. They were eager for His blood and led Him out to die, loaded with the cross. Do you recall how the high priest brought the scapegoat and put both his hands on its head, confessing the sins of the people that those sins might be laid on the goat and cease from the people? Then the goat was led away into the wilderness. It carried away the sins of the people. Now we see Jesus brought before the priests and rulers, who pronounce Him guilty. God Himself imputes our sins to Him: "The Lord hath laid on Him the iniquity of us all" (Isaiah 53:6). "He was made sin for us" (2 Corinthians 5:21). As the substitute for our guilt, bearing our sin on His shoulders, represented by the cross, we see the great Scapegoat led away by the appointed officers of justice. As you look at the cross on His shoulders, does it represent your sin? There is one way you can tell whether He carried your sin or not. Have you laid your hand on His head, confessed your sin, and trusted in Him? Then your sin does not lie on you. It has all been transferred to Christ, and He bears it on His shoulder as a load heavier than the cross.

April 4

"For he hath made him to be sin for us, who knew no sin; that we might be made the righteousness of God in him" (2 Corinthians 5:21).

Mourning Christian, why do you weep? Are you mourning over your own corruptions? Look to your perfect Lord, and remember you are complete in Him. You are in God's sight as perfect as if you had never sinned. More than that, the Lord our righteousness has put a divine garment on you so that you have more than the righteousness of man—you have the righteousness of God. You who are mourning by reason of inbred sin and depravity, remember, none of your sins can condemn you. You have learned to hate sin, but you have also learned that sin is not yours—it was laid on Christ's head. Your standing is not in yourself—it is in Christ. Your acceptance is not in yourself but in your Lord. You are as much accepted of God today, with all your sinfulness, as you will be when you stand before His throne, free from all corruption. Lay hold on this precious thought, *perfection in Christ!* For you are complete in Him. With your Savior's garment on, you are as holy as the Holy One. It is Christ who died and was risen again, who is at the right hand of God making intercession for us. When your time comes, you will rise up where Jesus sits and reign at His right hand, even as He has overcome and has sat down at His Father's right hand. All this because the divine Lord "was made to be sin for us, who knew no sin; that we might be made the righteousness of God in him" (2 Corinthians 5:21).

"On him they laid the cross, that he might bear it after Jesus" (Luke 23:26).

We see in Simon's carrying the cross a picture of the work of the Church throughout all generations. The Church is the cross-bearer after Jesus, and He did not suffer so as to exclude your suffering. He bears a cross, not that you may escape it, but that you may endure it. Christ exempts you from sin but not from sorrow. Remember that and expect to suffer. But let us comfort ourselves with this thought, that in our case, as in Simon's, it is not our cross but Christ's cross which we carry. When you are attacked for your piety, when your religion brings the trial of cruel mocking on you, then remember it is not your cross but Christ's cross which you carry. How delightful it is to carry the cross of our Lord Jesus! You carry the cross after Him. You have blessed company. Your path is marked with the footprints of your Lord. The mark of His blood-red shoulder is upon that heavy burden. It is His cross, and He goes before you as a shepherd goes before his sheep. Take up your cross daily and follow Him. Do not forget, also, that you bear this cross in partnership. You only carry the light end of the cross. Christ bore the heavier end. And remember, though Simon had to bear the cross for only a little while, it gave him lasting honor. Even so the cross we carry is only for a little while, and then we will receive the crown, the glory.

"Let us go forth therefore unto him without the camp" (Hebrews 13:13).

Jesus, bearing His cross, went forth to suffer. The Christian's reason for leaving the camp of the world's sin and religion is not because he loves to be different but because Jesus did so. The disciple must follow his Master. Christ was "not of the world." His life and His testimony were a constant protest against conformity with the world. Jesus would have His people go forth without the camp for their own sanctification. You cannot grow in grace to any high degree while you are conformed to the world. The life of separation may be a path of sorrow, but it is the highway of safety. The separated life may cost you many pangs, and make every day a battle, yet it is a happy life after all. No joy can excel that of the soldier of Christ. Jesus reveals Himself so graciously and gives such sweet refreshment that the warrior feels more calm and peace in his daily strife than others in their hours of rest. The highway of holiness is the highway of communion. It is thus we will hope to win the crown if we are enabled by divine grace faithfully to follow Christ without the camp. The crown of glory will follow the cross of separation. A moment's shame will be well recompensed by eternal honor. A little while of witness-bearing will seem nothing when we are forever with the Lord.

April 7

"O ye sons of men, how long will ye turn my glory into shame" (Psalm 4:2).

What honors did the blinded people of Israel award their long-expected King? (1.) They gave him a procession of honor in which Roman legionaries, Jewish priests, men and women, took a part, He Himself bearing His cross. This is the triumph which the world awards to Him who comes to overthrow man's direct foes. Shouts of ridicule are His only acclamations, and cruel taunts are His only praise. (2.) They presented Him with the wine of honor. Instead of a golden cup of generous wine, they offered Him the criminal's stupefying death-draught, which He refused. Afterwards when He cried, "I thirst" (John 19:28), they gave Him vinegar mixed with gall, thrust to His mouth on a sponge. Oh, what wretched, detestable inhospitality to the King's Son. (3.) He was provided with a guard of honor, who showed their esteem of Him by gambling over His garments, which they had seized as their booty. (4.) A throne of honor was found for Him on the bloody tree. The cross was, in fact, the full expression of the world's feeling toward Him. (5.) The title of honor was nominally "King of the Jews." But the blinded nation distinctly repudiated that title and really called Him "King of thieves" by placing Jesus in the place of highest shame between two thieves. His glory was thus in all things turned into shame by the sons of men, but it will yet gladden the eyes of saints and angels, world without end.

April 8

*"If they do these things in a green tree, what
shall be done in the dry"* (Luke 23:31).

When God saw Jesus in the sinner's place, He
did not spare Him. When He finds the unregenerate without Christ, He will not spare them. Oh,
sinner, Jesus was led away by His enemies; so will
you be dragged away to the place appointed for
you. Jesus was deserted by God; and if He, who
was only imputedly a sinner, was deserted, how
much more will you be! "Eloi, Eloi, lama,
sabachthani?" (See Mark 15:34.) What an awful
shriek! But what will be your cry when you say,
"O God! O God! Why have you forsaken me?" The
answer will come back, "Because ye have set at
nought all my counsel, and would none of my
reproof: I also will laugh at your calamity; I will
mock when your fear cometh" (Proverbs 1:25-
26). If God spared not His own Son, how much
less will He spare you! Self-righteous sinners, who
would stand in your place when God says, Awake,
O sword, against the man that rejected Me; smite
him, and let him feel the pain forever? Jesus was
spit on. Sinner, what shame will be yours? We
cannot sum up in one word all the mass of sorrows
which met on the head of Jesus, who died for us.
Therefore, it is impossible for us to tell you what
oceans of grief must roll over your spirit if you die
as you are now. By the agonies of Christ, by His
wounds and by His blood, do not bring on yourselves the wrath to come! Trust in the Son of God,
and you will never die.

April 9

"And there followed him a great company of people, and of women, which also bewailed and lamented him" (Luke 23:27).

Among the riotous mob which hounded the Redeemer to His doom, there were some gracious souls whose bitter anguish was released in wailing and lamentations—fit music to accompany that march of woe. When my soul can, in imagination, see the Savior bearing His cross to Calvary, it joins the godly women and weeps with them; for, indeed, there is true cause for grief. My sins were the scourges which lacerated those blessed shoulders and crowned those thorn-bleeding brow. My sins cried, "Crucify Him! Crucify Him!" and laid the cross on His gracious shoulders. His being led forth to die is sorrow enough for one eternity, but my having been His murderer is more grief than one poor fountain of tears can express. Why those women loved and wept is not hard to guess. They could not have had greater reasons for love and grief than my heart has. Nain's widow saw her son restored—but I myself have been raised to newness of life. Peter's wife's mother was cured of the fever—but I was healed of the greater plague of sin. Seven devils were cast out of Magdalene—but a whole legion were cast out of me. Mary and Martha were favored with visits—but He dwells with me. His mother bore His body—but He is formed in me the hope of glory. Let me not be behind the holy women in gratitude or sorrow.

April 10

"The place which is called Calvary" (Luke 23:33).

The hill of comfort is the hill of Calvary; the house of consolation is built with the wood of the cross; the temple of heavenly blessing is founded on the riven rock—riven by the spear which pierced His side. No scene in sacred history ever gladdens the soul like Calvary's tragedy. Light springs from the midday-midnight of Golgotha, and every herb of the field blooms sweetly beneath the shadow of the once accursed tree. In that place of thirst, grace has dug a fountain which ever gushes with waters pure as crystal, each drop capable of alleviating the woes of mankind. You who have had your seasons of conflict will confess that it was not at Olivet that you found comfort, not on the hill of Sinai, nor on Tabor; but Gethsemane, Gabbatha, and Golgotha have been a means of comfort to you. The bitter herbs of Gethsemane have often taken away the bitterness of your life; the scourge of Gabbatha has often scourged away your cares, and the groans of Calvary put all other groans to flight. Thus Calvary yields us comfort rare and rich. We never would have known Christ's love in all its heights and depths if He had not died. We could not guess the Father's deep affection if He had not given His Son to die.

"I am poured out like water, and all my bones are out of joint" (Psalm 22:14).

Did earth or heaven ever behold a sadder spectacle of woe? In soul and body, our Lord felt Himself to be weak as water poured on the ground. The placing of the cross in its socket had shaken Him with great violence, had strained all the ligaments, had pained every nerve, and more or less dislocated all His bones. Burdened with His own weight, the Sufferer felt the strain increasing every moment of those six long hours. His sense of faintness and general weakness was overpowering, while to His own consciousness He became nothing but a mass of misery and swooning sickness. How faint He must have been when He saw the dread vision of the wrath of God and felt it in His own soul! To us, sensations such as our Lord endured would have been insupportable, and kind unconsciousness would have come to our rescue. But in His case, He was wounded and felt the sword. He drained the cup and tasted every drop. As we kneel before our now ascended Savior's throne, let us remember well the way by which He prepared it as a throne of grace for us. Let us, in spirit, drink of His cup that we may be strengthened for our hour of heaviness whenever it may come.

"My heart is like wax; it is melted in the midst of my bowels" (Psalm 22:14).

Our blessed Lord experienced a terrible sinking and melting of soul. "The spirit of a man will sustain his infirmity, but a wounded spirit who can bear?" (Proverbs 18:14). Deep depression of spirit is the most grievous of all trials. Believer, humbly adore the King of glory as having more mental distress and inward anguish than anyone among us. As our faithful High Priest, He can be touched with a feeling of our infirmities. Especially let those of us whose sadness springs directly from the withdrawal of a present sense of our Father's love enter into near and intimate communion with Jesus. Do not give way to despair, since through this dark room the Master has passed before us. Our souls may sometimes long and faint and thirst to behold the light of the Lord's countenance. Come in, strong and deep love of Jesus, like the sea at the flood in spring tides, drown all my sins, wash out all my cares, lift up my earth-bound soul, and float it right up to my Lord's feet. There let me lie, a poor broken shell, washed up by His love, having no virtue or value. Only venturing to whisper to Him that if He will put His ear to me, He will hear within my heart faint echoes of the vast waves of His own love which have brought me where it is my delight to lie, even at His feet forever.

April 13

"A bundle of myrrh is my well-beloved unto me" (Song of Solomon 1:13).

Myrrh may well be chosen as the type of Jesus on account of its preciousness, its perfume, its pleasantness, its healing, preserving, disinfecting qualities, and its connection with sacrifice. But why is He compared to "a *bundle* of myrrh?" First, for *plenty*. He is not a drop of it; He is a treasure chest full. He is not a sprig or a flower of it, but a whole bundle. There is enough in Christ for all my necessities. "In him dwelleth all the fulness of the Godhead bodily" (Colossians 2:9). Everything needful is in Him. Take Jesus in His different characters, and you will see a marvelous variety—Prophet, Priest, King, Husband, Friend, Shepherd. View Him in His virtue, gentleness, courage, self-denial, love, faithfulness, truth, righteousness—everywhere He is a bundle of preciousness. He is a "bundle of myrhh" for *preservation*—not loose myrrh, to be dropped on the floor or trodden on, but myrrh tied up, myrrh to be stored in a treasure chest. We must value Him as our best treasure. We must prize His words and His ordinances. Moreover, Jesus is a "bundle of myrrh" for *speciality*. The emblem suggests the idea of distinguishing, discriminating grace. From before the foundation of the world, He was set apart for His people. He gives forth His perfume only to those who understand how to enter into communion with Him, and how to have close dealings with Him. Happy are you who can say, "A bundle of myrrh is my well-beloved unto me."

"All they that see me laugh me to scorn: they shoot out the lip, they shake the head" (Psalm 22:7).

Mockery was a great ingredient in our Lord's woe. Judas mocked Him in the garden; the chief priests and scribes laughed Him to scorn; Herod set Him at nought; the servants and the soldiers jeered at Him and brutally insulted Him; Pilate and his guards ridiculed His royalty; and on the tree, all sorts of horrid jests and hideous taunts were hurled at Him. Ridicule is always hard to bear, but when we are in intense pain, it is so heartless and cruel that it cuts us to the quick. Imagine the Savior crucified, racked with the anguish far beyond all mortal guess, and then picture that motley multitude, all wagging their heads or thrusting out their lips in bitterest contempt of one poor suffering victim! Surely there must have been something more in the crucified One than they could see, or else such a great and mingled crowd would not unanimously have honored Him with such contempt. Was it not evil confessing, in the very moment of its greatest apparent triumph, that after all it could do no more than mock at that victorious goodness which was then reigning on the cross? O Jesus, despised and rejected of men, how could You die for men who treated You so cruelly? We, too, have despised You in the days of our obstinance, and even since our new birth we have set the world on high in our hearts. Yet You bleed to heal our wounds and die to give us life.

April 15

"My God, my God, why hast thou forsaken me" (Psalm 22:1).

No other place so well shows the griefs of Christ as Calvary, and no other moment at Calvary is so full of agony as that in which His cry rends the air—"My God, my God, why hast thou forsaken me?" At this moment, physical weakness was united with acute mental torture from the shame and disgrace through which He had to pass. To make His grief culminate with emphasis, He suffered spiritual agony surpassing all expression, resulting from the departure of His Father's presence. This was the black midnight of His horror. It was then that He descended the abyss of suffering. No man can enter into the full meaning of these words. Some of us think at times that we could cry, "My God, my God, why hast thou forsaken me?" There are seasons when the brightness of our Father's smile is eclipsed by clouds and darkness, but let us remember that God never does really forsake us. It is only a *seeming* forsaking of us, but in Christ's case it was a *real* forsaking. In our case, our cry is often dictated by unbelief. In His case, it was the utterance of a dreadful fact, for God had really turned away from Him for a season. Since even the thought that He has forsaken us gives us agony, what must the woe of the Savior have been when He exclaimed, "My God, my God, why hast thou forsaken me?"

April 16

"The precious blood of Christ" (1 Peter 1:19).

Standing at the foot of the cross, we see hands, feet, and side, all distilling crimson streams of precious blood. It is "precious" because of its redeeming and atoning power. By it the sins of Christ's people are atoned for; they are redeemed from under the law; they are reconciled to God; they are made one with Him. Christ's blood is also "precious" in its cleansing power. It "cleanseth from all sin" (1 John 1:7). "Though your sins be as scarlet, they shall be as white as snow" (Isaiah 1:18). Through Jesus' blood there is not a spot left on any believer. The precious blood, which makes us clean, removes the stains of abundant iniquity and permits us to stand accepted in the Beloved, notwithstanding the many ways in which we have rebelled against our God! The blood of Christ is likewise "precious" in its preserving power. We are safe from the destroying angel under the sprinkled blood. Remember, it is God's *seeing* the blood that is the true reason for our being spared. The blood of Christ is "precious" also in its sanctifying influence. There is no motive for holiness so great as that which streams from the veins of Jesus. And "precious," unspeakably precious, is this blood, because it has an overcoming power. It is written, "They overcame through the blood of the Lamb" (Revelation 12:11). The blood of Jesus! Sin dies at its presence, death ceases to be death, and heaven's gates are opened.

"We are come to the blood of sprinkling, that speaketh better things than that of Abel" (Hebrews 12:24).

Reader, have *you* come to the blood of sprinkling? The question is not whether you have come to a knowledge of doctrine or an observance of ceremonies or to a certain form of experience, but have you come to the blood of Jesus? The blood of Jesus is the life of all vital godliness. If you have truly come to Jesus, we know how you came—the Holy Spirit sweetly brought you there. You came to the blood of sprinkling with no merits of your own. Guilty, lost, and helpless, you came to take that blood, and that blood alone, as your everlasting hope. You came to the cross of Christ with a trembling and an aching heart. Oh, what a precious sound it was for you to hear the voice of the blood of Jesus! The dropping of His blood is as the music of heaven to the penitent sons of earth. We are full of sin, but the Savior bids us lift our eyes to Him, and, as we gaze on His streaming wounds, each drop of blood, as it falls, cries, "It is finished; I have made an end of sin; I have brought in everlasting righteousness." Oh, sweet language of the precious blood of Jesus! If you have come to that blood once, you will come to it constantly. It is only by daily coming to Christ alone that you will find joy and comfort.

"She bound the scarlet line in the window"
(Joshua 2:21).

Rahab depended on the promise of the spies for her preservation. She looked on them as the representatives of the God of Israel. Her faith was simple and firm, but it was very obedient. To tie the scarlet line in the window was a trivial act in itself, but she dared not run the risk of omitting it. Come, my soul, is there not here a lesson for you? Have you been attentive to all your Lord's will, even though some of His commands should seem nonessential? Have you observed in His own way the two ordinances of believers' baptism and the Lord's Supper? Have I implicitly trusted in the precious blood of Jesus? Can I look out toward the Dead Sea of my sins, or the Jerusalem of my hopes, without seeing the blood? The passer-by can see a cord of a conspicuous color if it hangs from the window. It will be well for me if my life makes the atonement conspicuous to all onlookers. What is there to be ashamed of? Let men or devils gaze if they will. The blood is my boast and my song. My soul, there is One who will see that scarlet line, even when from weakness of faith you cannot see it yourself. Jehovah, the Avenger, will see it and pass over you. Jericho's walls fell flat. Rahab's house was on the wall, and yet it stood unmoved. My nature is built into the wall of humanity; and yet, when destruction smites the race, I will be secure. My soul, tie the scarlet thread in the window afresh and rest in peace.

"Behold, the veil of the temple was rent in twain from the top to the bottom" (Matthew 27:51).

The rending of so strong and thick a veil was not intended merely as a display of power—many lessons were taught us. The old law of ordinances was put away. When Jesus died, the sacrifices were all finished. That tear also revealed all the hidden things of the old dispensation: the mercy-seat could now be seen, and the glory of God gleamed forth above it. By the death of our Lord Jesus, we have a clear revelation of God. He was not like Moses who put a veil over his face. Life and immortality are now brought to light, and things which have been hidden since the foundation of the world are manifest in Him. The annual ceremony of atonement was thus abolished. The atoning blood, which was once every year sprinkled within the veil, was now offered once for all by the great High Priest. No blood of bullocks or of lambs is needed now, for Jesus has entered within the veil with His own blood. Access to God is now permitted and is the privilege of every believer in Christ Jesus. There is no small space laid open through which we may peer at the mercy-seat, but the tear reaches from the top to the bottom. We may come with boldness to the throne of the heavenly grace. Our Lord is the key to heaven. Let us enter in with Him into the heavenly places and sit with Him there until our common enemies are made His footstool.

"That through death he might destroy him that had the power of death" (Hebrews 2:14).

Child of God, cease to fear dying. Living near the cross of Calvary you may think of death with pleasure. Welcome it when it comes with intense delight. It is sweet to die in the Lord. It is a covenant-blessing to sleep in Jesus. Death is no longer banishment. It is a return from exile, a going home to the many mansions where the loved ones already dwell. The distance between glorified spirits in heaven and militant saints on earth seems great, but it is not so. We are not far from home—a moment will bring us there. How long will that soul be tossed on the waves before it comes to that sea which knows no storm? Listen to the answer: "Absent from the body, present with the Lord" (2 Corinthians 5:8). Like that ship of old, on the lake of Galilee, a storm had tossed it; but Jesus said, "Peace, be still," and immediately it came to the land. Do not think that a long period intervenes between the instant of death and the eternity of glory. When the eyes close on earth, they open in heaven. Child of God, what is there for you to fear in death, seeing that through the death of your Lord its curse and sting are destroyed? It is a Jacob's ladder whose foot is in the dark grave, but its top reaches to glory everlasting!

"I know that my Redeemer liveth" (Job 19:25).

The marrow of Job's comfort lies in that little word "my"—"my Redeemer," and in the fact that the Redeemer lives. Oh, to get hold of a living Christ. Do not be content until by faith you can say, "Yes, I cast myself on my living Lord, and He is mine." You may think it is presumption to say, "He lives as *my* Redeemer;" yet, remember, if you have but faith as a grain of mustard seed, that little faith entitles you to say it. But there is also another word here, expressive of Job's strong confidence—"I *know.*" To say, "I hope so, I trust so," is comfortable; and there are thousands in the fold of Jesus who hardly ever get much further. But to reach the essence of consolation you must say, "I know." Ifs and buts are sure murderers of peace and comfort. Doubts are dreary things in time of sorrow. If I have any suspicion that Christ is not mine, then there is vinegar mingled with the gall of death. But if I know that Jesus lives for me, then darkness is not dark. Even the night is light about me. Surely if Job, in those ages before the coming and advent of Christ, could say, "I know," we should not speak less positively. A living Redeemer, truly mine, is joy unspeakable.

"Him hath God exalted" (Acts 5:31).

Jesus, our Lord, once crucified, dead and buried, now sits on the throne of glory. The highest place that heaven affords is His by undisputed right. He is exalted at the Father's right hand. As Jehovah, He has eminent glories in which finite creatures cannot share. As the Mediator, He wears in heaven the honors which are the heritage of all the saints. It is delightful to reflect how close Christ's union is with His people. We are actually one with Him. We are members of His body, and His exaltation is our exaltation. He has a crown, and He gives us crowns too. He has a throne, but He is not content with having a throne to Himself. On His right hand there must be His bride arrayed in gold. He cannot be glorified without His bride. Look up to Jesus now. Let the eye of your faith behold Him with many crowns on His head. You will one day be like Him, when you will see Him as He is. You will not be as great as He is, or as divine, but you will still, in a measure, share the same honors and enjoy the same happiness and the same dignity which He possesses. Be content to live unknown for a little while. You will reign with Christ, for He has made us kings and priests unto God, and we will reign forever and ever. What a wonderful thought for the children of God! We have Christ for our glorious representative in heaven's courts now. Soon He will come and receive us to Himself, to be with Him there, to behold His glory, and to share in His joy.

"Nay, in all these things we are more than conquerors through him that loved us" (Romans 8:37).

We go to Christ for forgiveness, and then too often look to ourselves for power to fight our sins. Paul thus rebukes us: "O foolish Galatians, who hath bewitched you, that ye should not obey the truth? This only would I learn of you: Received ye the Spirit by the works of the law, or by the hearing of faith? Are ye so foolish? Having begun in the Spirit, are ye now made perfect by the flesh" (Galatians 3:1-3). Take your sins to Christ's cross, for the old man can only be crucified there. We are crucified with Him. For instance, how would you go about overcoming a bad temper? It is very possible you have never tried the right way of going to Jesus with it. How did I get salvation? I came to Jesus just as I was, and I trusted Him to save me. I must kill my angry temper in the same way. It is the only way I can ever kill it. I must go to the cross with it and say to Jesus, "Lord, I trust you to deliver me from it." This is the only way to give it a death-blow. Are you covetous? Do you feel the world entangling you? You may struggle against this evil as long as you please, but only the blood of Jesus will deliver you from your sinful ways. Give it to Christ. Your prayers, repentances, and tears—all of them put together—are worth nothing apart from Jesus. None but Jesus can do helpless sinners good—or helpless saints either. If you are to be a conqueror, it *must* be through Him.

"And because of all this we make a sure covenant" (Nehemiah 9:38).

There are many occasions when we may have a desire to renew our covenant with God. After recovery from sickness, when, like Hezekiah, we have had a new term of years added to our life, we may fitly do it. After any deliverance from trouble, when our joys bud forth anew, let us again visit the foot of the cross and renew our consecration. Especially, let us do this after any sin which has grieved the Holy Spirit or brought dishonor on the cause of God. Let us then look to that blood which can make us whiter than snow and again offer ourselves to the Lord. We should not only let our troubles confirm our dedication to God, but our prosperity should do the same. If we ever meet with occasions which deserve to be called "crowning mercies," then surely, if He has crowned us, we should also crown our God. If we would learn to profit by our prosperity, we would not need so much adversity. Have we received some blessing which we little expected? Has the Lord put our feet in a large room? Can we sing of His mercies? Then let us put our hand on the horns of the altar now and say, "Bind me here, my God; bind me here with cords forever." Let us make with Him a sure covenant because of our gratitude to Jesus.

"Rise up, my love, my fair one, and come away" (Song of Solomon 2:10).

I hear the voice of my Beloved! He speaks to me! He bids me, "Rise up," and well He may, for I have long enough been lying among the pots of worldliness. He is risen, and I am risen in Him. Why then should I cleave to the dust? From lower loves, desires, pursuits, and aspirations, I would rise toward Him. He calls me by the sweet title of "My love," and He counts me fair. If He has exalted me and thinks I am beautiful, how can I linger and find congenial associates among the sons of men? He bids me, "Come away." Farther and farther from everything selfish He calls me. "Come away" has no harsh sound to my ear, for what is there to hold me in this wilderness of vanity and sin? Oh, my Lord, I would, if it were possible, have neither eyes nor ears nor heart for sin. To come to You is to come home from exile, to come to land out of the raging storm, to come to rest after long labor, to come to the goal of my desires and the summit of my wishes. But Lord, how can a stone rise? How can a lump of clay come away from the horrible pit? Your grace can do it. Send Your Holy Spirit to kindle sacred flames of love in my heart, and I will continue to rise until I leave earthly life behind me and indeed come away.

"This do in remembrance of me" (1 Corinthians 11:24).

It appears almost impossible that those who have been redeemed by the blood of the dying Lamb and have been loved with an everlasting love by the eternal Son of God, would forget their gracious Savior. Forget Him who never forgot us? Forget Him who poured His blood forth for our sins? Forget Him who loved us even to the death? Can it be possible? Yes, it is not only possible, but conscience confesses that it is too sadly a fault with all of us, that we allow Him to be as wayfaring man tarrying but for a night. He whom we should make the abiding tenant of our memories is but a visitor. The cross where one would think that memory would linger, and unmindfulness would be an unknown intruder, is desecrated by the feet of forgetfulness. Do you find yourselves forgetful of Jesus? Some creature steals away your heart, and you are unmindful of Him. Some earthly business engrosses your attention when you should fix your eye steadily on the cross. It is the incessant turmoil of the world, the constant attraction of earthly things, which takes away the soul from Christ. We must be determined that whatever else we let slip through our fingers and from our minds, we will hold fast to Jesus.

April 27

"God, even our own God" (Psalm 46:6).

It is strange how little use we make of the spiritual blessings which God gives us, but it is stranger still how little use we make of God Himself. How seldom do we ask counsel of the Lord! How often do we go about our business without seeking His guidance! In our troubles how constantly we strive to bear our burdens ourselves, instead of casting them on the Lord that He may sustain us! This is not because we may not, for the Lord seems to say, "I am yours, soul; come and make use of Me as you will. You may freely come to My store; you are welcome." It is our own fault if we do not avail ourselves of our God. Since you have such a friend, and He invites you, draw from Him daily. There is no reason for lack while you have God to go to. Never fear or faint while you have God to help you. He can supply you with all. Let me urge you to make use of your God. Make use of Him in prayer. Go to Him often, because He is your God. Tell Him all your needs. Use Him by faith at all times. If some circumstance has clouded your way, use God as your direction. If some strong enemy has troubled you, find in Jehovah a shield; for He is guidance and protection to His people. If you have lost your way in the maze of life, use Him as a guide, for He will direct you. "God, even our own God, shall bless us."

"Remember the word unto thy servant, upon which thou hast caused me to hope" (Psalm 119:49).

Whatever your need may be, you may readily find a promise in the Bible regarding it. Are you weary? Here is the promise—"He giveth power to the faint" (Isaiah 40:29). When you read such a promise, take it back to the great Promiser, and ask Him to fulfill His own Word. Are you seeking Christ and thirsting for closer communion with Him? This promise shines like a star on you— "Blessed are they that hunger and thirst after righteousness, for they shall be filled" (Matthew 5:6). Take that promise to the throne continually. Go to God over and over again with this—"Lord, You said it; do as You said." Are you distressed because of sin and burdened with the heavy load of your iniquities? Listen to these words—"I, even I, am he that blotteth out thy transgressions, and will no more remember thy sins" (Isaiah 43:25). Are you afraid you may not be able to hold on until the end? If that is your state, take this word of grace to the throne and plead it: "The mountains shall depart, and the hills be removed; but my kindness shall not depart from thee" (Isaiah 54:10). If you have lost the sweet sense of the Savior's presence and are seeking Him with a sorrowful heart, remember the promises: "Return unto me, and I will return unto you" (Malachi 3:7). Base your faith on God's own Word. Whatever your fears or wants, go to your heavenly Father saying, "Remember the word unto thy servant, upon which thou hast caused me to hope."

"Thou art my hope in the day of evil" (Jeremiah 42:17).

The path of the Christian is not always bright with sunshine. He has his seasons of darkness and of storm. True, it is written in God's Word, "Her ways are ways of pleasantness, and all her paths are peace" (Proverbs 3:17). It is a great truth that trust in God brings a man happiness below as well as bliss above. Experience tells us that the course of the just is "as the shining light, that shineth more and more unto the perfect day" (Proverbs 4:18). Sometimes, however, that light is eclipsed. At certain periods, clouds cover the believer's sun, and he walks in darkness and sees no light. There are many who have rejoiced in the presence of God for a season. They have walked along the "green pastures" by the side of the "still waters," but suddenly they find the glorious sky is clouded. They say, "Surely, if I were a child of God, this would not happen." Oh, do not say this. The best of God's saints must experience trials. The dearest of His children must bear the cross. No Christian has enjoyed perpetual prosperity. Perhaps the Lord allotted you a smooth and unclouded path at first because you were weak and timid. Now that you are stronger in the spiritual life you must enter on the rougher experience of God's full-grown children. We need winds and tempest to exercise our faith, to tear off the rotten bough of self-dependence, and to root us more firmly in Christ. The day of evil reveals to us the value of our glorious hope.

April 30

"And all the children of Israel murmured" (Numbers 14:2).

There are murmurers among Christians now, as there were in the camp of Israel. There are those who, when the rod falls, cry out against the afflictive dispensation. They ask, "Why am I afflicted? What have I done to be chastened like this?" Allow me a word with you who murmur. Why should you murmur against the dispensations of your heavenly Father? Can He treat you more harshly than you deserve? Consider what a rebel you once were, but He pardoned you! Surely, if He in His wisdom sees fit to chasten you, you should not complain. Does not that proud, rebellious spirit of yours prove that your heart is not thoroughly sanctified? Those murmuring words are contrary to the holy, submissive nature of God's children. Is not the correction needed? But if you murmur against the chastening, take heed, for it will go hard with murmurers. But know one thing—"He doth not afflict willingly, nor grieve the children of men" (Lamentations 3:33). All His corrections are sent in love, to purify you, and to draw you nearer to Himself. Surely it must help you bear the chastening if you are able to recognize your Father's hand. For "whom the Lord loveth He chasteneth, and scourgeth every son whom He receiveth. If ye endure chastening, God dealeth with you as with sons" (Hebrews 12:6-7). "Neither murmur ye as some of them also murmured and were destroyed of the destroyer" (1 Corinthians 10:10).

"His cheeks are as a bed of spices, as sweet flowers" (Song of Solomon 5:13).

The flowery month is here! March winds and April showers have done their work, and the earth is clothed with beauty. To you the "beds of spices" are well known. You have often smelled the perfume of the "sweet flowers." Go at once to your Beloved and find in Him all loveliness and all joy. That cheek once so rudely smitten with a rod, often wet with tears of sympathy, and then defiled with spittle—that cheek, as it smiles with mercy, is a fragrant aroma to my heart. You did not hide Your face from shame and spitting, O Lord Jesus, and therefore I will find my dearest delight in praising You. Those cheeks were furrowed by the plow of grief and crimsoned with red lines of blood from Your thorn-crowned temples; such marks of love unbounded cannot but charm my soul far more than "pillars of perfume." In Jesus I find not only fragrance, but a bed of spices; not one flower, but all manner of sweet flowers. He is to me my rose and my lily, my hearts-ease and my cluster of camphor. When He is with me, it is May all year round. My soul goes forth to wash its happy face in the morning-dew of His grace and to solace itself with the singing of the birds of His promises. Precious Lord Jesus, let me know the blessedness which dwells in abiding, unbroken fellowship with You.

"I pray not that thou shouldest take them out of the world" (John 17:15).

It is a sweet and blessed event which will occur to all believers in God's own time—the going home to be with Jesus. In a few more years, the Lord's soldiers who are now fighting the good fight of faith will be through with conflict and enter into the joy of their Lord. But although Christ prays that His people may eventually be with Him where He is, He does not ask that they be taken at once from this world to heaven. He wishes them to stay here. He leaves us in His Father's hands, until, like shocks of corn fully ripe, we will each be gathered into our Master's garner. To abide in the flesh is needful for others, if not profitable for ourselves. Jesus asks that we be kept from evil, but He never asks for us to be admitted to the inheritance in glory until we are of full age. Christians often want to die when they have any trouble. Ask them why, and they will tell you, "Because we would be with the Lord." We fear it is not so much because they are longing to be with the Lord, as it is their desire to get rid of their troubles. Otherwise, they would feel the same wish to die at other times, when not under the pressure of trial. Now it is quite right to desire to depart, if we can do it in the same spirit that Paul did. To be with Christ is far better. But the wish to escape from trouble is a selfish one. Let your wish be to glorify God by your life here as long as He pleases. Even though it is in the midst of toil, conflict, and suffering, and allow Him to say when "it is enough."

"In the world ye shall have tribulation" (John 16:33).

Are you asking the reason for this, believer? Look upward to your heavenly Father and behold Him pure and holy. You are to be like Him one day. Will you be conformed to His image easily? Will you require much refining? Will it be an easy thing to get rid of your corruptions and make you perfect, even as your Father which is in heaven is perfect? Next, Christian, turn your eye downward. Do you know what foes you have beneath your feet? You were once a servant of Satan, and no king will willingly lose his subjects. Do you think that Satan will let you alone? No, he will always be at you, for he "goeth about like a roaring lion, seeking whom he may devour" (1 Peter 5:8). Expect trouble, Christian. Look around you. You are in an enemy's country, a stranger and a sojourner. The world is not your friend. If it is, then you are not God's friend, for he who is the friend of the world is the enemy of God. Be assured that you will find enemies everywhere. When you sleep, think that you are resting on the battlefield. When you walk, suspect an ambush in every hedge. As mosquitos are said to bite strangers more than natives, so will the trials of earth be sharpest to you. Lastly, look within your own heart and observe what is there. Sin and self are still within. Expect trouble. But do not despair because God said, "I will be with thee in trouble; I will deliver thee and honor thee" (Psalm 91:15).

"Shall a man make gods unto himself, and they are no gods?" (Jeremiah 41:20).

One great troublesome sin of ancient Israel was idolatry. Spiritual Israel, however, has a tendency to lean in the same direction. Self, in various forms, struggles to place the chosen ones under its dominion. Favorite children are often the cause of much sin in believers. The Lord is grieved when He sees us doting on them in the above measure. Spoiled children may live to be as great a curse to us as Absalom was to David. If Christians desire to grow thorns to stuff their sleepless pillows, let them dote on their dear ones. Why are we so vain? We pity the poor heathen who adores a god of stone, and yet we worship a god of flesh. Where is the vast superiority between a god of flesh and one of stone? The principle is the same in either case; only in ours, the crime is more aggravated because we have more light and sin in the face of it. The heathen bows to a false deity, but he has never known the true God. We commit two evils. We forsake the living God and turn to idols. May the Lord purge us all from this grievous iniquity.

"I will be their God, and they shall be my people" (2 Corinthians 6:16).

What a sweet title—"My people"! What a cheering revelation—"their God"! The whole world is God's. But of those He has chosen, whom He has purchased for Himself, He says what He does not say of others—"My people." In this word there is the idea of ownership. All the nations upon earth are His. The whole world is in His power. Yet, His people, His chosen, are His special possession. He has done more for them than others. He bought them with His blood. He brought them close to Himself. He has loved them with an everlasting love. Dear friends, can you, by faith, see yourselves in that number? Can you look up to heaven and say, "My Lord and my God?" Can you read your name written in precious blood? Can you, by humble faith, lay hold of Jesus' garments and say, "My Christ"? If you can, then God says of you and of others like you, "My people." If God is your God, and Christ is your Christ, the Lord pays special attention to you. You are the object of His choice, accepted in His beloved Son.

"We dwell in him" (1 John 4:13).

Do you want a house for your soul? Do you ask, "What is the price?" It is something less than proud human nature would like to give. It is without money and without price. Would you like to pay a respectable rent? Would you love to do something to win Christ? Then you cannot have the house, for it is without price. Will you take my Master's house on a lease for all eternity, with nothing to pay for it but the rent of loving and serving Him forever? Will you take Jesus and dwell in Him? See, this house is furnished with all you want. It is filled with more riches than you will spend as long as you live. Here you can have intimate communion with Christ and feast on His love. In it, when weary, you can find rest with Jesus. From it, you can look out and see heaven itself. Will you have the house? If you are houseless, you will say, "I would like to have the house. May I have it?" Yes, the key is, "Come to Jesus." "But," you say, "I am too shabby for such a house." Never mind, for there are garments inside. If you feel guilty and condemned, Christ will make you good enough for the house in time. He will wash you and cleanse you, and you will be able to sing, "We dwell in Him." Dwelling in Him, you have not only a perfect and secure house, but an everlasting one. When this world melts like a dream, our house will live and stand more imperishable than marble, more solid than granite, self-existent as God, for it is God Himself. "We dwell in him."

"Multitudes followed him, and he healed them all" (Matthew 12:15).

What a multitude of hideous sickness must have thrust itself under the eye of Jesus! Yet, we do not read that He was disgusted. What a variety of evils must have met at His feet! Yet, He was ready for every new shape of evil and was victor over it in every form. It did not matter if it was fever, palsy, madness, leprosy, or blindness—all knew the power of His word and fled at His command. It is even so this morning. Whatever my own case may be, the beloved Physician can heal me. Whatever may be the state of others whom I may remember in prayer, I have hope in Jesus that He will heal them of their diseases. My friend, I have hope for all when I remember the healing power of my Lord. He still dispenses His grace and works wonders among the sons of men. Let me go to Him at once in earnest. Let me praise Him this morning as I remember how He performed His spiritual cures by taking on Himself our sicknesses. "By his stripes we are healed" (Isaiah 53:5). The Church on earth is full of souls healed by our beloved Physician. The inhabitants of heaven itself confess that He healed them all. Come, then, publish abroad the virtue of His grace, and let it be "to the Lord for a name; for an everlasting sign which shall not be cut off" (Isaiah 55:13).

May 8

"He that was healed wist not who it was" (John 5:13).

Years are short to the happy and healthy, but thirty-eight years of disease must have dragged into a long time for the poor, impotent man. When Jesus healed him by a word while he lay at the pool of Bethesda, he was delightfully aware of a change. Likewise, the sinner who has been paralyzed with despair is very conscious of the change when the Lord Jesus speaks the word of power and gives joy and peace in believing. The evil removed is too great to be removed without our discerning it. The change brought about is too marvelous not to be noticed. Yet, the poor man was ignorant of the Author of his cure. He did not know the sacredness of His person on the errand which brought Him among men. We must not hastily condemn men for lack of knowledge. Where we can see the faith which saves the soul, we must believe that salvation has been bestowed. The Holy Spirit makes men penitent long before He makes them divine. Ignorance is, however, an evil. This poor man was tantalized by the Pharisees and was unable to cope with them. It is good to be able to answer opposition, but we cannot do so if we do not know the Lord Jesus clearly and with understanding. His ignorance, however, was soon cured when he was visited by the Lord in the temple. After that gracious manifestation, he was found testifying that it was Jesus who had made him whole.

"Who hath blessed us with all spiritual bless-ings" (Ephesians 1:3).

All the goodness of the past, the present, and the future, Christ bestows on His people. In the mysterious ages of the past, the Lord Jesus was His Father's first elect. He had from all eternity the prerogatives of Sonship. By adoption and regeneration, He has elevated us to Sonship also. The eternal covenant, based on suretyship and confirmed by oath, is ours. In the everlasting settlements of predestinating wisdom and omnipotent decree, the eye of the Lord Jesus was ever fixed on us. The marvelous incarnation of the God of heaven, with all the amazing condescension and humiliation which attended it, is ours. The bloody sweat, the scourge, and the cross are ours forever. Whatever blissful consequences flow from perfect obedience, finished atonement, resurrection, ascension, or intercession, are all ours by His own gift. Upon His breastplate He is now bearing our names. He employs His dominion over principalities and powers for those who trust in Him. His high estate is as much at our service as was His condition of abasement. He who gave Himself for us in the depths of woe and death, does not withdraw the grant now that He is enthroned in the highest heavens.

"But now is Christ risen from the dead" (1 Corinthians 15:20).

Christianity rests on the fact that Christ is risen from the dead. "If Christ be not risen, then is our preaching vain, and your faith is also vain. . . .ye are yet in your sins" (1 Corinthians 15:14-17). The divinity of Christ finds its surest proof in His resurrection, since He was "declared to be the Son of God with power, according to the spirit of holiness, by the resurrection from the dead" (Romans 1:4). Christ's sovereignty and deity depends on His resurrection, "for to this end Christ both died, and rose, and revived, that he might be Lord both of the dead and living" (Romans 14:9). Our justification, that choice blessing of the covenant, is linked with Christ's triumphant victory over death and the grave. "He was delivered for our offenses, and was raised again for our justification" (Romans 4:25). Our very regeneration is connected with His resurrection. We are "begotten again unto a lively hope by the resurrection of Jesus Christ from the dead" (1 Peter 1:3). And most certainly our ultimate resurrection rests here. "If the Spirit of him that raised up Jesus from the dead dwell in you, he that raised up Christ from the dead shall also quicken your mortal bodies by his Spirit that dwelleth in you" (Romans 8:11). If Christ is not risen, then we will not rise. But if He is risen, then they who are asleep in Christ have not perished, but in their flesh will surely behold their God. The silver thread of resurrection runs through all the believer's blessings, from his regeneration onward to his eternal glory, and binds them together.

"I am with you alway" (Matthew 28:20).

It is good to know there is One who is always the same and who is always with us. It is good there is one stable rock in the midst of the billows of the sea of life. Oh, my soul, set not your affections on rusting, moth-eaten, decaying treasures, but set your heart on Him who abides forever faithful to you. Do not build your house on the moving quicksands of a deceitful world, but found your hopes on this Rock which stands immovably secure. Put everything in Christ. Set all your affections on His person, all your hope in His merit, all your trust in His efficacious blood, and all your joy in His presence so you may laugh at loss and defy destruction. Remember that the day is coming when nothing will be left but the black, cold earth. Death's extinguisher must soon put out your candle. Oh, how sweet to have sunlight when the candle is gone! The dark flood must soon roll between you and all you have. Wed your heart then to Him who will never leave you. Trust yourself to Him who will go with you through the black and surging current of death's stream, will land you safely on the celestial shore, and will make you sit with Him in heavenly places forever. Tell your secrets to the Friend who sticks closer than a brother. Trust all your concerns to Him who never can be taken from you, who will never leave you, and who will never let you leave Him, even "Jesus Christ, the same yesterday, and today, and forever" (Hebrews 13:8). "Lo, I am with you alway" (Matthew 28:20) is enough for my soul to live on.

May 12

"And will manifest myself to him" (John 14:21).

The Lord Jesus gives special revelations of Himself to His people. Even if Scripture did not declare this, there are many of the children of God who could testify to the truth of it from their own experience. In the biographies of eminent saints, you will find many instances recorded in which Jesus has been pleased, in a very special manner, to speak to their souls and to unfold the wonders of His person. Their souls have been so steeped in happiness that they thought themselves to be in heaven. Even though they were not there, they were on the threshold of it. When Jesus manifests Himself to His people, it has a holy influence on the believer's heart. One effect will be *humility*. If a man says, "I have had such and such spiritual communications, I am a great man," he has never had any communion with Jesus at all. "God hath respect unto the lowly; but the proud he knoweth afar off" (Psalm 138:6). Another effect will be *happiness;* for in God's presence there are pleasures forevermore. *Holiness* will be sure to follow. A man who has no holiness has never had this manifestation. Some men profess a great deal, but we must not believe anyone unless we see that his deeds answer to what he says. "Be not deceived, God is not mocked" (Galatians 6:7). He will not bestow His favors upon the wicked. While He will not cast away a perfect man, neither will He respect an evildoer.

"Weeping may endure for a night, but joy cometh in the morning" (Psalm 30:5).

Christian, if you are in a time of trial, think of the future. Lift up your heart with the thought of the coming of your Lord. Be patient because He comes with clouds descending. Be patient! The Husbandman waits until He reaps His harvest. Jesus has said, "Behold, I come quickly; and my reward is with me, to give to every man according as his work shall be" (Revelation 22:12). Your life may be full of troubles now, but it will soon be free from care. Your garments may be soiled with dust now, but they will be white soon. Wait a little longer. How trivial our trials will seem when we look back on them! Looking at them here in the present, they seem immense. Let us go on boldly. If the night is dark, the morning is coming, which is more than they can say who are shut up in the darkness of hell. Do you know what it is to live on expectation—to anticipate heaven? Happy believer, it may be all dark now, but it will soon be light. It may be all trial now, but it will soon be all happiness! What does it matter though "weeping may endure for a night," when "joy cometh in the morning"?

"Joint heirs with Christ" (Romans 8:17).

As heir of all things, Jesus is the sole proprietor of the vast creation of God. He has permitted us to claim the whole world as ours by virtue of that deed of joint-heirship which the Lord has ratified with His chosen people. The golden streets of paradise, the pearly gates, the river of life, the transcendent bliss, and the unutterable glory are, by our blessed Lord, given to us for our everlasting possession. All that He has He shares with His people. Crown the head, and the whole body shares the honor. Behold here is the reward of every Christian conqueror! Christ's throne, crown, scepter, palace, treasure, robes, and heritage are yours. Christ deems His happiness completed by His people sharing it. "The glory which thou gavest me have I given them" (John 17:22). "These things have I spoken unto you, that my joy might remain in you, and that your joy might be full" (John 15:11). The honors of His Kingdom are more pleasing, because His people appear with Him in glory. More valuable to Him are His conquests, since they have taught His people to overcome. He delights in His throne because on it there is a place for them. He rejoices in His royal robes, since over them His skirts are spread. He delights all the more in His joy because He calls them to enter into it.

"All that believe are justified" (Acts 13:39).

The believer in Christ receives a present justification. Faith does not produce this fruit by and by, but now. Since justification is the result of faith, it is given to the soul in the moment when it accepts Him. Are they who stand before the throne of God justified now? So are we, as truly and as clearly justified as they who walk in white and sing melodious praises to celestial harps. The thief on the cross was justified the moment he turned the eye of faith to Jesus. Paul the aged, after years of service, was not more justified than was the thief with no service at all. We are *today* accepted in the Beloved, *today* absolved from sin, *today* acquitted. God supplies us in our journeying to and fro. We are pardoned *now*; *now* our sins are put away; *now* we stand in the sight of God accepted as though we had never been guilty. "There is therefore now no condemnation to them which are in Christ Jesus" (Romans 8:1). There is not a sin in the Book of God, even now, against one of His people. Who can lay anything to their charge? There is neither speck nor spot nor wrinkle nor any such thing remaining on any believer. Let present privilege awaken us to present duty; and now, while life lasts, let us spend and be spent for our sweet Lord Jesus.

"Who giveth us richly all things to enjoy" (1 Timothy 6:17).

Our Lord Jesus is ever giving and does not for a solitary instant withdraw His hand. As long as there is a vessel of grace not yet full to the brim, the oil will not stop. The rain of His grace is always dropping. The river of His bounty is ever-flowing, and the well-spring of His love is constantly overflowing. As the King can never die, so His grace can never fail. Daily we pluck His fruit, and daily His branches bend down to our hand with a fresh store of mercy. There are seven feast days in His weeks. Who has ever returned from His door unblessed? Who has ever risen from His table unsatisfied? His mercies are new every morning and fresh every evening. Who can know the number of His benefits or recount the list of His bounties? The countless stars are like the standard bearers of a more innumerable host of blessings. Who can count the dust of the benefits which He bestowed on Jacob or tell the number of the fourth part of His mercies toward Israel? How will my soul extol Him who daily loads us with benefits and who crowns us with lovingkindness? Oh, that my praise could be as ceaseless as His bounty!

"So to walk even as he walked" (1 John 2:6).

Why should Christians imitate Christ? They should do it for *their own sakes*. If they desire to be in a healthy state of soul—if they would escape the sickness of sin and enjoy the vigor of growing grace, let Jesus be their model. There is nothing which can so assist you to walk toward heaven with good speed, as wearing the image of Jesus on your heart to rule all its actions. It is when, by the power of the Holy Spirit, you are enabled to walk with Jesus in His very footsteps, that you are most happy and most known to be the sons of God. Next, for *faith's sake,* strive to be like Jesus. Faith has been sorely shot at by cruel enemies but has not been wounded half as dangerously by its enemies as by its friends. Who made those wounds in the fair hand of godliness? The professor who used the dagger of hypocrisy. The man who enters the fold, being nothing but a wolf in sheep's clothing, and worries the flock more than the lion outside. There is no weapon half as deadly as a Judas-kiss. Inconsistent professors injure the gospel more than the sneering critic or the infidel. But especially for *Christ's own sake*, imitate His example. Christian, do you love your Savior? Is His name precious to you? Would you see the kingdom of the world become His? Is it your desire that He should be glorified? Are you longing for souls to be won to Him? If so, imitate Jesus. Be an epistle of Christ, known and read of all men.

"In him dwelleth all the fulness of the God-head bodily. And ye are complete in him" (Colossians 2:9-10).

All the attributes of Christ, as God and man, are at our disposal. He cannot endow us with the attributes of deity, but He has done all that can be done. How vast His grace, how firm His faithfulness, how unchangeable, how infinite His power, how limitless is His knowledge! All these are made the pillars of the temple of salvation by the Lord Jesus, and all are covenanted to us as our inheritance. The whole of Christ, in His adorable character as the Son of God, is given to us to enjoy. His wisdom is our direction, His knowledge our instruction, His power our protection, His justice our surety, His love our comfort, and His mercy our solace. He holds back nothing from us. Instead, He opens the recesses of the Mountain of God and bids us dig in the mines for the hidden treasures. "Everything is yours," He says, "Be filled and satisfied with the goodness of the Lord." Oh, how sweet to behold Jesus and to call on Him with the certain confidence that in seeking His love or power, we are only asking for what He already faithfully promised!

"I have seen servants upon horses, and princes walking as servants upon the earth" (Ecclesiastes 10:7).

Upstarts frequently usurp the highest places, while the truly great pine away in obscurity. This is a riddle in providence whose solution will one day gladden the hearts of the upright, but it is a common fact that none of us should murmur if it should fall to our own lot. When our Lord was on earth, He walked the footpath of weariness and service as the Servant of servants. The world is upside down. Therefore, the first are last, and the last first. When the wheel turns, those who are lowest rise, and the highest sink. Have patience believer! Eternity will right the wrongs of time. Grace must reign as a prince and make the members of the body instruments of righteousness. The Holy Spirit loves order, and He therefore sets our powers and faculties in due rank and place, giving the highest room to those spiritual faculties which link us with the great King. Let us not disturb the divine arrangement but ask for grace that we may keep our bodies under subjection. We were not recreated to allow our passions to rule over us, but that we, as kings, may reign in Christ Jesus over the triple kingdom of our spirit, soul, and body, to the glory of God the Father.

"Marvellous lovingkindness" (Psalm 17:7).

When we give our hearts with our alms, we give well; but we often fail in this respect. Not so our Master and our Lord. His favors are always performed with the love of His heart. He does not send us the cold meat and the broken pieces from the table of His luxury. Instead, He dips our morsel in His own dish, seasoned with the spices of His fragrant affections. He will come into our homes on His errands of kindness and will not act as some visitors do in the poor man's cottage. He will sit by our side and not despise our poverty. What comforting words come from His gracious lips! What embraces of affection He bestows upon us! It is impossible to doubt the sincerity of His love, for there is a bleeding heart stamped on the face of all His charitable donations. He gives liberally and upbraideth not with not one hint that we are burdensome to Him. He instead rejoices in His mercy and presses us to His bosom while He is pouring out His life for us. There is a sweetness in His honeycomb which could not be in it unless the very essence of His soul's affection had been mingled with it. May we continually taste and know the blessedness of it!

"If so be ye have tasted that the Lord is gracious" (1 Peter 2:3).

"If"—then there is a possibility that some may not have tasted that the Lord is gracious. There is no spiritual favor which is not a matter for heart searching. But while this should be a matter of earnest and prayerful inquiry, no one should be content while there is any such thing as an "if" about his having tasted that the Lord is gracious. A jealous and holy distrust of self may give rise to the question even in the believer's heart, but the continuance of such a doubt would be an evil. We must not rest without a desperate struggle to clasp the Savior in the arms of faith and say, "I know whom I have believed, and I am persuaded that he is able to keep that which I have committed unto him" (2 Timothy 1:12). Let nothing satisfy you until, by the infallible witness of the Holy Spirit bearing witness with your spirit, you are certified that you are a child of God. Do not trifle here. Let no "perhaps" or "if" or "maybe" satisfy your soul. Get the sure mercies of David. Advance beyond these dreary "ifs." Abide no more in the wilderness of doubts and fears. Cross the Jordan of distrust and enter the Canaan of peace, where the Canaanite still lingers, but where the land does not cease to flow with milk and honey.

"He led them forth by the right way" (Psalm 107:7).

Changes often lead the anxious believer to inquire, "Why is it like this with me? I looked for light, but darkness came. I looked for peace but experienced trouble. I said in my heart, 'My mountain stands firm; I will never be moved.' It was only yesterday that I could read my title clear. Today, my hopes are clouded. Is this part of God's plan for me? Can this be the way in which God would bring me to heaven?" Yes, it could be. The eclipse of your faith, the darkness of your mind, the fainting of your hope—all these things are part of God's method of making you ready for the great inheritance which you will soon receive. These trials are for the testing and strengthening of your faith—they are waves that wash you farther upon the rock—they are winds which waft your ship more swiftly toward the desired haven. According to David's words, so it might be said of you, "So he bringeth them to their desired haven" (Psalm 107:30). By honor and dishonor, by evil report and by good report, by plenty and by poverty, by joy and by distress, by persecution and by peace, by all these things is the life of your soul maintained. Do not think, believer, that your sorrows are out of God's plan; they are necessary parts of it. "We must, through much tribulation, enter the kingdom" (Acts 14:22). Learn then to "count it all joy when ye fall into divers temptations" (James 1:2).

"The Lord will perfect that which concerneth me" (Psalm 138:8).

The confidence which the psalmist expressed here was a divine confidence. He did not say, "I have grace enough to perfect that which concerneth me—my faith is so steady that it will not stagger—my love is so warm that it will never grow cold—my resolution is so firm that nothing can move it." No, his dependence was on the Lord alone. If we indulge in any confidence which is not grounded on the Rock of Ages, our confidence is worse than a dream. It will fall on us and cover us with its ruins, to our sorrow and confusion. All that nature spins, time will unravel, to the eternal confusion of all who are clothed therein. The psalmist was wise. He rested on nothing short of the Lord's work. It is the Lord who has begun the good work within us. It is He who has carried it on. If He does not finish it, it never will be complete. This is our confidence, the Lord who began will perfect. Our confidence must not be in what *we* have done, but entirely in what *the Lord* will do. Unbelief insinuates that You will never be able to stand. Yes, we would indeed perish if left to our own strength. But thanks be to God, He will perfect that which concerns us and bring us to the desired haven. We can never be too confident when we confide in Him alone.

"Blessed be God, which hath not turned away my prayer" (Psalm 66:20).

In looking back on the character of our prayers, if we do it honestly, we will be filled with wonder that God ever answered them. There may be some who think their prayers are worthy of acceptance—as the Pharisee did. The true Christian, in a more enlightened retrospect, weeps over his prayers. If he could retrace his steps, he would desire to pray more earnestly. Remember, Christian, how cold your prayers have been. In your prayer closet you should have wrestled as Jacob did. Instead, your petitions have been faint and few—far removed from that humble, believing, persevering faith which cries, "I will not let thee go except thou bless me" (Genesis 32:26). Yet, wonderful to say, God has heard these cold prayers of yours. Not only has He heard, but He has answered them. Reflect, also, how infrequently you have prayed. God has not ceased to bless. It is marvelous that the Lord should regard those intermittent prayers which come and go with our necessities. What a God He is to hear the prayers of those who come to Him when they have pressing needs but neglect Him when they have received a mercy. They approach Him when they are forced to come but forget to address Him when mercies are plentiful and sorrows are few! Let His gracious kindness in hearing such prayers touch our hearts, so that we may henceforth be found "praying always with all prayer and supplication in the spirit" (Ephesians 6:18).

May 25

"Forsake me not, O Lord" (Psalm 38:21).

We frequently pray that God will not forsake us in times of trial and temptation, but we forget that we need to use this prayer at all times. There is no moment of our life, however holy, in which we can do without His constant upholding. Whether in light or in darkness, in communion or in temptation, we need the prayer, "Forsake me not, O Lord. Hold me up, and I shall be safe." A little child, while learning to walk, always needs aid. The ship left by the pilot drifts at once from her course. We cannot do without continued aid from above. Father, do not forsake Your child, lest he fall by the hand of the enemy. Shepherd, do not forsake Your lamb, lest he wander from the safety of the fold. Do not forsake me in my joys, lest they absorb my heart. Do not forsake me in my sorrows, lest I murmur against You. Do not forsake me, for without You I am weak, but with You I am strong. Do not forsake me, for my path is dangerous and full of snares. I cannot do without Your guidance. "Be not far from me, O Lord, for trouble is near, for there is none to help" (Psalm 22:11). "Leave me not, neither forsake me, O God of my salvation" (Psalm 27:9).

May 26

"Cast thy burden upon the Lord, and he shall sustain thee" (Psalm 55:22).

Worry, if carried to excess, has the nature of sin in it. The precept to avoid worry is repeated frequently by our Savior. It is reiterated by the apostles. It is a principle which cannot be neglected without involving transgression. We labor to take on ourselves our weary burden, as if He were unable or unwilling to take it for us. This disobedience to His principle, this unbelief in His Word, is all sinful. More than this, worry often leads to acts of sin. He who cannot calmly leave his affairs in God's hand is very likely to be tempted to use wrong means to help himself. This sin leads to forsaking God as our Counselor and resorting instead to human wisdom. This is going to the "broken cistern" instead of to the "fountain;" a sin which was laid against Israel of old. Anxiety makes us doubt God's lovingkindness, and our love for Him grows cold. We feel mistrust and grieve the Spirit of God, so that our prayers become hindered, our consistent example marred, and our life one of self-seeking. Thus, lack of confidence in God leads us to wander far from Him. If we cast each burden as it comes on Him and we are "careful for nothing" because He undertakes to care for us, it will keep us close to Him and strengthen us against such temptation. "Thou wilt keep him in perfect peace whose mind is stayed on thee because he trusteth in thee" (Isaiah 26:3).

"So Mephibosheth dwelt in Jerusalem: for he did eat continually at the king's table; and was lame on both his feet" (2 Samuel 9:13).

Mephibosheth was no great ornament to a royal table, yet he had a continual place at David's table because the king could see in his face the features of the beloved Jonathan. Like Mephibosheth, we may cry to the King of Glory, "What is thy servant, that thou shouldst look upon such a dead dog as I am?" (2 Samuel 9:8). But still the Lord indulges us in communion with Himself, because He sees in our countenances the remembrance of His dearly-beloved Jesus. Such is the love which the Father bears to His only begotten. For His sake He raises His lowly brethren from poverty to courtly companionship, noble rank, and royal provision. Their deformity shall not rob them of their privileges. Lameness is no bar to sonship. The cripple is as much the heir as if he could run like Asahel. Yet, grievous disability may mar the persons of the best-loved saints. Saints whose faith is weak and whose knowledge is slender are great losers. They are exposed to many enemies and cannot follow the king everywhere he goes. Bad nursing in their spiritual infancy often causes converts to fall into a despondency from which they never recover. Lord, help the lame to leap like a hart and satisfy all Your people with the bread of your table!

"Whom he justified, them he also glorified" (Romans 8:30).

Believer, here is a precious truth for you. You may be poor or suffering, but for encouragement take a review of your "calling" and the consequences that flow from it. Especially that blessed result spoken of here. As surely as you are God's child today, so surely will all your trials be at an end. Your weary head will wear the crown of glory, and hand of labor will grasp the palm branch of victory. Do not lament your troubles, but rather rejoice that before long you will be where "there shall be neither sorrow nor crying, neither shall there be any more pain" (Revelation 21:4). The chariots of fire are at your door, and a moment will suffice to bear you to the glorified. The everlasting song is almost on your lips. The portals of heaven stand open for you. If He has called you, nothing can divide you from His love. Distress cannot sever the bond. The fire of persecution cannot burn the link. The hammer of hell cannot break the chain. You are secure. That voice which called you at first will call you again from earth to heaven, from death's dark gloom to immortality's unuttered splendors. Rest assured; the heart of Him who has justified you beats with infinite love toward you. You will soon be with the glorified, where your portion is. You are only waiting here to be made meet for the inheritance. Once that is done, the wings of angels will lift you far away to the mount of peace, joy, and blessedness where you will rest forever and ever.

"Thou hatest wickedness" (Psalm 45:7).

Be ye angry and sin not. There can hardly be goodness in a man if he is not angry at sin. He that loves truth must hate every false way. How our Lord Jesus hated it when the temptation came. Three times it assailed Him in different forms, but He met it with "Get thee behind me, Satan" (Mark 8:33). He hated it when temptation came to others. He showed His hate more often in tears of pity than in words of rebuke. Yet, what language could be more stern, more Elijah-like, than the words, "Woe unto you, Scribes and Pharisees, hypocrites! for ye devour widows' houses, and for a pretense make long prayers" (Matthew 23:14). He hated wickedness so much that He bled on the cross to destroy it. He rose that He might forever trample it beneath His feet. Christ is in the gospel, and that gospel is opposed to wickedness in every shape. Wickedness arrays itself in fair garments and imitates the language of holiness. But the precepts of Jesus, like His famous scourge of small cords, chase it out of the temple and will not tolerate it in the Church. When our Redeemer comes to be our Judge, His words will manifest His abhorrence of iniquity. As perfect as is His righteousness, so complete will be the destruction of every form of wickedness. Oh, glorious champion of right and destroyer of wrong, for this cause has God, even your God, anointed you with the oil of gladness.

"Take us the foxes, the little foxes that spoil the vines" (Song of Solomon 2:15).

A little thorn may cause much suffering. A little cloud may hide the sun. Little foxes spoil the vines, and little sins do mischief to the tender heart. These little sins burrow in the soul and make it full of that which is hateful to Christ, so that He will hold no comfortable fellowship and communion with us. A great sin cannot destroy a Christian, but a little sin can make him miserable. Jesus will not walk with His people unless they drive out every known sin. He says, "If ye keep my commandments, ye shall abide in my love, even as I have kept my Father's commandments and abide in his love" (John 15:10). Some Christians very seldom enjoy their Savior's presence. Why is this? Surely it must be an affliction for a tender child to be separated from his father. How can you be the spouse of Christ and be content without His company? Ask the question—What has driven Christ from me? If you want to live with Christ, walk with Christ, and have fellowship with Christ, take heed of the little foxes that spoil the vines. Our vines have tender grapes. Jesus invites you to go with Him. He will surely, like Samson, easily take the foxes at once. Go with Him to the hunting.

"The king also himself passed over the brook Kidron" (2 Samuel 15:23).

David passed that gloomy brook when fleeing from his traitor son. The man after God's own heart was not exempt from trouble. In fact, his life was full of it. He was both the Lord's anointed and the Lord's afflicted. Why then should we expect to escape? Why should we complain as though some strange thing had happened to us? The King of kings Himself was not favored with a more cheerful or royal road. He passed over the filthy ditch of Kidron through which the filth of Jerusalem flowed. God had one Son without sin, but not a single child without the rod. It is a great joy to believe that Jesus has been tempted in all points like we are. What is our Kidron this morning? Is it a faithless friend, a sad bereavement, or a slanderous reproach? The King has passed over all these. Is it bodily pain, poverty, persecution, or contempt? Over each of these Kidrons, the King has gone before us. "In all our afflictions he was afflicted" (Isaiah 63:9). The idea of strangeness in our trials must be banished at once and forever. He, who is the Head of all saints, knows by experience the grief which we think so peculiar. David's Lord arose victorious from the grave. Let us then be of good courage, for we will be victorious also. We will draw water out of the wells of salvation with joy, though for a season we have to pass by the noxious streams of sin and sorrow. Have courage, soldiers of the Cross. The King Himself triumphed after going over Kidron, and so will you.

"The evening and the morning were the first day" (Genesis 1:5).

Did light and darkness divide the realm of time in the first day? Then little wonder is it if I also have changes in my circumstances from the sunshine of prosperity to the midnight of adversity. I must expect at seasons to mourn the absence of my former joys and to seek my Beloved in the night. I'm not alone in this, for all the Lord's beloved ones have had to sing the mingled song of judgment and of mercy, of trial and deliverance, of mourning and of delight. It is one of the arrangements of divine providence that day and night will not cease, either in the spiritual or natural creation, until we reach the land of which it is written, "There is no night there" (Revelation 22:5). What our heavenly Father ordains is wise and good. What then, my soul, is best for you to do? Learn first to be content with this divine order. Praise the Lord for the sun of joy when it rises and for the gloom of evening as it falls. There is beauty both in sunrise and sunset. Like the nightingale, pour forth your notes at all hours. Believe that the night is as useful as the day. The stars of promise shine forth gloriously amid the darkness of grief. Continue your service under all changes. Continue in your calling as the Lord's servant until He suddenly appears in His glory.

"For the flesh lusteth against the Spirit, and the Spirit against the flesh" (Galatians 5:17).

There is a constant struggle between the old nature and the new in every believer's heart. The old nature is very active and loses no opportunity of plying all the weapons of its deadly armory against new-born grace. On the other hand, the new nature is ever on the watch to resist and destroy its enemy. Grace within us will employ prayer, faith, hope, and love to cast out evil. It puts on the "whole armor of God" and wrestles earnestly. These two opposing natures will never cease to struggle so long as we are in this world. With Jesus, who is always with us, the new-born nature is more than a match for its foes. Are you fighting with the adversary today? Are Satan, the world, and the flesh all against you? Do not be discouraged. Fight on! For God Himself is with you. *Jehovah Nissi* is your banner, and *Jehovah Rophi* is the healer of your wounds. You will overcome, for who can defeat omnipotence? Fight on, looking to Jesus. Although the conflict may be long and hard, the victory will be sweet. Jesus, the Captain of our salvation, assures us that we will eventually become more than conquerors through Him who loves us.

"These were potters, and those that dwelt among plants and hedges: there they dwelt with the king for his work" (1 Chronicles 4:23).

Potters were not the very highest grade of workers, but the king needed potters. Therefore, they were in royal service even though the material they worked on was nothing but clay. We, too, may be engaged in the most menial part of the Lord's work, but it is a great privilege to do anything for the King. Those who dwelt among plants and hedges had rough, rustic, hedging and ditching work to do. They may have desired to live in the city amid its refinement, but they kept their appointed places because they also were doing the king's work. The place of our habitation is fixed. We are not to leave it out of whim, but we are to seek to serve the Lord in it by being a blessing to those among whom we reside. These potters and gardeners had royal company, for they dwelt with the king. No menial occupation can keep us from communion with our divine Lord. In visiting crowded dwellings, workplaces, or jails, we may go *with the King*. In all works of faith, we may count on Jesus' fellowship. When we are in His work, we are confident of His approval. You unknown workers who are occupied for your Lord amid the dirt and wretchedness of the lowest of the low, be of good cheer for jewels have been found on dunghills, earthen pots have been filled with heavenly treasure, and ill weeds have been transformed into precious flowers. Dwell with the King for His work, and when He writes His chronicles your name will be recorded.

June 4

"The kindness and love of God our Saviour" (Titus 3:4).

How sweet it is to behold the Savior communing with His own beloved people! Let your mind consider for an instant the history of the Redeemer's love, and a thousand acts of affection will suggest themselves. When we meditate on this amazing love, our soul may well faint for joy. Who can endure such a weight of love? That partial sense of it which the Holy Spirit is sometimes pleased to afford is more than the soul can contain. How glorious must be a complete view of it! When our soul is able to discern all the Savior's gifts, have wisdom to estimate them, and time to meditate upon them, we will then be able to commune with Jesus more closely. But who can imagine the sweetness of such fellowship? It may be one of the things which has not entered into the heart of man, but which God has prepared for them that love Him. Oh, to burst open the door of our Joseph's granaries and see the plenty which He has stored up for us! This will overwhelm us with love. By faith we see, as in a glass darkly, the reflected image of His unbounded treasures. But when we actually see the heavenly things themselves, with our own eyes, how deep will be the stream of fellowship in which our soul will bathe itself!

"The Lord shut him in" (Genesis 7:16).

Noah was shut in *away from all the world* by the hand of divine love. We are not of the world, even as our Lord Jesus was not of the world. We cannot enter into the sin and pursuits of the multitude. We cannot play with the children of darkness, for our heavenly Father has shut us in. Noah was shut in with his God. "Come thou into the ark" was the Lord's invitation by which He clearly showed that He Himself intended to dwell in the ark with His servant and his family. The chosen are enclosed in the same circle which contains God in the Person of the Father, Son, and Spirit. Let us never be inattentive to that gracious call. Come, my people, enter into your chambers. Shut your doors behind you and hide yourself for a little moment. Noah was so shut in that no evil could reach him. Floods only lifted him heavenward, and winds only wafted him on his way. Outside of the ark all was ruin, but inside all was rest and peace. Without Christ we perish, but in Christ Jesus there is perfect safety. Noah was so shut in that he did not even desire to come out. Those who are in Christ Jesus are in Him forever. Eternal faithfulness has shut them in. In the last days, the Master of the house will rise up and shut the door. It will be in vain for mere philosophers to knock and cry, "Lord, Lord, open unto us." That same door which shuts in the wise virgins will shut out the foolish forever. Lord, shut me in by your grace.

June 6

"Behold, I am vile" (Job 40:4).

Lost sinner, I have a word of encouragement for you! You think you cannot come to God because you are vile. There is not a saint living on earth who has not been made to feel that he is vile. If Job, Isaiah, and Paul were all obliged to say, I am vile, will you be ashamed to join in the same confession? If divine grace does not eradicate all sin from the believer, how do you hope to do it yourself? If God loves His people while they are yet vile, do you think your vileness will prevent His loving you? Believe on Jesus. Jesus calls you just as you are! Even now say, "You have died for sinners. I am a sinner. Lord Jesus, sprinkle your blood on me." If you confess your sin, you will find pardon. If, now, with all your heart, you will say, "I am vile; wash me," you will be washed *now*. You can rise from reading this morning's portion with all your sins pardoned. Although you woke this morning with every sin that man has ever committed on your head, you will rest tonight accepted in the Beloved. Once degraded with the rags of sin, you will be adorned with a robe of righteousness and appear white as the angels are. For *now* is the accepted time. If you believe on Him who justifies the ungodly, you are saved. May the Holy Spirit give you saving faith in Him who receives the vilest.

June 7

"Ye that love the Lord, hate evil" (Psalm 97:10).

You have good reason to hate evil. Consider what harm it has already brought you. Sin blinds you so that you cannot see the beauty of the Savior. It made you deaf so that you could not hear the Redeemer's tender invitations. Sin turned your feet into the way of death and poured poison into the very fountain of your being. It tainted your heart and made it "deceitful above all things, and desperately wicked" (Jeremiah 17:9). You were an heir of wrath even as others. You ran with the multitude to do evil. Such were all of us. But Paul reminds us, "but ye are washed, but ye are sanctified, but ye are justified in the name of the Lord Jesus, and by the Spirit of our God" (1 Corinthians 6:11). We have good reason for hating evil when we look back and trace its deadly workings. Our soul would have been lost had not omnipotent love interfered to redeem us. Even now it is an active enemy, ever watching to do us harm. Therefore, hate evil, Christian, unless you desire trouble. Live a happy life and die a peaceful death. Walk in all the ways of holiness, hating evil, even to the end. If you truly love your Savior and would honor Him, then hate evil. When you spend ample time with Jesus, it is impossible for you to be at peace with sin.

"There fell down many slain, because the war was of God" (1 Chronicles 5:22).

Warrior, fighting under the banner of the Lord Jesus, observe this verse with holy joy; for as it was in the days of old, so it is now. If the war is of God, the victory is sure. The sons of Reuben, the Gadites, and half the tribe of Manasseh could barely muster forty-five thousand fighting men. Yet, in their war with the Hagarites, they slew "men a hundred thousand." They cried to God in the battle, and He interceded for them because they put their trust in Him. If we go forth in Jehovah's name, the Lord of Hosts is with us as our Captain. They did not neglect buckler, sword, and bow, neither did they place their trust in these weapons. We must use all fitting means, but our confidence must rest in the Lord alone. He is the sword and the shield of His people. The great reason for their extraordinary success lay in the fact that "the war was of God." Beloved, in fighting with sin without and within, with error doctrinal or practical, with spiritual wickedness in high places or low places, with devils and the devil's allies, you are waging Jehovah's war. The battle is the Lord's, and He will deliver His enemies into our hands.

"The Lord hath done great things for us, whereof we are glad" (Psalm 126:3).

Some Christians are sadly prone to look on the dark side of everything and to dwell more on what they have gone through than on what God has done for them. Ask for their impression of the Christian life, and they will describe their continual conflicts, their deep afflictions, their sad adversities, and the sinfulness of their hearts with scarcely any allusion to the mercy and help which God has given them. But a Christian whose soul is in a healthy state will come forward joyously and say, "I will speak, not about myself, but to the honor of my God. He brought me up out of a horrible pit and out of the miry clay. He set my feet on a rock and established my goings. He put a new song in my mouth, even praise to our God. The Lord has done great things for me, whereof I am glad." Such an abstract of experience as this is the very best that any child of God can present. It is true that we endure trials, but it is just as true that we are delivered out of them. In looking back, it would be wrong to deny that we have had trials, but it would be equally wicked to forget that we have been through them safely and profitably. The deeper our troubles, the louder our thanks to God who has led us through all and preserved us until now.

"We live unto the Lord" (Romans 14:8).

If God had willed it, each of us might have entered heaven at the moment of conversion. It was not absolutely necessary for our preparation for immortality that we should tarry here. He could have changed us from imperfection to perfection and taken us to heaven at once. Why then are we here? Would God keep His children out of paradise a single moment longer than was necessary? Why is the army of the living God still on the battlefield, when one charge might give them the victory? The answer is—They are here that they may *"live unto the Lord"* and bring others to know His love. We remain on earth as sowers to scatter good seed; as plowmen to break up the fallow ground; as heralds publishing salvation. We are here as the "salt of the earth," to be a blessing to the world. We are here to glorify Christ in our daily life. We are here as workers for Him and as workers together with Him. Let us see that our life answers its end. Let us live earnest, useful, holy lives to the praise of the glory of His grace.

"We love him because he first loved us" (1 John 4:19).

There is no light in the planet but that which proceeds from the sun, and there is no true love for Jesus in the heart but that which comes from the Lord Jesus Himself. From this overflowing fountain of the infinite love of God, all our love for God springs. This is a certain truth, that we love Him for no other reason than because He first loved us. Our love for Him is the fair offspring of His love for us. Anyone may have cold admiration when studying the works of God. The warmth of love can only be kindled in the heart by God's Spirit. How marvelous that when we had rebelled against Him, He would by a display of such amazing love, seek to draw us back. We would never have had a grain of love toward God unless it had been sown in us by the sweet seed of His love for us. Love, then, has for its parent the love of God shed abroad in the heart; but after it is divinely born, it must be divinely nourished. Love is not a plant which will flourish naturally in human soil. It must be watered from above. Love for Jesus is a flower of delicate nature. If it received no nourishment but that which could be drawn from the rock of our hearts, it would soon wither. As love comes from heaven, so it must feed on heavenly bread. It cannot exist in the wilderness unless it is fed by manna from on high. Love must feed on love. The very soul and life of our love for God is His love for us.

"Thou art weighed in the balances and found wanting" (Daniel 5:27).

It is well to frequently weigh ourselves in the scale of God's Word. You will find it a holy exercise to read daily some psalm of David. As you meditate on each verse, ask yourself, "Can I say this? Have I felt as David felt? Has my heart ever been broken on account of sin, as his was when he penned his penitential psalms? Has my soul been full of true confidence in the hour of difficulty? Do I take the cup of salvation and call on the name of the Lord?" As you read ask yourself how far you are conformed to His likeness. Endeavor to discover whether you have the meekness, the humility, the lovely spirit which He constantly displayed. Then, read the epistles to see whether you can go with the apostle in what he said of his experience. Have you ever cried out as he did— "O wretched man that I am! who shall deliver me from the body of this death" (Romans 7:24). Have you seemed to yourself the chief of sinners and less than the least of all saints? Could you join with him and say, "For me to live is Christ, and to die is gain" (Philippians 1:21). If we thus read God's Word as a test of our spiritual condition, we will have good reason to stop many times and say, "Lord, give me true penitence. Give me real faith, warmer zeal, and more fervent love. Make me more like Jesus. Let me no longer be found wanting when weighed in the balances of the sanctuary, lest I be found wanting in the scales of judgment."

"Whosoever will, let him take the water of life freely" (Revelation 22:17).

Jesus says, "Take freely." He wants no payment or preparation. He seeks no recommendation from our virtuous emotions. You have no belief and no repentance. Come to Him, and He will give them to you. Come just as you are. He gives Himself to needy ones. We can hardly imagine anyone so foolish as to stand before a drinking fountain and to cry, "I cannot drink because I do not have enough money." However poor the man is, the fountain is there for him to freely drink of it. Thirsty people whether they are dressed in silk or in broadcloth, do not look for any warrant for drinking. The fountain itself is their warrant for taking its water freely. Perhaps the only persons who need go thirsty are those who think it would demean them to drink at a common fountain. Instead, they pass by with parched lips. Oh, how many there are who are rich in their own good works and cannot therefore come to Christ! "I will not be saved," they say, "in the same way as the harlot or the profane. What? Go to heaven in the same way as a chimneysweep? Is there no pathway to glory but the path which led the thief there? I will not be saved that way." Such proud boasters must remain without the living water, but, "Whosoever will, let him take the water of life freely."

"Delight thyself also in the Lord" (Psalm 37:4).

The teaching of these words must seem very surprising to those who are strangers to vital godliness. But to the sincere believer it is only the repetition of a recognized truth. The life of the believer is described as a delight in God, and we are certified of the great fact that true religion overflows with happiness and joy. Ungodly persons and nominal Christians never look on religion as a joyful thing. To them it is service, duty, or necessity but never pleasure or delight. If they attend to religion at all, it is either that they may gain thereby or because they dare not do otherwise. The thought of delight in religion is so strange to most men that no two words in their language stand farther apart than "holiness" and "delight." But believers who know Christ understand that delight and faith are so blessedly united that the gates of hell cannot prevail to separate them. They who love God with all their hearts find that His ways are ways of pleasantness and all His paths are peace. Our faith is no fetter, and our profession is no bondage. We are not dragged to holiness or driven to duty. No, our piety is our pleasure, our hope is our happiness, and our duty is our delight.

June 15

"And Sarah said, God hath made me to laugh, so that all that hear will laugh with me" (Genesis 21:6).

It was far above the power of nature and even contrary to its laws that the aged Sarah should be honored with a son. It is also beyond all ordinary rules that I, a sinner, should find grace to bear the indwelling Spirit of the Lord Jesus in my soul. I, whose nature was as dry, withered, barren, and accursed as a howling wilderness, have been made to bring forth fruit unto holiness. My mouth is filled with joyous laughter because of the grace which I have received from the Lord. I have found Jesus, the promised seed, and He is mine forever. This day I will lift up psalms of triumph to the Lord, who has remembered my low estate. "My heart rejoiceth in the Lord, mine horn is exalted in the Lord: my mouth is enlarged over mine enemies; because I rejoice in thy salvation" (1 Samuel 2:1). I surprise my family with my abundant peace. I delight my friends with my ever-increasing happiness. I edify the Church with my grateful confessions. I even impress the world with the cheerfulness of my daily conversation. The Lord Jesus is a deep sea of joy. My soul will dive therein and will be swallowed up in the delights of His companionship. Sarah looked on her Isaac and laughed with excess of rapture, and all her friends laughed with her. You, my soul, look on Jesus and bid heaven and earth unite in your unspeakable joy.

June 16

"And I give unto them eternal life, and they shall never perish" (John 10:28).

The Christian should never think or speak lightly of unbelief. For a child of God to mistrust His love, His truth, His faithfulness must be greatly displeasing to Him. How can we ever grieve Him by doubting His upholding grace? Christian, it is contrary to every promise of God's precious Word that you would ever be forgotten or left to perish. If it could be so, how could He be true who has said, "Can a woman forget her sucking child, that she should not have compassion on the son of her womb? Yea, they may forget, yet will I never forget thee" (Isaiah 49:15). What would be the value of the promise: "The mountains shall depart, and the hills be removed; but my kindness shall not depart from thee, neither shall the covenant of my peace be removed, saith the Lord that hath mercy on thee?" (Isaiah 54:10). Where would be the truth of Christ's words: "I give unto my sheep eternal life; and they shall never perish, neither shall any man pluck them out of my hand. My father which gave them me is greater than all, and no man is able to pluck them out of my Father's hand?" (John 10:29). Where is the veracity of God, His honor, His power, His grace, His covenant, His oath, if any of those who have put their trust in Christ should nevertheless be cast away? Banish those unbelieving fears which so dishonor God. Remember it is sinful to doubt His Word wherein He has promised you that you will never perish.

"Help, Lord" (Psalm 12:1).

David mourned the fewness of faithful men and therefore lifted up his heart in supplication. When the creature failed, he flew to the Creator. He evidently felt his own weakness, or he would not have cried for help. But at the same time, he intended honestly to exert himself for the cause of truth, for the word "help" is inapplicable where we ourselves do nothing. The psalmist runs straight to his God with a well-considered prayer. He knows what he is seeking and where to seek it. Lord, teach us to pray in the same blessed manner. The occasions for the use of this prayer are frequent. How suitable it is in providential afflictions for tried believers who find all helpers failing them. Students in doctrinal difficulties may often obtain aid by lifting up this cry of "Help, Lord," to the Holy Spirit, the great Teacher. Spiritual warriors in inward conflicts may send to the throne for reinforcements, and this will be a model for their request. Workers in heavenly labor may thus obtain grace in time of need. Seeking sinners in doubts and alarms may offer up the same weighty supplications. In fact, in all cases, times, and places, this will serve the turn of needy souls. "Help, Lord," will suit us living and dying, suffering or laboring, rejoicing or sorrowing. In Him our help is found. Let us not be slack to cry to Him. The answer to the prayer is certain, if it is sincerely offered through Jesus. The Lord's character assures us that He will not leave His people. His gift of Jesus is a pledge of every good thing.

"Thy Redeemer" (Isaiah 54:5).

Jesus the Redeemer is ours forever. He is king for us, priest for us, and prophet for us. Whenever we read a new title for our Redeemer, let us appropriate Him as ours in that name also. He is the Shepherd, the Captain, the Prince, and the Prophet. Jesus has no dignity which He will not employ for our exaltation and no prerogative which He will not exercise for our defense. His fullness in the Godhead is our unfailing, inexhaustible treasure house. His manhood also, which He took on Him for us, is ours in all its perfection. To us our gracious Lord communicates the spotless virtue of a stainless character. On us He bestows the reward procured by obedient submission and incessant service. He bequeaths us His manger that we may learn how God came down to man. His cross teaches us how man may go up to God. All His thoughts, emotions, actions, utterances, miracles, and intercessions were for us. He trod the road of sorrow on our behalf and has given us as His heavenly legacy the full results of all the labors of His life. Oh, my soul, by the power of the Holy Spirit, call Him your Redeemer this morning.

June 19

"And they were all filled with the Holy Ghost" (Acts 2:4).

It is a rich blessing to be filled with the Holy Spirit. It would be impossible to over-estimate the consequences of this sacred filling of the soul. Life, comfort, light, purity, power, peace, and many other precious blessings are inseparable from the Spirit's presence. As sacred oil, He anoints the head of the believer, sets him apart to the priesthood of saints, and gives him grace to execute his office right. As the only truly purifying water, He cleanses us from the power of sin and sanctifies us, working in us to do the Lord's good pleasure. As the light, He manifested to us at first our lost estate. Now He reveals the Lord Jesus to us and in us and guides us in the way of righteousness. Enlightened by His pure celestial ray, we are no more darkness, but light in the Lord. He is the sacrificial flame by which we are enabled to offer our whole souls as a living sacrifice to God. As heavenly dew, He removes our barrenness and fertilizes our lives. As the dove, with wings of peaceful love, He broods over His Church and over the souls of believers. As the Comforter, He dispels the cares and doubts which mar the peace of His beloved. He descends on the chosen and bears witness to their sonship by working in them a filial spirit by which they cry, Abba, Father. As the wind, He brings the breath of life to men. Blowing where He wills, He performs the quickening operations by which the spiritual creation is animated and sustained. Pray to God that we might feel His presence this day and every day.

"For, lo, I will command, and I will sift the house of Israel among all nations, like as corn is sifted in a sieve, yet shall not the least grain fall upon the earth" (Amos 9:9).

Every sifting comes by divine command and permission. Satan had to ask for permission before he could lay a finger on Job. Satan may hold the sieve, hoping to destroy the corn; but the overruling hand of the Master is accomplishing the purity of the grain by the very process which the enemy intended to be destructive. Be comforted by the blessed fact that the Lord directs the sieve to His own glory and to your eternal profit. The Lord Jesus will surely use the fan which is in His hand and will divide the precious from the vile. In the sieve true weight alone has power. Husks and chaff, being devoid of substance, must fly before the wind, and only solid corn will remain. Observe the complete safety of the Lord's wheat. Even the smallest grain has a promise of preservation. God Himself sifts in all places, in all nations, and in the most effectual manner. Yet through all of this, not the smallest, lightest, or most shriveled grain is permitted to fall to the ground. Every individual believer is precious in the sight of the Lord, and He will not lose one of His redeemed people. No matter how little we may be, if we are the Lord's, we may rejoice that we are preserved in Christ Jesus.

"Thou art fairer than the children of men" (Psalm 45:2).

Jesus is altogether complete. He is a picture of beauty and a breastplate of glory. In Him all the things of good repute are in their proper places and assist in adorning each other. Not one feature in His glorious person attracts attention at the expense of others. But He is perfectly and altogether lovely. Oh, Jesus, Your power, Your grace, Your justice, Your tenderness, Your truth, Your majesty, and Your immutability, make up such a God-man, as neither heaven nor earth has seen elsewhere. Your infancy, Your eternity, Your sufferings, Your triumphs, Your death, and Your immortality are all woven in one gorgeous tapestry without seam or rent. You are music without discord. You are many and yet not divided. You are all things and yet not diverse. As all the colors blend into one resplendent rainbow, so all the glories of heaven and earth meet in You and unite so wondrously, that there is none like You in all things. If all the virtues of the most excellent were bound in one bundle, they could not rival You. You have been anointed with the holy oil of myrrh and cassia, which Your God has reserved for you alone. As for Your fragrance, it is as the holy perfume, the like of which none other can ever mingle. Even with the art of the apothecary, each spice is fragrant, but the compound is divine.

"He shall build the temple of the Lord; and he shall bear the glory" (Zechariah 6:13).

Christ Himself is the builder of His spiritual temple. He has built it on the mountains of His unchangeable affection, His omnipotent grace, and His infallible truthfulness. But as it was in Solomon's temple, so in this. The materials need to be made ready. The cedars of Lebanon are not framed for the building. They are not cut down, shaped, and made into those planks of cedar, whose odoriferous beauty will make glad the courts of the Lord's house in Paradise. The rough stones are still in the quarry. They must be hewn and squared. All this is Christ's own work. Each individual believer is being prepared, polished, and made ready for his place in the temple. But Christ's own hand performs the preparation work. Afflictions cannot sanctify, except as they are used by Him to this end. Our prayers and efforts cannot make us ready for heaven apart from the hand of Jesus, who fashions our hearts. In the building of Solomon's temple, there was neither hammer nor axe nor any tool of iron heard in the house, because all was brought perfectly ready for the exact spot it was to occupy. So it is with the temple which Jesus builds—the making ready is all done on earth. When we reach heaven, there will be no sanctifying us there, no squaring us with afflictions, no planing us with suffering.

"Ephraim is a cake not turned" (Hosea 7:8).

A pancake not turned is unbaked on one side. Ephraim was like this in many respects. He had areas in his life that were untouched by divine grace. Although there was some partial obedience, there was much rebellion left. Are you thorough in the things of God? Has grace gone through the very center of your being? To be sanctified in your spirit, soul, and body should be your aim and prayer. There must not be the appearance of holiness in one place and reigning sin in another, or you, too, will be a cake not turned. The assumed appearance of superior sanctity frequently accompanies a total absence of all vital godliness. The saint in public is sometimes a devil in private. He deals in flour by day and in soot by night. The cake which is burned on one side is dough on the other. If it is so with me, O Lord, turn me! Turn my unsanctified nature to the fire of Your love and let it feel the sacred glow. Let my burned side cool a little while I learn of my own weakness and desire heat when I am removed from Your heavenly flame. Let me not be found a double-minded man, but one entirely under the powerful influence of reigning grace. I know if I am left like a cake unturned and am not on both sides the subject of Your grace, I must be consumed forever amid everlasting burnings.

"A certain woman of the company lifted up her voice, and said unto him, Blessed is the womb that bare thee, and the paps which thou hast sucked. But he said, Yea rather, blessed are they that hear the word of God, and keep it." (Luke 11:27-28).

It is fondly imagined by some that it must have involved very special privileges to have been the mother of our Lord. They suppose that she had the benefit of looking into His very heart in a way in which we cannot hope to do. We do not know that Mary knew more than others. She does not appear from anything we read in the gospels to have been a better-instructed believer than any other of Christ's disciples. All that she knew, we also may discover. Do you wonder that we should say so? Here is a text to prove it: "The secret of the Lord is with them that fear him, and he will show them his covenant" (Psalm 25:14). Remember the Master's words: "Henceforth I call you not servants; for the servant knoweth not what his Lord doeth: but I have called you friends; for all things that I have heard of my Father I have made known unto you" (John 15:15). This divine Revealer of secrets tells us His heart and keeps nothing back which is profitable to us. Therefore, we will not ignorantly cry out, "Blessed is the womb that bare thee." We will instead intelligently bless God that, having heard the Word and kept it, we have as true an acquaintance with the secrets of His heart as Mary was supposed to have obtained. How happy we are to have this privilege!

June 25

"Get thee up into the high mountain" (Isaiah 40:9).

Our knowledge of Christ is somewhat like climbing a mountain. When you are at the base you see very little. The mountain itself appears to be half as high as it really is. Confined in a little valley, you discover scarcely anything but the rippling brooks as they descend into the stream at the foot of the mountain. Climb the first rising knoll, and the valley lengthens and widens beneath your feet. Go higher, and you see the country for four or five miles round and are delighted with the widening prospect. Mount still, and the scene enlarges; until at last, you are on the summit. The Christian life is of the same order. When we first believe in Christ, we see little of Him. The higher we climb, the more we discover of His beauties. But who has ever gained the summit? Who has known all the heights and depths of the love of Christ which passes knowledge? Paul, when grown old, sitting gray-haired, shivering in a dungeon in Rome, could say with greater emphasis than we can, "I know whom I have believed." Each experience had been like the climbing of a hill, each trial had been like ascending another summit, and his death seemed like gaining the top of the mountain. From there he could see the faithfulness and the love of Him to whom he had committed his soul. Get up, dear friend, to the high mountain.

"Art thou become like unto us" (Isaiah 14:10).

What must be the apostate's doom when his naked soul appears before God? How will he bear that voice, "Depart, ye cursed; you have rejected Me, and I reject you; you have played the harlot and departed from Me. I also have banished you forever from My presence and will not have mercy on you"? What will be this wretch's shame at the last great day when, before assembled multitudes, the apostate will be unmasked? No greater eagerness will ever be seen among Satanic tormentors than in that day when devils drag the hypocrite's soul down to perdition. Bunyan pictures this with massive but awful grandeur of poetry when he speaks of the back way to hell. Seven devils bound the wretch with nine cords and dragged him from the road to heaven, in which he had professed to walk, and thrust him through the back door into hell. Mind that back way to hell! Examine yourselves whether you are in the faith. Look well to your state and see whether you be in Christ or not. It is the easiest thing in the world to give a lenient verdict when one's self is to be tried. Be just to all, but be rigorous to yourself. Remember, if it is not a rock on which you build, when the house falls, great will be the fall of it. May the Lord give you sincerity, constancy, and firmness; and in no day, however evil, may you be led to turn aside.

June 27

"Only ye shall not go very far away" (Exodus 8:28).

This is a crafty word from the Pharaoh. If the poor bondaged Israelites must go out of Egypt, then he bargains with them that it will not be very far away—at least not far enough to escape the terror of his arms and the observation of his spies. After the same fashion, the world would have us be more charitable and not carry matters with too severe a hand. Death to the world and burial with Christ are experiences which carnal minds treat with ridicule. Worldly wisdom recommends the path of compromise and talks of moderation. According to this carnal policy, purity is admitted to be very desirable, but we are warned against being too precise. Truth is of course to be followed, but error is not to be severely denounced. "Yes," says the world, "be spiritually minded by all means, but do not deny yourself a little frivolity. What's the good of criticizing something when it is so fashionable and everybody does it?" Multitudes of professing Christians yield to this cunning advice to their own eternal ruin. If we would follow the Lord wholly, we must go right away into the wilderness and leave the carnal world behind us. We must leave its maxims, pleasures, and religion and go far away to the place where the Lord calls His sanctified ones. When the town is on fire, our house cannot be too far from the flames. To all true believers, let the trumpet-call be sounded, "Come ye out from among them; be ye separate" (2 Corinthians 6:17).

June 28

"Looking unto Jesus" (Hebrews 12:2).

It is the Holy Spirit's work to turn our eyes away from self to Jesus. Satan's work is just the opposite of this. He is constantly trying to make us regard ourselves instead of Christ. Satan implants thoughts about self, and we will never find comfort of assurance by looking within. But the Holy Spirit turns our eyes entirely away from self. He tells us that we are nothing, but that "Christ is all in all" (Colossians 3:11). Remember, therefore, it is not your hold on Christ that saves you—it is Christ. It is not even faith in Christ, though that be the instrument—it is Christ's blood and merits. Therefore, look not so much to your hand with which you are grasping Christ, as to look at Christ Himself. Look to Jesus, the source of your hope, the author and finisher of your faith. We will never find happiness by looking at our prayers, our doings, or our feelings. It is what *Jesus* is, not what *we* are, that gives rest to the soul. If we would at once overcome Satan and have peace with God, it must be by "looking unto Jesus." Simply keep your eye on Him. Let His death, His sufferings, His merits, His glories, and His intercession be fresh on your mind. When you wake in the morning, look to Him. When you lie down at night, look to Him. He will never fail you!

June 29

"Them also which sleep in Jesus will God bring with him" (1 Thessalonians 4:14).

Do not think that the soul sleeps in insensibility. "Today shalt thou be with me in Paradise" is the whisper of Christ to every dying saint. They "sleep in Jesus," but their souls are before the throne of God, praising Him day and night in His temple, singing hallelujahs to Him who washed them from their sins in His blood. The body sleeps in its lonely bed of dirt beneath the coverlet of grass. But what is this sleep? The idea connected with sleep is *rest,* and that is the thought which the Spirit of God would convey to us. Sleep shuts the door of the soul and bids all intruders to wait for a while. The toil-worn believer quietly sleeps like a weary child who slumbers on his mother's breast. Happy are they who die in the Lord. They rest from their labors, and their works follow them. Guarded by angel watchers, curtained by eternal mysteries, their earthly bodies sleep on, until the fullness of time brings the fullness of redemption. They went to their rest with the furrowed brow and the wasted features, but they will wake up in beauty and glory. The shriveled seed, so destitute of form and comeliness, rises from the dust a beautiful flower. The winter of the grave gives way to the spring of redemption and the summer of glory. Blessed are those who "sleep in Jesus."

"And the glory which thou gavest me I have given them" (John 17:22).

Behold the unsurpassed openhandedness of the Lord Jesus for He has given us His all. Although a tithe of His possessions would have made a universe of angels rich beyond all thought, He was not content until He had given us all that He had. We would have been satisfied if He had allowed us to eat the crumbs of His bounty beneath the table of His mercy; but He will do nothing by halves. He makes us sit with Him and share the feast. Had Jesus given us some small pension from His royal chambers, we would have had cause to love Him eternally. But no, He wants His bride to be as rich as Himself. He will not have a glory or a grace in which she will not share. He has not been content with less than making us joint-heirs with Himself, so that we might have equal possessions. He gives His people the keys to every room in His house. He gives them full liberty to take all that He has to be their own. Christ has put the flask of His love and grace to the believer's lip and bidden him drink forever. If the believer could drain it, he is welcome to do so; but since he cannot exhaust it, he is bidden to drink abundantly, for it is all his own. What truer proof of fellowship can heaven or earth afford?

July 1

"In summer and in winter shall it be" (Zechariah 14:8).

The streams of living water which flow from Jerusalem are not dried up by the parching heat of sultry midsummer anymore than they were frozen by the cold winds of blustering winter. Rejoice, Oh my soul, that you are spared to testify of the faithfulness of the Lord. The seasons change and you change, but your Lord remains the same. The streams of His love are as deep, as broad, and as full as ever. The heat of business cares and scorching trials make me need the cooling influences of the river of His grace. Job said his brothers were like deceitful brooks, but he found his God to be an overflowing river of consolation. The Nile is the great confidence of Egypt, but its floods are variable. Our Lord is always the same. By turning the course of the Euphrates, Cyrus took the city of Babylon; but no power, human or infernal, can divert the current of divine grace. The tracks of ancient rivers have been found all dry and desolate; but the streams which take their rise on the mountains of divine sovereignty and infinite love will always be full to the brim. Generations melt away, but the course of grace is unaltered. My soul, how blessed you are to be led beside such still waters! Never wander to other streams or you might hear the Lord's rebuke.

"Our heart shall rejoice in him" (Psalm 33:21).

The fact that Christians can rejoice, even in the deepest distress, is a blessing. The waves may roll over them, but their souls soon rise to the surface and see the light of God's countenance. They have a bouyancy about them which keeps their head always above the water and helps them to sing amid the tempest. Trouble does not necessarily bring consolation with it to the believer, but the presence of the Son of God in the trial with him fills his heart with joy. He is sick and suffering, but Jesus visits him. The cold, chilly waters of Jordan are gathering about him up to his neck. Jesus puts His arms around him and cries, "Fear not, beloved; to die is to be blessed; the waters of death have their fountain-head in heaven; they are not bitter; they are sweet as nectar, for they flow from the throne of God." As the departing saint wades through the stream, the billows gather around him, and heart and flesh fail him, the same voice sounds in his ear, "Fear not; I am with thee; be not dismayed; I am thy God" (Isaiah 41:10). As he nears the borders of the infinite unknown, Jesus says, "Fear not, little flock; for it is your Father's good pleasure to give you the kingdom" (Luke 12:32). Thus strengthened and consoled, the believer is not afraid to die. He is even willing to depart, for he has seen Jesus as the morning star and longs to gaze on Him as the sun in His strength. Truly, the presence of Jesus is all the heaven we desire.

July 3

"The ill-favoured and lean-fleshed kine did eat up the seven well-favoured and fat kine" (Genesis 41:4).

Pharaoh's dream has too often been my waking experience. My days of sloth have ruinously destroyed all that I had achieved in times of zealous industry. My seasons of coldness have frozen all the genial glow of my periods of fervency and enthusiasm. My fits of wordliness have thrown me back from my advances in the divine life. I need to beware of lean prayers, lean praises, lean duties, and lean experiences, for these will eat up the fat of my comfort and peace. If I neglect prayer for a short time, I lose all the spirituality to which I had attained. If I draw no fresh supplies from heaven, the old corn in my granary is soon consumed by the famine which rages in my soul. How anxious I am to have no lean-fleshed days, no ill-favored hours! If every day I journeyed toward the goal of my desires I would soon reach it, but backsliding leaves me still far off from the prize of my high calling and robs me of the advances which I had so laboriously made. The only way in which all my days can be like the healthy cattle is to feed in the right meadow and to spend time with the Lord in His service, in His company, in His fear, and in His way. Why wouldn't every year be richer than the past, in love, usefulness, and joy? I have had more experience of my Lord and should be more like Him. O Lord, keep the curse of leanness of soul far from me.

July 4

"Sanctify them through thy truth" (John 17:17).

Sanctification begins in regeneration. The Spirit of God infuses into man that new living principle by which he becomes a new creature in Christ Jesus. This work, which begins in the new birth, is carried on in two ways: mortification, where the lusts of the flesh are subdued and kept under; and vivification, by which the life which God has put within us is made a well of water springing up to everlasting life. This is carried on every day in what is called perseverance, by which the Christian is preserved and continued in a gracious state and is made to abound in good works to the praise and glory of God. While the Spirit of God is the author of sanctification, there is a visible agency employed which must not be forgotten. "Sanctify them," said Jesus, "through thy truth. Thy word is truth" (John 17:17). Many passages of Scripture prove that the instrument of our sanctification is the Word of God. The Spirit of God brings to our minds the precepts and doctrines of truth and applies them with power. These are heard in the ear but received in the heart. They work in us to will and to do of God's good pleasure. The Word is the sanctifier. If we do not hear or read the truth, we will not grow in sanctification. "Thy word is a lamp unto my feet and a light unto my path" (Psalm 119:105).

"Called to be saints" (Romans 1:7)

We tend to regard the apostolic saints as if they were saints in a more special manner than the other children of God. All are saints whom God has called by His grace and sanctified by His Spirit. The nearer a man lives to God, the more intensely he mourns over his own evil heart. The more his Master honors him in His service, the more also does his evil flesh tease him daily. The fact is, if we had seen the apostle Paul, we would have thought him remarkably like the rest of the chosen family. If we had talked with him, we would have said, "We find that his experience and ours are much the same. He is more faithful, more holy, and more deeply taught than we are, but he has the same trials to endure." Do not look on the ancient saints as being exempt from infirmities or sins. Do not regard them with that mystic reverence which will almost make us idolaters. Their holiness is attainable even by us. We are called to be saints by that same voice which constrained them to their high vocation. It is a Christian's duty to force his way into the inner circle of saintship. We have the same light that they had, and the same grace is accessible to us. Why should we rest satisfied until we have equaled them in heavenly character? They lived *with* Jesus and *for* Jesus. Therefore, they grew *like* Jesus. Let us live by the same Spirit as they did, "looking unto Jesus," and our saintship will soon be apparent.

"Whoso hearkeneth unto me shall dwell safely, and shall be quiet from fear of evil" (Proverbs 1:33).

The Israelites provoked the Most High by their continued idolatry. He punished them by withholding both dew and rain, so that their land was visited by a sore famine. But while He did this, He took care that His own chosen ones would be secure. If all other brooks are dry, yet there will be one reserved for Elijah. When that fails, God will still preserve for him a place of sustenance. The Lord had not simply one Elijah, but He had a remnant who were hidden by fifties in a cave. Though the whole land was subject to famine, yet these fifties in the cave were fed from Ahab's table by the faithful, God-fearing steward, Obadiah. Let us draw from this the inference that, come what may, God's people are safe. Let convulsions shake the solid earth, and let the skies themselves be rent in two. Yet, amid the wreck of worlds the believer will be as secure as in the calmest hour of rest. If God cannot save His people under heaven, He will save them in heaven. If the world becomes too hot to hold them, then heaven will be the place of their reception and their safety. Be confident when you hear of wars and rumors of wars. Let no agitation distress you, but be quiet from fear of evil. Whatever comes on the earth, you, beneath the broad wings of Jehovah, will be secure.

July 7

"Brethren, pray for us" (1 Thessalonians 5:25).

We implore every Christian household to grant this fervent request first uttered by an apostle. A very heavy responsibility rests on all ministers of the gospel. As officers in Christ's army, they are the special targets of the enmity of men and devils. Their sacred calling involves temptations from which you are exempt. Above all, it too often draws them away from personal enjoyment of truth into a ministerial and official consideration of it. They observe very sad backslidings, and their hearts are wounded. They see millions perishing, and their spirits sink. They want to profit from their preaching. They desire to be a blessing to your children. They long to be useful both to saints and sinners. Therefore, dear friends, intercede for those in the ministry. You do not look to them but to the Master for spiritual blessings. Yet, how many times has He given those blessings through His ministers! Ask, then, again and again, that they may be the earthen vessels into which the Lord may put the treasures of the gospel. The whole company of missionaries, ministers, teachers, and students, in the name of Jesus, beseech you—"Brethren, pray for us."

"Tell me, I pray thee, wherein thy great strength lieth" (Judges 16:6).

Where lies the secret strength of faith? It lies in the food it feeds on. Faith studies *what the promise is*—an emanation of divine grace, an overflowing of the great heart of God. Faith says, "My God gave this promise out of love and grace; therefore, I am certain His Word will be fulfilled." Then faith thinks, "Who is the author of this promise?" It remembers that it is God, who cannot lie—God omnipotent and God immutable. Faith, therefore concludes that the promise must be fulfilled. It remembers why the promise was *given*—namely, for God's glory. He will never stain His own character or mar the luster of His own crown. Therefore, the promise must and will stand. Then faith also considers the amazing *work of Christ* as being a clear proof of the Father's intention to fulfill His Word. "He that spared not his own Son, but freely delivered him up for us all, how shall he not with him also freely give us all things?" (Romans 8:32). Faith looks back on *the past* and remembers that God never failed it. Faith recollects times of great peril when deliverance came and hours of awful need when its strength was found. It cries, "Hitherto the Lord has helped me, and He will help me still." Thus faith can say with assurance, "Surely goodness and mercy shall follow me all the days of my life!" (Psalm 23:6).

July 9

"Forget not all his benefits" (Psalm 103:2).

It is delightful to observe the hand of God in the lives of ancient saints, His goodness in delivering them, His mercy in pardoning them, and His faithfulness in keeping His covenant with them. But it is even more interesting for us to mark the hand of God in our own lives. We do our Lord an injustice when we suppose that He performed all His mighty acts for those in the early time but does not perform wonders for the saints who are now on the earth. Let us review our own lives. Surely in these we may discover some happy incidents, refreshing to ourselves and glorifying to our God. Have you had no deliverances? Have you passed through rivers supported by the divine presence? Have you walked through fires unharmed? Have you had no manifestations? Have you had choice favors? Has God never listened to you and answered your requests? Surely the goodness of God has been the same to us as to the saints of old. Let us weave His mercies into a song. Let our souls give forth music as sweet and as exhilarating as came from David's harp while we praise the Lord whose mercy endureth forever.

"Fellow-citizens with the saints" (Ephesians 2:19).

What is meant by our being citizens in heaven? It means that we are under heaven's government. Christ, the King of heaven, reigns in our hearts. Our daily prayer is, "Thy will be done on earth as it is in heaven" (Matthew 6:10). The proclamations issued from the throne of glory are freely received by us. We cheerfully obey the decrees of the Great King. Then, as citizens of the New Jerusalem, we share heaven's honors. The glory which belongs to beautified saints belongs to us, for we are already sons of God. We have Christ for our Brother, God for our Father, and a crown of immortality for our reward. We share the honors of citizenship. We have common rights to all the property of heaven. Also, as citizens of heaven, we enjoy its delights. Do they there rejoice over sinners that repent—prodigals that have returned? So do we. Do they chant glories of triumphant grace? We do the same. Do they cast their crowns at Jesus' feet? We cast our honors there too. Are they charmed with His smile? It is not less sweet to us who dwell below. Do they look forward, waiting for His second advent? We also look and long for His appearing. Since we are *citizens of heaven,* let our walk and actions be consistent with our high dignity.

July 11

"After that ye have suffered awhile, make you perfect, stablish, strengthen, settle you" (1 Peter 5:10).

You have seen the rainbow as it spans the plain. It is beautiful, but it passes away. The fair colors give way to the fleecy clouds, and the sky is no longer brilliant with the tints of heaven. It is not *established*. How can it be? How can a glorious show made up of transitory sunbeams and passing raindrops remain? The graces of the Christian character must not resemble the rainbow in its transitory beauty. Seek, believer, that every good thing you have may be an established, settled thing. May your character not be a writing on the sand but an inscription on the rock. Be rooted and grounded in love. May your whole life be so settled and established that all the blasts of hell and all the storms of earth will never be able to remove you. Notice how this blessing of being established in the faith is gained. The apostle's words point us to *suffering* as the means employed—*"After that ye have suffered awhile."* It is of no use to hope that we will be well rooted if no rough winds pass over us. Do not shrink from the tempestuous winds of trial, but take comfort, believing that by their rough discipline God is fulfilling this benediction to you.

"Sanctified by God the Father" (Jude 1); *"Sanctified in Christ Jesus"* (1 Corinthians 1:2); *"Through sanctification of the Spirit"* (1 Peter 1:2).

How unwisely do those believers talk who make preferences in the Persons of the Trinity. They think of Jesus as if He were the embodiment of everything lovely and gracious, while the Father they regard as severely just and destitute of kindness. Equally wrong are those who magnify the decree of the Father and the atonement of the Son so as to depreciate the work of the Spirit. In deeds of grace, none of the Persons of the Trinity act apart from the rest. They are as united in their deeds as in their essence. In their love toward the chosen, they are one. In the actions which flow from that great central source, they are still undivided. Especially notice this in the matter of sanctification. While we may without mistake speak of sanctification as the work of the Spirit, we must take heed that we do not view it as if the Father and the Son had no part therein. It is correct to speak of sanctification as the work of the Father, of the Son, and of the Spirit. Jehovah said, "Let *us* make man in our own image after our likeness" (Genesis 1:26) and thus we are "His workmanship, created in Christ Jesus unto good works, which God hath before ordained that we should walk in them" (Ephesians 2:10). See the value which God sets on real holiness. You, as the follower of Christ, must also set a high value on holiness—on purity of life and godliness of conversation. Let us begin today to live in a manner that will manifest the work of the Triune God in us.

July 13

"God said to Jonah, Doest thou well to be angry" (Jonah 4:9).

Anger is not always sinful, but it has a tendency to run wild. Whenever it displays itself, we should be quick to question its character with this inquiry, "Doest thou well to be angry?" It may be that we can answer, "Yes." Very frequently anger is the madman's firebrand, but sometimes it is Elijah's fire from heaven. We do well when we are angry with sin because of the wrong which it commits against our good and gracious God. We are rightfully angry with ourselves if we remain so foolish after so much divine instruction. He who is not angry at transgression becomes a partaker in it. Sin is a loathsome and hateful thing, and no renewed heart can patiently endure it. God Himself is angry with the wicked every day. It is written in His Word, "Ye that love the Lord, hate evil" (Psalm 97:10). Far more frequently it is to be feared that our anger is not commendable or even justifiable. Then we must answer, "No." Why should we be fretful with children, irritable with workers, or irate with friends? Is such anger honorable to our Christian profession or glorifying to God? It is the old evil heart seeking to gain dominion. We should resist it with all the might of our new-born nature. Many believers give way to temper as though it were useless to attempt resistance. But let the believer remember that he must be a conqueror in every point, or else he cannot be crowned. If we cannot control our tempers, what has grace done for us? We must not make natural infirmity an excuse for sin. We must ask the Lord to crucify our tempers and renew us in gentleness and meekness after His own image.

July 14

"If thou lift up thy tool upon it, thou hast polluted it" (Exodus 20:25).

God's altar was to be built of unhewn stones, so that no trace of human skill or labor might be seen on it. Human wisdom delights to trim and arrange the doctrines of the cross into a system more artificial and more congenial with the depraved tastes of fallen nature. Instead of improving the gospel, carnal wisdom pollutes it until it becomes another gospel and not the truth of God at all. All alterations and amendments of the Lord's own Word are defilements. The proud heart of man is very anxious to have a hand in the justification of the soul before God. Preparations for Christ are dreamed of, humblings and repentings are trusted in, good works are cried up, and natural ability is much boasted. The Lord alone must be exalted in the work of atonement, and not a single mark of man's chisel or hammer will be endured. There is an inherent blasphemy in seeking to add to what Christ Jesus in His dying moments declared to be finished. Trembling sinner, put away your tools and fall on your knees in humble supplication. Accept the Lord Jesus to be the altar of your atonement, and rest in Him alone. Many believers may take warning from this morning's text as to the doctrines which they believe. There is far too much inclination among Christians to reconcile the truths of revelation. This is a form of irreverence and unbelief. Strive against it, and receive truth as you find it. Rejoice that the doctrines of the Word are unhewn stones and are all the more fit to build an altar for the Lord.

"The fire shall ever be burning upon the altar; it shall never go out" (Leviticus 6:13).

Keep the altar of private prayer burning. This is the very life of all piety. Burn here the fat of your sacrifices. Let your private devotions be, if possible, regular, frequent, and undisturbed. Effectual prayer availeth much. Have you nothing to pray for? Let us suggest the Church, the ministry, your own soul, your children, your relations, your neighbors, your country, and the cause of God and truth throughout the world. Let us examine ourselves on this important matter. Do we engage in private devotion with lukewarmness? Is the fire of devotion burning dimly in our hearts? If so, be alarmed at this sign of decay. Let us ask for the spirit of grace and of supplication. Let us set apart special periods for extraordinary prayer. For if this fire should be smothered beneath the ashes of a worldly conformity, it will dim the fire on the family altar and lessen our influence both in the Church and in the world. The text will also apply to the altar of the heart. This is a golden altar indeed. God loves to see the hearts of His people glowing toward Himself. Let us give God our hearts, blazing with love and seeking His grace, that the fire may never be quenched. It will not burn if the Lord does not keep it burning. Many adversaries will attempt to extinguish it. Let us use Scriptures as fuel for our heart's fire; they are live coals. Let us attend sermons, but above all let us be much alone with Jesus.

July 16

"They gathered manna every morning" (Exodus 16:21).

Labor to maintain a sense of your entire dependence on the Lord's good will and pleasure for the continuance of your richest enjoyments. Never try to live on the old manna or seek to find help in the world. All must come from Jesus. Old anointings will not suffice to impart unction to your spirit. Your head must have fresh oil poured on it from the golden horn of the sanctuary, or it will cease from its glory. Today you may be on the summit of the mount of God, but He who has put you there must keep you there, or you will sink. Your mountain only stands firm when He settles it in its place. If He hides His face, you will soon be troubled. Only Jesus can supply the joy of your heart, the light of your eyes, and the strength of your life. Comfort lies in His hand. Our Lord is determined that we will feel and recognize this hourly dependence, for He only permits us to pray for daily bread. He only promises that "as thy days, so shall thy strength be" (Deuteronomy 33:25). Is it not best for us that it should be so, that we may often approach His throne and constantly be reminded of His love? Oh, how rich the grace which supplies us so continually and does not refrain itself because of our ingratitude! The golden shower never ceases, the cloud of blessing hovers continually above our habitation. O Lord Jesus, we would bow at Your feet, conscious of our utter inability to do anything without You.

July 17

"Knowing, brethren beloved, your election of God" (1 Thessalonians 1:4).

Many people want to know their election before they look to Christ. But they cannot because it is only discovered by looking to Jesus. Do you think you are a lost, guilty sinner? Go straight to the cross of Christ and tell Jesus so. Tell Him that you have read in the Bible, "Him that cometh unto me I will in no wise cast out" (John 6:37). Look to Jesus and believe on Him, and you will prove your election directly. For as surely as you believe, you are elect. If you have given yourself wholly to Christ and trust Him, then you are one of God's chosen ones. But if you stop and say, "I want to know first whether I am elect," you do not know what you have asked. Go to Jesus just as you are. Leave all curious inquiry about election alone. Go straight to Christ and you will know your election. The assurance of the Holy Spirit will be given to you so that you will be able to say, "I know whom I have believed, and am persuaded that he is able to keep that which I have committed unto him" (2 Timothy 1:12). Christ was at the everlasting council. He can tell you whether you were chosen or not. But you cannot find it out in any other way. Go and put your trust in Him, and His answer will be, "I have loved thee with an everlasting love; therefore with lovingkindness have I drawn thee" (Jeremiah 31:3). There will be no doubt about His having chosen *you*, when you have chosen *Him*.

"They shall go hindmost with their standards"
(Numbers 2:31).

The camp of Dan brought up the rear when the
armies of Israel were on the march. The Danites
occupied the hindmost place. But what did the
position matter since they were as truly part of the
host as were the foremost tribes? They followed
the same fiery cloudy pillar. They ate the same
manna, drank of the same spiritual rock, and journeyed to the same inheritance. Come, my heart,
cheer up, though last and least, it is your privilege
to be in the army and to fare as those who lead.
Someone must be hindmost in honor and esteem.
Someone must do menial work for Jesus, and why
not I? The Danites occupied a very useful place.
Stragglers have to be picked up on the march, and
lost property has to be gathered from the field.
Fiery spirits may dash forward over untrodden
paths to learn fresh truth and win more souls to
Jesus. But some of a more conservative spirit may
be engaged in reminding the Church of her
ancient faith and restoring her fainting sons. Every
position has its duties, and the slowly moving children of God will find their peculiar state an eminent blessing to the whole host. The rear guard is a
place of danger. There are foes behind us as well
as before us. Attacks may come from any quarter.
The experienced Christian will find much work
for his weapons in aiding those poor, doubting,
and wavering souls who are hindmost in faith,
knowledge, and joy. These must not be left
unaided. My soul, tenderly watch to help the hindmost this day.

"The Lord our God hath showed us his glory" (Deuteronomy 5:24).

How will the glory of God be manifested to such fallen creatures as we are? Man's eye is not single. He always has a side glance toward his own honor and too high an estimate of his own powers. He is not qualified to behold the glory of the Lord. It is clear, then, that self must get out of the way that there may be room for God to be exalted. This is the reason He allows His people to experience straits and difficulties. Being made conscious of their own folly and weakness, they will be fit to behold the majesty of God when He comes forth to work their deliverance. He whose life is one even and smooth path will see little of the glory of the Lord. He has few occasions of self-emptying and, therefore, little fitness for being filled with the revelation of God. Among the huge waves of bereavement, poverty, temptation, and reproach, we learn the power of Jehovah because we feel the littleness of man. Thank God, then, if you have been led by a rough road. This has given you your experience of God's greatness and lovingkindness. Your troubles have enriched you with a wealth of knowledge to be gained by no other means. Praise God that you have not been left to the darkness and ignorance which continued prosperity might have involved. In the fight of affliction you have been capacitated to excel in His glory because of His wonderful dealings with you.

"The earnest of our inheritance" (Ephesians 1:14).

Oh, what enlightenment, what joys, what consolation, what delight of heart is experienced by that man who has learned to feed on Jesus alone. Yet, the realization which we have of Christ's preciousness is, in this life, imperfect at best. As an old writer has said, " 'Tis but a taste!' " We have tasted that the Lord is gracious, but we do not yet know *how* good and gracious He is. What we know of His sweetness makes us long for more. We have enjoyed the first-fruits of the Spirit, and they have set us hungering and thirsting for the fullness of the heavenly vintage. We groan within ourselves, waiting for the adoption. Here we see the manna falling small like coriander seed, but there we will eat the bread of heaven. We are beginners in spiritual education. Although we have learned the first letters of the alphabet, we cannot read words yet, much less put sentences together. We have many ungratified desires at present, but soon every wish will be satisfied. Within time you will be rid of all your trials and troubles. Your eyes, now filled with tears, will weep no longer. You will gaze in ineffable rapture on the splendor of Him who sits on the throne. You will share in His triumph. You will be co-heir with Him who is the Heir of all things.

"The daughter of Jerusalem hath shaken her head at thee" (Isaiah 37:22).

Reassured by the Word of the Lord, the poor, trembling citizens of Zion grew bold and shook their heads at Sennacherib's boastful threats. Strong faith enables the servants of God to look with calm contempt on their most haughty foes. We know that our enemies are attempting impossibilities. They seek to destroy the eternal life which cannot die while Jesus lives. They seek to overthrow the citadel against which the gates of hell will not prevail. We know their weakness. What are they but men? And what is man but a worm? When the Lord arises, they will fly as chaff before the wind and be consumed as crackling thorns. Their utter powerlessness to do damage to the cause of God and His truth may make the weakest soldiers in Zion's ranks laugh them to scorn. Above all, we know that the Most High is with us. When He dresses Himself for battle, where are His enemies? His rod of iron will dash them in pieces like a potter's vessel, and their very remembrance will perish from the earth. The Kingdom is safe in the King's hands. Let us shout for joy for the Lord reigns, and His foes will be as straw for the dunghill.

July 22

"I am married unto you" (Jeremiah 3:14).

Christ Jesus is joined to His people in marriage. In love He espoused His Church as a chaste virgin long before she fell under the yoke of bondage. Full of burning affection, He toiled like Jacob for Rachel, until the whole of her purchase-money had been paid. Now, having sought her by His Spirit and brought her to know and love Him, He awaits the glorious hour when their mutual bliss will be consummated at the marriage-supper of the Lamb. The glorious Bridegroom has not yet presented His betrothed, perfect and complete, before the Majesty of heaven. She is still a wanderer in a world of woe, a dweller in the tents of Kedar. But she is even now the bride, the spouse of Jesus, dear to His heart, precious in His sight, written on His hands, and united with His person. On earth He exercises toward her all the affectionate offices of Husband. He makes rich provision for her needs, pays all her debts, allows her to assume His name and to share in all His wealth. He will never act otherwise to her. He will never mention the word divorce, for "He hateth putting away" (Malachi 2:16). Death must sever the conjugal tie between the most loving mortals, but it cannot divide the links of this immortal marriage. In heaven they marry not but are as the angels of God. Yet, there is this one marvelous exception to the rule, for in heaven Christ and His Church will celebrate their joyous nuptials.

"Even thou wast as one of them" (Obadiah 1:11).

Special stress in the sentence before us is laid on the word *thou*. A bad action may be all the worse because of the person who has committed it. When God's chosen people sin, we sin with an emphasis. If an angel should lay his hand on us when we are doing evil, he need not use any other rebuke than the question, "What dost thou here?" Much forgiven, much delivered, much instructed, and much blessed, will we dare to put our hand to evil? God forbid! A few minutes of confession may be beneficial to you this morning. Have you ever behaved as the wicked? At an evening party, certain men laughed at an unclean joke. *You were as one of them, and it was not altogether offensive to your ears.* When hard things were spoken concerning the ways of God, you were bashfully silent and seemed to be *as one of them.* Is there any difference? Here we come to close quarters. Be honest with yourself and make sure that you are a new creature in Christ Jesus. When this is sure, walk jealously lest any would again be able to say, "Even you were as one of them." You would not desire to share their eternal doom, why be like them here? Side with the afflicted people of God and not with the world.

"Stand still, and see the salvation of the Lord" (Exodus 14:13).

These words contain God's command to the believer when he is brought into extraordinary difficulties. He cannot retreat or go forward. He is shut up on the right hand and on the left. What is he to do now? The Master's Word to him is, "Stand still." It will be well for him if at such times he listens only to his Master's word, for other and evil advisers come with their suggestions. Despair whispers, "Lie down and die; give it all up." But God would have us walk in cheerful courage and rejoice in His love and faithfulness. Cowardice says, "Retreat and go back to the world's way of acting. You cannot play the Christian's part. It is too difficult. Relinquish your principles." However much Satan may urge this course on you, you cannot follow it if you are a child of God. If you are called to stand still for a while, it is to renew your strength for some greater advance in due time. Hastiness cries, "Do something. Stir yourself because to stand still and wait is sheer idleness." Presumption boasts, "If the sea is before you, march into it and expect a miracle." But faith does not listen to presumption, despair, cowardice, or hastiness. It hears God say, "Stand still," and it stands immovable as a rock. "Stand still"—keep the posture of a man ready for action, expecting further orders, while cheerfully and patiently awaiting the directing voice. It will not be long before God will say to you, as distinctly as Moses said it to the people of Israel, "Go forward."

July 25

"He left his garment in her hand, and fled and got him out" (Genesis 39:12).

In contending with certain sins there remains no mode of victory but by flight. He who would be safe from acts of evil must run away from occasions of it. A covenant must be made with our eyes not even to look on the cause of temptation for such sins only need a spark to begin with and a blaze follows in an instant. Who would enter the leper's prison and sleep amid its horrible corruption? Only he who desires to be leprous himself would thus court contagion. If the mariner knew how to avoid a storm, he would do anything rather than run the risk of weathering it. Today I may be exposed to great peril; let me have the wisdom to keep out of it and avoid it. The wings of a dove may be of more use to me today than the jaws of a lion. It is true I may be an apparent loser by declining evil company, but I had better leave my cloak than lose my character. It is not needful that I be rich, but it is imperative for me to be pure. No ties of friendship, no chains of beauty, no flashings of talent, or no unfair ridicule must turn me from the wise resolve to flee from sin. I am to resist the devil, and he will flee from me; but the lusts of the flesh I must flee, or they will surely overcome me.

July 26

"Giving all diligence, add to your faith virtue, and to virtue knowledge" (2 Peter 1:5-6).

Take care that your faith is of the right kind—that it is not a mere belief of doctrine but a simple faith depending on Christ alone. Give diligent heed to your courage that you may, with a consciousness of right, go on boldly. Study well the Scriptures and get knowledge, for a knowledge of doctrine will tend to confirm faith. Try to understand God's Word; let it dwell in your heart richly. When you have done this, add to your knowledge temperance. Take heed to your body; be temperate without. Take heed to your soul; be temperate within. Get temperance of lip, life, heart, and thought. Add to this, by God's Holy Spirit, patience. Ask Him to give you that patience which endures affliction; which, when it is tried, will come forth as gold. Array yourself with patience that you may not murmur or be depressed in your afflictions. When that grace is won, look to godliness. Godliness is something more than religion. Make God's glory your object in life. To that add brotherly love. Have a love for all the saints. To that add charity which opens its arms to all men and loves their souls. When you are adorned with these jewels, you will come to know by clearest evidence your calling and election. Remember, lukewarmness and doubting very naturally go hand in hand.

"Exceeding great and precious promises" (2 Peter 1:4).

If you know the preciousness of the promises and enjoy them in your own heart, take time to meditate on them. Thinking over the hallowed words will often be the prelude to their fulfillment. Many a Christian who has thirsted for the promise has found the sought after blessing gently distilling into his soul while he is meditating on the promise. He rejoiced that he was led to lay the promise near his heart. But besides meditating on the promises, receive them as being the very words of God. Speak to your soul thus: "If I were dealing with a man's promise, I would carefully consider the ability and the character of the man who had covenanted with me. So with the promise of God. My eye must not be so much fixed on the greatness of the mercy as on the greatness of the Promiser. My soul, it is God, even your God, who cannot lie, and who speaks to you. This Word of His which you are now considering is as true as His own existence. He is an unchangeable God. He has not altered the thing which has gone out of His mouth or called back one single consolatory sentence. It is the God who made the heavens and the earth who has spoken. He cannot fail in wisdom as to the time when He will bestow the favors because He knows when it is best to give and when better to withhold. Therefore, I will and must believe the promise." If we meditate on the promises and consider the Promiser, we will experience their sweetness and obtain their fulfillment.

"So foolish was I, and ignorant: I was as a beast before thee" (Psalm 73:22).

Remember, this is the confession of the man after God's own heart. In telling us his inner life, he writes, "So foolish was I, and ignorant." The word *foolish,* here, means more than it signifies in ordinary language. David, in a former verse of the Psalm, writes, "I was envious of the foolish when I saw the prosperity of the wicked." This shows that the folly he intended had sin in it. He puts himself down as being *foolish.* It was sinful folly, a folly which was to be condemned because of its perverseness, for he had been envious of the present prosperity of the ungodly—forgetful of the dreadful end awaiting them. Are we better than David that we should call ourselves wise? Do we profess that we have attained perfection or have been so chastened that the rod has taken all our stubbornness out of us? This would be pride indeed! Look back believer. Think of your doubting God when He has been so faithful to you. Think how often you have chosen sin because of its pleasure when that pleasure was a root of bitterness to you! Surely if we know our own heart, we must plead guilty to the indictment of a sinful folly and resolve that God will be our counsel and guide.

July 29

"Nevertheless, I am continually with thee" (Psalm 73:23).

Nevertheless—As if, notwithstanding all the foolishness and ignorance which David had just been confessing to God, not one atom the less was it true and certain that David was saved, accepted, and blessed by God's constant presence. Believer, endeavor in like spirit to say, "Nevertheless, since I belong to Christ I am continually with God!" He is always thinking of me for my good and I am continually on His mind. The Lord never sleeps, but He is perpetually watching over my welfare. I am continually in His hand so that none will be able to pluck me out. I am continually on His heart, worn there as a memorial, even as the high priest bore the names of the twelve tribes on his heart forever. God is always making providence work for our good. Suprising grace! You see me in Christ, and, though in myself abhorred, You behold me as wearing Christ's garments and washed in His blood. I stand accepted in His presence. I am continually in His favor. Here is comfort for the tried and afflicted soul who is troubled within. Look at the calm in Jesus. *"Nevertheless"*—say it in your heart and take the peace it gives. "Nevertheless, I am continually with thee."

"And when he thought thereon, he wept" (Mark 14:72).

Some feel that as long as Peter lived his tears flowed when he remembered how he denied his Lord. This may be so, for his sin was very great and grace in him had afterward done a perfect work. This same experience is common to all the redeemed family according to the degree in which the Spirit of God has removed the natural heart of stone. We, like Peter, remember our boastful promise: "Though all men forsake You, yet I will not." When we think of what we vowed to be and of what we have been, we may weep whole showers of grief. Can we, when we are reminded of our sins and their exceeding sinfulness, remain stolid and stubborn? Do we cry to the Lord for renewed assurances of pardoning love? May we never take a dry-eyed look at sin unless, before long, we have a tongue parched in the flames of hell. Peter thought of his Master's look of love. The Lord followed up the cock's warning voice with an admonitory look of sorrow, pity, and love. That glance was never out of Peter's mind so long as he lived. It was far more effectual than ten thousand sermons would have been without the Spirit. The penitent apostle would be sure to weep when he recollected the Savior's full forgiveness which restored him to his former place. To think that we have offended so kind and good a Lord is more than sufficient reason for constant weeping. Lord, smite our rocky hearts and make the waters flow.

"I in them" (John 17:23).

If such is the union which subsists between our souls and the person of our Lord, how deep and broad is the channel of our communion! This is no narrow pipe through which a thread-like stream may wind its way. It is a channel of amazing depth and breadth along whose glorious length a ponderous volume of living water may roll. This city of communion has many pearly gates. Each gate is thrown wide open, that we may enter assured of welcome. How much we are blessed in having so large an entrance! Had the Lord Jesus been far away from us, with many a stormy sea between, we would have longed to send a messenger to tell Him of our love and bring us tidings from His Father's house. See His kindness. He takes lodging with us and tabernacles in poor humble hearts. How foolish we are if we do not live in habitual communion with Him! When the road is long, dangerous, and difficult, we need not wonder that friends seldom meet each other. But when they live together, will Jonathan forget his David? A wife may, when her husband is on a journey, live many days without holding a conversation with him, but she could never be separated from him if she knew he was in one of the rooms of her own house. Seek your Lord for He is near. Embrace Him for He is your Brother. Hold Him fast for He is your Husband. Press Him to your heart for He is of your own flesh.

"Let me now go to the field, and glean ears of corn" (Ruth 2:2).

Downcast and troubled Christian, come and glean today in the broad field of promise. Here are abundant promises which exactly meet your wants. Take this one: "He will not break the bruised reed, nor quench the smoking flax" (Matthew 12:20). Does that suit your case? A reed, helpless and weak, yet, He will not break you but will restore and strengthen you. You are like the smoking flax. No light or warmth can come from you, but He will not quench you. Would you glean another ear? "Come unto me, all ye that labor and are heavy laden, and I will give you rest" (Matthew 11:28). What soft words! Your heart is tender, and the Master knows it. Therefore, He speaks so gently to you. Will you obey Him and come to Him now? Take another ear of corn: "Fear not, thou worm Jacob; I will help thee, saith the Lord and thy Redeemer, the Holy One of Israel" (Isaiah 41:14). How can you be afraid when He offers this wonderful assurance? You may gather ten thousand such golden ears as these: "I have blotted out thy sins like a cloud, and like a thick cloud thy transgressions" (Isaiah 44:22). Or this: "Though your sins be as scarlet, they shall be as wool; though they be red like crimson, they shall be whiter than snow" (Isaiah 1:18). Our Master's field is very rich. They lie before you believer! Gather them up, make them your own, for Jesus bids you take them. Do not be afraid—only believe! Grasp these sweet promises, thresh them out by meditation, and feed on them with joy.

"Who worketh all things after the counsel of his own will" (Ephesians 1:12).

Our belief in God's wisdom supposes that He has a settled purpose and plan in the work of salvation. What would creation have been without His design? In every bone, joint, muscle, sinew, gland, and blood vessel, you see the presence of a God working everything according to the design of infinite wisdom. And will God be present in creation, ruling over all, and not in grace? Will the new creation have the fickle genius of free will to preside over it when divine counsel rules the old creation? Look at Providence! Even the hairs of your head are all numbered. God weighs the mountains of our grief in scales and the hills of our tribulation in balances. And will there be a God in providence and not in grace? No! He knows the end from the beginning. He sees, in its appointed place, not merely the cornerstone which He has laid in fair colors in the blood of His dear Son, but He beholds in their ordained position each of the chosen stones taken out of the quarry of nature and polished by His grace. He has in His mind a clear knowledge of every stone which will be laid in its prepared space, how vast the divide will be, and when the topstone will be brought forth with shoutings of, "Grace! Grace! unto it." At the last it will be clearly seen that, in every chosen vessel of mercy, Jehovah did as He willed with His own. In every part of the work of grace, He accomplished His purpose and glorified His own name.

August 3

"The Lamb is the light thereof" (Revelation 21:23).

Quietly contemplate the Lamb as the light of heaven. Light in Scripture is the emblem of joy. The joy of the saints in heaven is comprised in this: Jesus chose us, loved us, bought us, cleansed us, robed us, kept us, and glorified us. We are here entirely through the Lord Jesus. Light is also the cause of beauty. Without light, no radiance flashes from the sapphire, and no peaceful ray proceeds from the pearl. Thus, all the beauty of the saints above comes from Jesus. As planets, they reflect the light of the Sun of Righteousness. They live as beams proceeding from the central orb. If He withdrew, they must die. If His glory were veiled, their glory must expire. Light is also the emblem of knowledge. In heaven our knowledge will be perfect, but the Lord Jesus Himself will be the fountain of it. Dark providences which were never understood before will then be clearly seen. All that puzzles us now will become plain to us in the light of the Lamb. Oh, what glorifying of the God of love! Light also means manifestation. Light manifests. In this world it does not yet appear what we will be. What a transformation! We were stained with sin; but with one touch of His finger, we are bright as the sun and clear as crystal. Oh, what a manifestation! All this proceeds from the exalted Lamb. Oh, to be present and to see Him in His own light, the King of kings and Lord of lords!

"The people that do know their God shall be strong" (Daniel 11:32).

Every believer understands that to know God is the highest and best form of knowledge. This spiritual knowledge is a source of strength to the Christian. It strengthens his faith. Believers are constantly spoken of in the Scriptures as being persons who are enlightened and taught of the Lord. They are said to have an unction from the Holy One, and it is the Spirit's peculiar office to lead them into all truth. Knowledge strengthens love as well as faith. Knowledge opens the door; and then through that door, we see our Savior. Or, to use another similitude, knowledge paints the portrait of Jesus; and when we see that portrait, then we love Him. We cannot love a Christ whom we do not know, at least in some degree. If we know little of the excellencies of Jesus, what He has done for us and what He is doing now, we cannot love Him much. But the more we know Him, the more we will love Him. Knowledge also strengthens hope. How can we hope for a thing if we do not know of its existence? Knowledge supplies us reasons for patience. There is not a single grace of the Christian which, under God, will not be fostered and brought to perfection by holy knowledge. How important it is that we grow not only in grace but in the knowledge of our Lord and Savior Jesus Christ!

"We know that all things work together for good to them that love God" (Romans 8:28).

On some points a believer is absolutely sure. He knows, for instance, that God sits in the stern-sheets of the vessel when it rocks most. He believes that an invisible hand is always on the world's tiller and that wherever providence may drift, Jehovah steers it. That reassuring knowledge prepares him for everything. He looks over the raging waters, sees the Spirit of Jesus treading the billows, and hears a voice saying, "It is I; be not afraid" (Mark 6:50). He knows, too, that God is always wise. Knowing this, he is confident that there can be no accidents and no mistakes. He can say, "If I would lose all I have, it is better to lose than to have, if God so wills." "We know that all things work together for good to them that love God." The Christian does not merely hold this as a theory, but *he knows it* as a matter of fact. Everything has worked for good as yet. Every event as yet has worked out the most divinely blessed results; and so, believing that God rules all, that He governs wisely, that He brings good out of evil, the believer's heart is assured. He is able to calmly meet each trial as it comes. The believer can, in the spirit of true resignation, pray, "Send me what You will, my God, so long as it comes from You. There never came an ill portion from Your table to any of Your children."

"Watchman, what of the night?" (Isaiah 21:11)

What enemies are abroad? What heresy must I guard against? Sins creep from their lurking-places when the darkness reigns. I must mount the watch-tower and watch in prayer. Our heavenly Protector foresees all the attacks which are about to be made on us. When Satan desires evil for us, He prays for us that our faith will not fail when we are sifted as wheat. What weather is coming for the Church? We must care for the Church with anxious love. Let us observe the signs of the times and prepare for conflict. "Watchman, what of the night?" What stars are visible? What precious promises suit our present case? You sound the alarm and give us the consolation, also. Christ, the polestar, is ever fixed in His place, and all the stars are secure in the right hand of their Lord. But, watchman, when comes the morning? The Bridegroom tarries. Are there no signs of His coming forth as the Sun of Righteousness? Has not the morning star arisen as the pledge of day? When will the day dawn and the shadows flee away? O Jesus, come in Spirit to my sighing heart and make it sing for joy.

"The upright love thee" (Song of Solomon 1:4).

Believers love Jesus with a deeper affection than they dare to give to any other being. They would sooner lose father and mother than part with Christ. They hold all earthly comforts with a loose hand, but they carry Him locked in their bosoms. They voluntarily deny themselves for His sake, but they are not to be driven to deny *Him*. It is scant love which the fire of persecution can dry up. The true believer's love is a deeper stream than this. Men have labored to divide the faithful from their Master, but their attempts have been fruitless in every age. Neither crowns of honor nor frowns of anger have untied this knot. This is no everyday attachment which the world's power may at length dissolve. Neither man nor devil has found a key which opens this lock. Never has the craft of Satan been more at fault than when he has exercised it in seeking to tear apart this union of two divinely welded hearts. It is written, and nothing can blot out the sentence, "The upright love thee." The intensity of the love of the upright, however, is not so much to be judged by what it appears as by what the upright long for. It is our daily lament that we cannot love enough. If only our hearts were capable of holding more and reaching farther. Measure our love by our intentions, and it is high indeed. If only we could give all the love in all hearts, in one great mass, to Him who is altogether lovely!

"They weave the spider's web" (Isaiah 59:5).

See the spider's web and behold in it a most suggestive picture of the hypocrite's religion. It is meant to catch his prey. Foolish persons are easily entrapped by the loud professions of pretenders, and even the more judicious cannot always escape. Custom, reputation, praise, advancement, and other flies are the small game which hypocrites take in their nets. A spider's web is a marvel of skill. Look at it and admire the cunning hunter's wiles. Is not a deceiver's religion equally amazing? How does he make so barefaced a lie appear to be truth? A spider's web comes from the creature's own bowels. The bee gathers her wax from flowers. The spider sucks no flowers, yet she spins out her material to any length. Even so hypocrites find their trust and hope within themselves. They lay their own foundation and hew out the pillars of their own house, refusing to be debtors to the sovereign grace of God. But a spider's web is very frail. It is not enduringly manufactured. It is no match for the servant's broom or the traveler's staff. Hypocritical cobwebs will soon come down when the broom of destruction begins its purifying work. This reminds us of one more thought—that such cobwebs are not to be endured in the Lord's house. He will see to it that they and those who spin them will be destroyed forever. Oh, my soul, be resting on something better than a spider's web. Let the Lord Jesus be your eternal hiding place.

"The city hath no need of the sun, neither of the moon, to shine in it" (Revelation 21:23).

In the better world, the inhabitants are independent of all creature comforts. They have no need of raiment. Their white robes never wear out, and they will never be defiled. They need no medicine to heal diseases. They need no sleep to refresh themselves. They rest not day or night but untiringly praise Him In His temple. They need no social relationship to minister comfort. Whatever happiness they may derive from association with their fellows is not essential to their bliss, for their Lord's society is enough for their largest desires. They need no teachers there. They doubtless commune with one another concerning the things of God, but they will all be taught of the Lord. Ours are the alms at the king's gate, but they feast at the table itself. Here we lean on the friendly arm, but there they lean on their Beloved. Here we must have the help of our companions, but there they find all they want in Christ Jesus. Here the angels bring us blessings, but we will not need messengers from heaven then. We will not need Gabriels there to bring love-notes from God, for there we will see Him face to face. What a glorious hour when God and not His creatures—when the Lord and not His works—will be our daily joy! Our souls will then have attained the perfection of bliss.

"Christ, who is our life" (Colossians 3:4).

Paul's marvelously rich expression indicates that Christ is the *source* of our life. "You hath he quickened, who were dead in trespasses and sins" (Ephesians 2:1). That same voice which brought Lazarus out of the tomb raised us to newness of life. He is now the *substance* of our spiritual life. It is by His life that we live. He is in us. *Christ is the sustenance of our life.* "This is the bread which cometh down from heaven, that a man may eat thereof, and not die" (John 6:50). *Christ is the solace of our life.* All our true joys come from Him. In times of trouble, His presence is our consolation. There is nothing worth living for but Him, and His lovingkindness is better than life! *Christ is the object of our life.* As the soldier fights for his captain and is crowned in his captain's victory, so the believer contends for Christ and gets his triumph out of the triumphs of his Master. "For him to live is Christ" (Philippians 1:21). *Christ is the example of our life.* Where there is the same life within, there will be, to a great extent, the same developments without. If we live in near fellowship with the Lord Jesus, we will grow like Him. We will set Him before us as our divine copy, and we will seek to tread in His footsteps, until He becomes *the crown of our life* in glory.

August 11

"O that I were as in months past" (Job 29:2).

Some Christians look back on the past with pleasure but regard the present with dissatisfaction. Once they lived near to Jesus, but now they feel they have wandered from Him. They say, "O that I were as in months past!" They complain that they do not have peace of mind or that they have no enjoyment in the means of grace or that conscience is not so tender or that they have not so much zeal for God's glory. The causes of this mournful state of things are manifold. It may arise through a *neglect of prayer,* for a neglected prayer closet is the beginning of all spiritual decline. Or it may be the result of *idolatry.* The heart has been occupied with something else more than with God. The affections have been set on the things of earth instead of the things of heaven. A jealous God will not be content with a divided heart. He must be loved first and best. He will withdraw the sunshine of His presence from a cold, wandering heart. Or the cause may be found in *self-confidence* and *self-righteousness.* Pride is busy in the heart, and self is exalted instead of lying low at the foot of the cross. Christian, if you are not now as you "were in months past," do not rest satisfied with wishing for a return of former happiness, but go at once to seek your Maker and tell Him your sad state. Ask His grace and strength to help you walk more closely with Him. Humble yourself before Him, and He will lift you up. Do not sit down to sigh and lament. While the beloved Physician lives there is hope and certainty of recovery for the worst cases.

"The Lord reigneth, let the earth rejoice" (Psalm 97:1).

There is no cause for fear once we believe in this blessed scripture. On earth the Lord's power as readily controls the rage of the wicked as the rage of the sea. His love as easily refreshes the poor with mercy as the earth with showers. Majesty gleams in flashes of fire amid the tempest's horrors, and the glory of the Lord is seen in its grandeur in the fall of empires and the crash of thrones. In all our conflicts and tribulations, we may behold the hand of the divine King. In hell, evil spirits recognize with misery His undoubted supremacy. When permitted to roam abroad, it is with a chain at their heel. Death's darts are under the Lord's lock, and the grave's prisons have divine power as their warden. The terrible vengeance of the Judge of all the earth makes fiends cower and tremble, even as dogs in the kennel fear the hunter's whip. In heaven, none doubt the sovereignty of the eternal King, but all fall on their faces to do Him homage. Angels are His courtiers, the redeemed are His favorites, and all delight to serve Him day and night. May we soon reach the city of the great King.

"The cedars of Lebanon which he hath planted" (Psalm 104:16).

Lebanon's cedars are symbolic of the Christian in that they owe their planting entirely to the Lord. This is quite true of every child of God. He is not man-planted or self-planted but God-planted. The mysterious hand of the divine Spirit dropped the living seed into a heart which He had Himself prepared for its reception. Every true heir of heaven owns the great Husbandman as his planter. Moreover, the cedars of Lebanon are not dependent on man for their watering. They stand on the lofty rock, unmoistened by human irrigation, yet our heavenly Father supplies them. This is the way it is with the Christian who has learned to live by faith. He is independent of man, even in temporal things. He looks to the Lord his God for his continued maintenance and to Him alone. He is not a hot-house plant sheltered from temptation. He stands in the most exposed position. He has no shelter or protection, except the broad wings of the eternal God who always covers the cedars which He Himself has planted. Like cedars, believers are full of sap, having vitality enough to be ever green, even amid winter's snows. Lastly, the flourishing and majestic condition of the cedar is to the praise of God only. The Lord alone has been everything to the cedars. Therefore, David very sweetly puts it in one of the psalms, "Praise ye the Lord, fruitful trees and all cedars" (Psalm 148:9). In the believer there is nothing that can magnify man. He is planted, nourished, and protected by the Lord's own hand. To Him let all the glory be given.

"Thou, Lord, hast made me glad through thy work" (Psalm 92:4).

Do you believe that your sins are forgiven and that Christ has made a full atonement for them? Then what a joyful Christian you ought to be! You should live above the common trials and troubles of the world! Since sin is forgiven, can it matter what happens to you now? Luther said, "Smite, Lord, smite, for my sin is forgiven; if Thou hast but forgiven me, smite as hard as Thou wilt." Christian, if you are saved, be grateful and loving. Cling to that cross which took your sin away. Paul wrote, "I beseech you, therefore, by the mercies of God, that ye present your bodies a living sacrifice, holy, acceptable unto God, which is your reasonable service" (Romans 12:1). Do not let your zeal evaporate. Show your love. Love the brethren of Him who loved you. If there is a Mephibosheth anywhere who is lame, help him for Jonathan's sake. If there is a poor, tried believer, weep with him and bear his cross for the sake of Him who wept for you and carried your sins. Since you are forgiven, for Christ's sake, go and tell the joyful news of pardoning mercy to others. Do not be content with this blessing for yourself alone. Holy gladness and holy boldness will make you a good preacher, and all the world will be a pulpit for you to preach in. Cheerful holiness is the most forcible of sermons, but the Lord must give it to you. Seek it this morning before you go into the world. When it is the Lord's work in which we rejoice, we need not be afraid of being too glad.

"Isaac went out to meditate in the field at the eventide" (Genesis 24:63).

If those who spend so many hours in idle company, light reading, and useless pastimes could learn wisdom, they would find more interesting engagements in meditation than in the vanities which now have such charms for them. We would all know more, live nearer to God, and grow deeper in grace. Meditation chews the cud and extracts the real nutrition from the mental food gathered elsewhere. When Jesus is the theme, meditation is sweet indeed. Isaac found Rebecca while engaged in private thoughts. Very admirable was the choice of place. In the field we have innumerable texts for thought. From the cedar to the hyssop, from the soaring eagle to the chirping grasshopper, from the blue expanse of heaven to a drop of dew, all things are full of teaching. When the eye is divinely opened, that teaching flashes on the mind far more vividly than from written books. Our little rooms are neither so healthy, so suggestive, so agreeable, nor so inspiring as the fields. Let us count nothing common or unclean but feel that all created things point to their Maker, and the field will at once be hallowed. The glory of the setting sun excites our wonder, and the solemnity of approaching night awakens our awe. If the business of this day will permit it, it will be well, dear reader, if you can spare an hour to walk in the field in the evening. But if not, the Lord is in the town, too, and will meet with you in your room or in the crowded street. Let your heart go forth to meet Him.

"Give unto the Lord the glory due unto his name" (Psalm 29:2).

God's glory is the result of His nature and acts. He is glorious in His character for there is such a store of everything that is holy, good, and lovely in God that He must be glorious. The actions which flow from His character are also glorious. He intends that they should manifest to His creatures His goodness, mercy, and justice. He is equally concerned that the glory associated with them should be given only to Himself. There is nothing in ourselves in which we may glory. What do we have that we did not receive from God? Then how careful ought we to be to walk humbly before the Lord! The moment we glorify ourselves, since there is room for one glory only in the universe, we set ourselves up as rivals to the Most High. Will the dust of the desert strive with the whirlwind or the drops of the ocean struggle with the tempest? Give the Lord all the honor and glory that is due His name. Yet it is, perhaps, one of the hardest struggles of the Christian life to learn this sentence—"Not unto us, O Lord, not unto us, but unto thy name give glory" (Psalm 115:1). It is a lesson which God is teaching us. Let a Christian begin to boast, "I can do all things," without adding, "through Christ which strengtheneth me" (Philippians 4:13), and before long he will have to groan, "I can do nothing." When we do anything for the Lord, and He is pleased to accept our doings, let us lay our crown at His feet and exclaim, "Not I, but the grace of God which was with me!"

August 17

"The mercy of God" (Psalm 52:8).

Meditate a little on this tender mercy of the Lord. With a gentle, loving touch, He heals the broken in heart and binds up their wounds. It is a great mercy. There is nothing little in God. His mercy is like Himself—it is infinite. You cannot measure it. It is undeserved mercy, as indeed all true mercy must be, for deserved mercy is only a misnomer for justice. There was no right on the sinner's part to the kind consideration of the Most High. Had the rebel been doomed at once to eternal fire he would have merited the doom; and if delivered from wrath, sovereign love alone has found a cause, for there was none in the sinner himself. It is rich mercy. Some things are great but have little efficacy in them. This mercy is a cordial to your drooping spirits. It is manifold mercy. As Bunyan says, "All the flowers in God's garden are double." There is no single mercy. You may think you have only one mercy, but you will find it to be a whole cluster of mercies. It is abounding mercy. Millions have received it. Yet, far from its being exhausted, it is as fresh, as full, and as free as ever. It is unfailing mercy. It will never leave you. If mercy is your friend, mercy will be with you in temptation to keep you from yielding, and it will be with you in trouble to prevent you from sinking. Mercy is with you while you are living, to be the light and life of your countenance. And when you are dying, mercy will be the joy of your soul when earthly comfort is ebbing fast.

"Strangers are come into the sanctuaries of the Lord's house" (Jeremiah 51:51).

On this account the faces of the Lord's people were covered with shame, for it was a terrible thing that men should intrude into the Holy Place reserved for the priests alone. Everywhere about us we see cause for sorrow. How many ungodly men are now being educated to enter into the ministry! How fearful it is that ordination would be placed on the unconverted and that among the more enlightened churches of our land there would be such laxity of discipline. If the thousands who will read this portion will all take this matter before the Lord Jesus this day, He will interfere and avert the evil which will come on His Church. To adulterate the Church is to pollute a well, to pour water on fire, to sow a fertile field with stones. May we all have grace to maintain in our own proper way the purity of the Church as being an assembly of believers and not an unsaved community of unconverted men. Our zeal must, however, begin at home. Let us examine ourselves as to our right to eat at the Lord's table. Let us see to it that we have our wedding garment on, lest we ourselves be intruders in the Lord's sanctuaries. Many are called, but few are chosen; the way is narrow, and the gate is straight. Oh, for grace to come to Jesus with the faith of God's elect! Heart searching is the duty of all who are baptized or come to the Lord's table. "Search me, O God, and know my heart: try me, and know my thoughts" (Psalm 139:23).

"He shall stand and feed in the strength of the Lord" (Micah 5:4).

Christ's reign in His Church is that of a Shepherd-King. He has supremacy, but it is the superiority of a wise and tender Shepherd over His needy and loving flock. He commands and receives obedience, but it is the willing obedience of the well-cared-for sheep rendered joyfully to their beloved Shepherd. He rules by the force of love and the energy of goodness. The great Head of the Church is actively engaged in providing for His people. He does not sit down on the throne in an empty state or hold a scepter without wielding it in government. No! He stands and feeds. The expression "feed," in the original, means to shepherdize, to do everything expected of a shepherd: to guide, watch, preserve, restore, and tend, as well as to feed. It is said, "He shall stand and feed;" not, "He shall feed now and then and leave His position;" not, "He shall one day grant a revival and then the next day leave His Church to barrenness." His eyes never slumber, and His hands never rest. His heart never ceases to beat with love, and His shoulders are never weary of carrying His people's burdens. Wherever Christ is, there is God; and whatever Christ does is the act of the Most High. It is a joyful truth to consider that He who stands today representing the interests of His people is God to whom every knee will bow. We are happy to belong to such a Shepherd. Let us worship and bow down before Him as the people of His pasture.

"The sweet psalmist of Israel" (2 Samuel 23:1).

Among all the saints whose lives are recorded, David possesses the most striking, varied, and instructive character. In his history, we meet with trials and temptations not to be discovered, as a whole, in other saints of ancient times, and he is all the more suggestive a type of our Lord. David knew the trials of all ranks and conditions of men. Kings have their troubles, and David wore a crown. The peasant has his cares, and David handled a shepherd's crook. The wanderer has many hardships, and David abode in the caves of Engedi. The psalmist was also tried in his friends. His counselor Ahithophel forsook him. "He which did eat of my bread, hath lifted up his heel against me" (Psalm 41:9). His worst foes were of his own household, and his children were his greatest affliction. The temptations of poverty and wealth, of honor and reproach, and of health and weakness all tried their power on him. David no sooner escaped from one trial than he fell into another. It is probably from this cause that David's psalms are so universally the delight of experienced Christians. Whatever our frame of mind, whether ecstasy or depression, David has exactly described our emotions. He was an able master of the human heart because he had been tutored in the best of all schools—the school of heartfelt, personal experience. As we are instructed in the same school, we increasingly appreciate David's psalms and find them to be green pastures. My soul, let David's experience cheer and counsel you this day.

"He that watereth shall be watered also himself" (Proverbs 11:25).

In this morning's scripture we are taught the great lesson that to get, we must give; to accumulate, we must scatter; to make ourselves happy, we must make others happy; and in order to become spiritually vigorous, we must seek the spiritual good of others. In watering others, we are watered ourselves. How? Our efforts to be useful bring out our powers for usefulness. We have latent talents and dormant faculties, which are brought to light by exercise. We do not know what tender sympathies we possess, until we try to dry the widow's tears and soothe the orphan's grief. We often find in attempting to teach others that we gain instruction for ourselves. What gracious lessons some of us have learned as we have attempted to help others. We went to teach the Scriptures and came away blushing that we knew so little of them. Watering others makes us humble. Our own comfort is also increased by our working for others. We endeavor to cheer them, and the consolation gladdens our own heart. Like the two men in the snow—one rubbed the other's limbs to keep him from dying, and in so doing kept his own blood in circulation and saved his own life. The poor widow of Sarepta gave from her scanty store for the prophet's wants, and from that day she never again knew what want was. Give, and it will be given to you, good measure, pressed down, and running over.

"I charge you, O daughters of Jerusalem, if ye find my beloved, that ye tell him that I am sick of love" (Song of Solomon 5:8).

Gracious souls are never perfectly at ease unless they are in a state of nearness to Christ. When they are away from Him, they lose their peace. The nearer to Him, the nearer they are to the perfect calm of heaven. The nearer to Him, the fuller the heart is, not only of peace, but of life, vigor, and joy, for these all depend on constant communion with Jesus. What the sun is to the day, what the moon is to the night, what the dew is to the flower, such is Jesus Christ to us. What bread is to the hungry, clothing to the naked, the shadow of a great rock to the traveler in a weary land, such is Jesus Christ to us. Supremely blessed are they who thirst after the Righteous One. Blessed is that hunger, since it comes from God. There is a hallowness about that hunger, since it sparkles among the beatitudes of our Lord. But the blessing involves a promise. Such hungry ones will be filled with what they are desiring. If Christ causes us to long after Himself, He will certainly satisfy those longings. When He does come to us, how sweet it will be!

August 23

"The voice of weeping shall be no more heard" (Isaiah 65:19).

The glorified weep no more, for all outward causes of grief are gone. There are no broken friendships or blighted prospects in heaven. Poverty, famine, peril, persecution, and slander are unknown there. They weep no more, for they are perfectly sanctified. No evil heart of unbelief prompts them to depart from the living God. They are without fault before His throne and are fully conformed to His image. Well may they cease to mourn who have ceased to sin. They weep no more, because all fear of change is past. They know that they are eternally secure. Sin is shut out, and they are shut in. They dwell within a city which will never be stormed. They bask in a sun which will never set. They drink of a river which will never dry, and they pluck fruit from a tree which will never wither. Countless cycles may revolve, but eternity will not be exhausted. While eternity endures, their immortality and blessedness will co-exist with it. They are forever with the Lord. They weep no more, because every desire is fulfilled. Imperfect as our present ideas are of the things which God has prepared for them that love Him, yet we know enough by the revelation of the Spirit to know the saints above are supremely blessed. The joy of Christ, which is an infinite fullness of delight, is in them. That same joyful rest remains for us. Before long the weeping willow will be exchanged for the palm branch of victory, and sorrow's dewdrops will be transformed into the pearls of everlasting bliss. "Wherefore comfort one another with these words" (1 Thessalonians 4:18).

"The breaker is come up before them" (Micah 2:13).

Because Jesus has gone before us, things are much different than they would have been had He never passed that way. He has conquered every foe that obstructed the way. Cheer up now. Not only has Christ traveled the road, but He has slain your enemies. Do you dread sin? He has nailed it to His cross. Do you fear death? He has been the death of death. Are you afraid of hell? He has barred it against the advent of any of His children. They will never see the gulf of perdition. Whatever foes may be before the Christian, they are all overcome. There are lions, but their teeth are broken; there are serpents, but their fangs are extracted; there are rivers, but they are bridged or fordable. The sword that has been forged against us is already blunted. The instruments of war which the enemy is preparing have already lost their point. God has taken away in the person of Christ all the power that anything can have to hurt us. Well then, you may go joyously along your journey, for all your enemies are conquered beforehand. You will, it is true, often engage in combat; but your fight will be with a vanquished foe. His head is under your foot. He may attempt to injure you, but his strength will not be sufficient for his malicious design. Your victory is certain.

"His fruit was sweet to my taste" (Song of Solomon 2:3).

Faith, in the Scripture, is spoken of as pertaining to all the senses. It is hearing. "Hear, and your soul shall live" (Isaiah 55:3). One of the first performances of faith is hearing. We hear the voice of God, not with the outward ear alone, but with the inward ear. We hear it as God's Word, and we believe it to be so; that is the *"hearing"* of faith. Then our mind looks on the truth as it is presented to us; that is to say, we understand it; we perceive its meaning. This is *sight*. "Unto them that look for him shall he appear the second time without sin unto salvation" (Hebrews 9:28). We begin to admire it and find how fragrant it is; that is faith in its *"smell."* Faith is smelling. "All thy garments smell of myrrh, aloes, and cassia" (Psalm 45:8). Then we appropriate the mercies which are prepared for us in Christ; that is faith in its *"touch."* By faith the woman came behind and touched the hem of Christ's garment, and by this we handle the things of the good word of life. Faith is equally the spirit's *taste*. "How sweet are thy words to my taste! yea, sweeter than honey to my lips" (Psalm 119:103). "Except ye eat the flesh of the Son of man, and drink his blood, ye have no life in you" (John 6:53). That which gives true enjoyment is the aspect of faith wherein Christ is received into us and made to be the food of our souls. It is then we sit under His shadow with great delight and find His fruit sweet to our taste.

August 26

"He hath commanded his covenant forever"
(Psalm 111:9).

The Lord's people delight in the covenant. It is an unfailing source of consolation to them as the Holy Spirit leads them into His banqueting house and waves His banner of love. They delight to contemplate *the antiquity* of that covenant, remembering that before planets ran their round, the interests of the saints were made secure in Christ Jesus. It is peculiarly pleasing to them to remember *the sureness* of the covenant. They delight to celebrate it as signed, sealed, and ratified in all things. It often makes their hearts dilate with joy to think of its *immutability,* as a covenant which neither time nor eternity, life nor death, will ever be able to violate—a covenant as old as eternity and as everlasting as the Rock of ages. They rejoice to feast on *the fullness* of this covenant, for they see all things provided for them in it. God is their portion, Christ their companion, the Spirit their Comforter, earth their lodge, and heaven their home. They see in it an inheritance reserved for every soul possessing salvation. How their souls were gladdened when they saw in the last will and testament of their divine Kinsman that it was bequeathed to them! More especially it is the pleasure of God's people to contemplate *the graciousness* of this covenant. They see that the law was made void because it was a covenant of works and depended on merit. But this they perceive to be enduring because grace is the basis. The covenant is a treasury of wealth, a fountain of life, a storehouse of salvation, a charter of peace, and a haven of joy.

August 27

"How long will it be ere they believe me?" (Numbers 14:11).

Strive, with all diligence, to keep out unbelief. Among hateful things it is the most to be abhorred. Its injurious nature is so venemous that he who exercises it, and he on whom it is exercised, are both hurt by it. In your case, believer, it is most wicked, for the mercies of your Lord in the past increase your guilt in doubting Him now. It is very cruel for a well-beloved wife to mistrust a kind and faithful husband. The sin is needless, foolish, and unwarranted. Jesus has never given the slightest ground for suspicion, and it is hard to be doubted by those to whom our conduct is uniformly affectionate and true. This is crowning His head with thorns of the sharpest kind. Jesus is the Son of the Highest and has unbounded wealth. It is shameful to doubt Omnipotence and distrust All-Sufficiency. The cattle on a thousand hills will suffice for our most hungry feeding, and the granaries of heaven are not likely to be emptied by our eating. If Christ were only a cistern, we might soon exhaust His fullness; but who can drain a fountain? Myriad spirits have drawn their supplies from Him, and not one of them has murmured at the scantiness of His resources. Put away this lying traitor unbelief, for his only errand is to cut the bonds of communion and make us mourn an absent Savior.

August 28

"Oil for the light" (Exodus 25:6).

My soul, how much you need this! Your lamp will not continue to burn long without it. You have no oil well springing up in your human nature. Even the consecrated lamps could not give light without oil. Under the most happy circumstances you cannot give light for another hour unless fresh oil of grace is given you. Not every oil could be used in the Lord's service. Neither the petroleum which exudes so plentifully from the earth nor the produce of fishes nor that extracted from nuts would be accepted. Only the best olive oil was selected. Pretended grace from natural goodness or imaginary grace from outward ceremonies will never serve the true saint of God. He knows that the Lord would not be pleased with these. He goes to the olive-press of Gethsemane and draws his supplies from Him who was crushed therein. The oil of gospel grace is pure, and hence the light which is fed thereon is clear and bright. Our churches are the Savior's golden candelabra. If they are to be lights in this dark world, they must have much holy oil. Let us pray for ourselves, our ministers, and our churches, that they may never lack oil for the light. Truth, holiness, joy, knowledge, and love are all beams of the sacred light. But we cannot exemplify them unless we receive oil from God the Holy Spirit in private.

"Have mercy upon me, O God" (Psalm 51:1).

When Dr. Carey was suffering from a serious illness, he was asked, "If this sickness would prove fatal, what passage would you select as the text for your funeral sermon?" He replied, "I feel that such a poor, sinful creature is unworthy to have anything said about him. But if a funeral sermon must be preached, let it be from the words, 'Have mercy upon me, O God, according to Thy lovingkindness; according unto the multitude of Thy tender mercies blot out my transgressions'" (Psalm 51:1). In the same spirit of humility, he directed in his will that the following inscription, and nothing more, should be cut on his gravestone:

WILLIAM CAREY, BORN AUGUST 17th, 1761;
DIED—.
"A wretched, poor, and helpless worm,
On Thy kind arms I fall."

The best of men are conscious, above all others, that they are men at the best. We need the Lord's mercy on our good works, our prayers, our preachings, our alms-givings, and our holiest things. The blood was not only sprinkled on the door-posts of Israel's houses, but on the sanctuary, the mercy seat, and the altar; as sin intrudes into our holiest things, the blood of Jesus is needed to purify them from defilement.

"Wait on the Lord" (Psalm 27:14).

Sometimes it takes years of teaching before we learn to *wait*. It is much easier to forge ahead than to stand still. There are hours of perplexity when the most willing spirit, anxiously desirous to serve the Lord, does not know what part to take. Then what will it do? Fly back in cowardice, turn to the right hand in fear, or rush forward in presumption? No, it must simply wait. *Wait in prayer*, however. Call on God and spread the case before Him. Tell Him your difficulty and plead His promise of aid. In dilemmas between one duty and another, it is sweet to be humble as a child and wait with simplicity of soul on the Lord. It is sure to be well with us when we are heartily willing to be guided by the will of God. But *wait in faith*. Express your unstaggering confidence in Him. Unfaithful, untrusting waiting is an insult to the Lord. Believe that He will come at the right time. The vision will come and will not tarry. *Wait in quiet patience,* not rebelling because you are under the affliction, but blessing your God for it. Never murmur as the children of Israel did against Moses. Never wish you could go back to the world again, but accept the case as it is and put it, without any self-will, into the hand of your covenant God, saying, "Now, Lord, not my will, but Yours be done. I do not know what to do. But I will wait until You drive back my foes. I will wait, for my heart is fixed on You alone, O God, and my spirit waits for You in the full conviction that You will be my joy and my salvation, my refuge and my strong tower."

August 31

"On mine arm shall they trust" (Isaiah 51:5).

In times of severe trial, the Christian has nothing on earth that he can trust and is therefore compelled to cast himself on his God alone. He must simply and entirely trust himself to the providence and care of God. When a man is so poor, so friendless, so helpless that he has nowhere else to turn, he flies into his Father's arms and is blessedly clasped therein! He will learn more of his Lord then than at any other time. Tempest-tossed believer, it is a happy trouble that drives you to your Father! Now that you have only your God to trust, see that you put your full confidence in Him. Do not dishonor your Lord and Master by unworthy doubts and fears; but be strong in faith, giving glory to God. Show rich men how rich you are in your poverty when the Lord God is your helper. Show the strong man how strong you are in your weakness when underneath you are the everlasting arms. Now is the time for feats of faith. Be strong and very courageous; God will certainly, as surely as He built the heavens and the earth, glorify Himself in your weakness and magnify His might in the midst of your distress. The grandeur of the arch of heaven would be spoiled if the sky were supported by a single visible column, and your faith would lose its glory if it rested on anything discernible by the carnal eye. May the Holy Spirit give you rest in Jesus this closing day of the month.

September 1

"Thou shalt guide me with thy counsel, and afterward receive me to glory" (Psalm 73:24).

The psalmist felt his need for divine guidance. He had just been discovering the foolishness of his own heart, and he resolved that God's counsel would henceforth guide him. A sense of our own folly is a great step toward being wise when it leads us to rely on the wisdom of the Lord. The blind man leans on his friend's arm and reaches home in safety. Likewise, we should give ourselves up implicitly to divine guidance, nothing doubting, assured that though we cannot see, it is always safe to trust the All-seeing God. *"Thou shalt"* is a blessed expression of confidence. He was sure that the Lord would not decline the condescending task. Be assured that your God will be your counselor and friend. He will guide you. He will direct all your ways. In His written Word you have this assurance in part fulfilled, for holy Scripture is His counsel to you. We have God's Word always to guide us! This is the unerring chart from the quicksands of destruction to the haven of salvation, mapped and marked by One who knows all the way. Bless You, O God, that we may trust You to guide us to the end! After this guidance through life, the psalmist anticipates a divine reception at last— *"And afterward receives me to glory"* (Psalm 73:24). What a thought for you, believer! *God* Himself will receive *you* to glory—*you!* Wandering, erring, straying, yet He will bring you safe at last to glory! This is your portion; live on it this day.

September 2

"But Simon's wife's mother lay sick of a fever, and anon they tell him of her" (Mark 1:30).

This little peep into the house of the apostolic fisherman is very interesting. We see at once that household joys and cares are no hindrance to the full exercise of the ministry. A few may decry marriage, but true Christianity and household life agree well together. Peter's house was probably a poor fisherman's hut, but the Lord of Glory entered it, lodged in it, and wrought a miracle in it. If this little book is read this morning in some humble cottage, let this fact encourage those who reside there to seek the company of King Jesus. God is in little huts more often than in rich palaces. Jesus is looking around your room now and is waiting to be gracious to you. Sickness had entered Simon's house, and fever in a deadly form had prostrated his mother-in-law. As soon as Jesus came they told Him of the sad affliction, and He hastened to the patient's bed. Do you have any sickness in the house this morning? You will find Jesus the best Physician by far. Go to Him at once and tell Him all about the matter. It concerns one of His people, and therefore it will not be trivial to Him. Observe that *at once* the Savior restored the sick woman. None can heal as He does. We know that believing prayer for the sick is far more likely to be followed by restoration than anything else in the world. Where this does not avail, we must meekly bow to His will by whom life and death are determined. The tender heart of Jesus waits to hear our griefs. Pour them into His patient ear.

September 3

"Thou whom my soul loveth" (Song of Solomon 1:7).

It is wonderful to be able to say of the Lord Jesus— *"Thou whom my soul loveth."* Many can only say they *hope* they love Him; they *trust* they love Him; but only a poor and shallow experience will be content to stay here. No one should give any rest to his spirit until he feels quite sure about this vitally important matter. We should not be satisfied with a superficial *hope* that Jesus loves us and with a bare trust that we love Him. The old saints spoke positively and plainly. Paul said, "I know whom I have believed" (2 Timothy 1:12). "I know that my Redeemer liveth," said Job. Get positive knowledge of your love for Jesus. True love for Christ is the Holy Spirit's work in every case. He is the cause of it. *Why* do we love Jesus? *Because He first loved us and gave Himself for us.* We have life through His death. We have peace through His blood. Though He was rich, for our sakes He became poor. *Why* do we love Jesus? Because of the *excellency of His person.* We are filled with a sense of His beauty! His greatness, goodness, and loveliness combine to enthrall the soul until it is so overcome with love that it exclaims, "Yea, He is altogether lovely." This is a blessed love—a love which binds the heart with chains softer than silk and firmer than stone!

"I will; be thou clean" (Mark 1:41).

Primeval darkness heard the Almighty command, "Let there be light," and immediately there was light. The Word of the Lord Jesus is equal in majesty to that ancient word of power. Redemption, like creation, has its word of might. Jesus speaks, and it is done. Leprosy yielded to no human remedies, but it fled at once at the Lord's "I will." The disease exhibited no hopeful signs or tokens of recovery. The sinner is in a plight more miserable than the leper. Let him go to Jesus, beseeching Him, and kneeling down to Him. Let him exercise what little faith he has, even if it can go no farther than, "Lord, if You will, You can make me clean." There need be no doubt as to the result. Jesus heals all who come and casts out none. In reading this morning's Scripture, notice that Jesus touched the leper. This unclean person had broken through the regulations of the ceremonial law and pressed into the house, but Jesus broke through the law Himself in order to meet him. Jesus Christ was made sin for us, although in Himself He knew no sin, that we might be made the righteousness of God in Him. If only poor sinners would go to Jesus, believing in the power of His blessed substitutionary work, they would soon learn the power of His gracious touch. That hand which multiplied the loaves, which saved sinking Peter, which upholds afflicted saints, which crowns believers—that same hand will touch every seeking sinner and in a moment make him clean. The love of Jesus is the source of salvation.

September 5

"Woe is me, that I sojourn in Mesech, that I dwell in the tents of Kedar!" (Psalm 120:5).

Even though you are a Christian, you have to live in the midst of an ungodly world, and it is of little use for you to cry, "Woe is me." Jesus did not pray that you would be taken out of the world. It is better to meet the difficulty in the Lord's strength and glorify Him in it. The enemy is always on the watch to detect inconsistency in your conduct; therefore, be very holy. Remember that the eyes of all are on you, and more is expected from you than from other men. Strive to give no occasion for blame. Let your goodness be the only fault they can discover in you. Seek to be useful as well as consistent. Perhaps you think, "If I were in a more favorable position, I might serve the Lord's cause; but I cannot do any good where I am." But the worse the people are among you, the more they need your example. If they are crooked, you should set them straight. If they are perverse, they need you to turn their proud heart to the truth. Where would the physicians be but where there are many sick? When you become weary of the strife and sin that meet you on every hand, remember that all the saints have endured the same trial. Some of them had to endanger their lives to the death, and you will not be crowned until you also have endured hardness as a good soldier of Jesus Christ. Therefore, "stand fast in the faith; quit you like men; be strong" (1 Corinthians 16:13).

"In the midst of a crooked and perverse nation, among whom ye shine as lights in the world" (Philippians 2:15).

A Christian man should so shine in his life that a person could not live with him a week without knowing the gospel. His conversation should be such that all who are around him would clearly perceive whose he is and whom he serves. People should see the image of Jesus reflected in his daily actions. Lights are intended for *guidance*. We are to help those around us who are in the dark. We are to hold forth the Word of life to them. We are to point sinners to the Savior and the weary to a divine resting place. Men sometimes read their Bibles and fail to understand them. We should be ready, like Philip, to instruct the inquirer in the meaning of God's Word, the way of salvation, and the life of godliness. Lights are also used for *warning*. Christian men should know that there are many false lights shining everywhere in the world, and therefore the right light is needed. The wreckers of Satan are always abroad, tempting the ungodly to sin under the name of pleasure. They hoist the wrong light. It is our responsibility to put up the true light on every dangerous rock, to point out every sin, and tell what it leads to so we may be clear of the blood of all men. Lights also have a very *cheering* influence and so have Christians. A Christian ought to be a comforter with kind words on his lips and sympathy in his heart. He should carry sunshine wherever he goes and diffuse happiness around him.

"And when they could not come nigh unto him for the press, they uncovered the roof where he was: and when they had broken it up, they let down the bed wherein the sick of the palsy lay" (Mark 2:4).

Faith is full of inventions. The house was full, a crowd blocked the door, but faith found a way of getting at the Lord and placing the palsied man before Him. If we cannot get sinners where Jesus is by ordinary methods, we must use extraordinary ones. It seems, according to Luke 5:19, that the roofing had to be removed, which would make dust and cause a measure of danger to those below. But where the case is very urgent, we must not mind running some risks and shocking some proprieties. Jesus was there to heal, and come what may, faith ventured all so that her poor paralyzed charge might have his sins forgiven. Oh, that we had more daring faith among us! Try today to perform some gallant act for the love of souls and the glory of the Lord. Cannot faith invent also and reach by some new means the outcasts who lie perishing around us? It was the presence of Jesus which excited victorious courage in the four bearers of the palsied man. Is the Lord not among us now? Have we seen His face this morning? Have we felt His healing power in our own souls? If so, let us, breaking through all impediments, labor to bring souls to Jesus. O Lord, make us quick to suggest methods of reaching Your sin-sick ones and bold to carry them out at all hazards.

"From me is thy fruit found" (Hosea 14:8).

The fruit of the branch is directly traceable to the root. Sever the connection, the branch dies, and no fruit is produced. By virtue of our union with Christ, we bring forth fruit. Every bunch of grapes has been first in the root. It has passed through the stem, flowed through the sap vessels, and fashioned itself externally into fruit. But it was first in the stem. Also, every good work was first in Christ, and then it is brought forth in us. Christian, prize this precious union in Christ, for it must be the source of all the fruitfulness which you can hope to know. If you were not joined to Jesus Christ, you would be a barren bough indeed. Our fruit comes from God. The fruit owes much to the root, but it also owes much to external influences. How much we owe to God's grace and providence! He provides us contantly with quickening, teaching, consolation, strength, or whatever else we need. To this we owe all of our usefulness or virtue. The gardener's sharp-edged knife promotes the fruitfulness of the tree by thinning the clusters and by cutting off superfluous shoots. So it is, Christian, with that pruning which the Lord gives to you. "My Father is the husbandman. Every branch in me that beareth not fruit he taketh away; and every branch that beareth fruit, he purgeth it, that it may bring forth more fruit" (John 15:2). Since our God is the author of our spiritual graces, let us give to Him all the glory of our salvation.

September 9

"I will answer thee, and show thee great and mighty things which thou knowest not" (Jeremiah 33:3).

There are different translations of these words. One version renders it, "I will show thee great and fortified things;" another, "great and reserved things." Now, there are reserved and special things in Christian experience. There are the common frames and feelings of repentance, faith, joy, and hope, which are enjoyed by the entire family. But there is an upper realm of rapture, of communion, and conscious union with Christ which is far from being the common dwelling-place of believers. Not all of us have John's high privilege to lean on Jesus' bosom or Paul's to be caught up into the third heaven. There are heights in knowledge of the things of God which the eagle's eye and philosophic thought has never seen. God alone can bear us there. But the chariot in which He takes us up, and the fiery steeds with which that chariot is dragged, are prevailing prayers. Prevailing prayer takes the Christian to Carmel and enables him to cover heaven with clouds of blessing and earth with floods of mercy. Prevailing prayer bears the Christian aloft and shows him the inheritance reserved. It elevates and transfigures us. If you desire to reach to something higher than ordinary, look to the Rock that is higher than you and gaze with the eye of faith through the window of persistent prayer. When you open the window on your side, it will not be bolted on the other!

September 10

"And he goeth up into a mountain, and calleth unto him whom he would: and they came unto him" (Mark 3:13).

Here was sovereignty. Impatient spirits may fret and fume because they are not called to the highest places in the ministry. But reader, rejoice that Jesus calls whom He will. If He calls me to be a doorkeeper in His house, I will cheerfully bless Him for His grace in permitting me to do anything in His service. The call of Christ's servants comes from above. Those whom He calls must go up the mountain to Him. They must seek to rise to His level by living in constant communion with Him. They may not be able to mount to classic honors or attain scholastic eminence, but they must, like Moses, go up into the mount and have constant communion with the unseen God. Jesus went apart to hold fellowship with the Father. We must enter into the same divine companionship if we would bless our fellow men. No wonder the apostles were clothed with power when they came down from the mountain where Jesus was. This morning we must endeavor to ascend the mount of communion that we may be ordained to the life-work for which we are set apart. Let us not see the face of man today until we have seen Jesus. We, too, will cast out devils and work wonders if we go down into the world girded with that divine energy which Christ alone can give. We *must* see Jesus. We must linger at the mercy-seat until we can truthfully say, "We were with Him in the Holy Mount."

"Be ye separate" (2 Corinthians 6:17).

The Christian, while *in* the world, is not to be *of* the world. To him, to live, should be Christ. Whether he eats or drinks or whatever he does, he should do all to God's glory. You may lay up treasure, but lay it up in heaven where neither moth nor rust corrupts or where thieves cannot break through or steal. You may strive to be rich, but let it be your ambition to be rich in faith and good works. You may have pleasure; but when you are merry, sing psalms and make melody in your heart to the Lord. In your spirit, as well as in your aim, you should differ from the world. Waiting humbly before God, always conscious of His presence, delighting in communion with Him, and seeking to know His will, you will prove that you are of the heavenly race. And you should be separate from the world in your actions. If a thing is right, though you lose by it, it must be done. If it is wrong, though you would gain by it, you must scorn the sin for your Master's sake. You must have no fellowship with the unfruitful works of darkness, but rather reprove them. Walk worthy of your high calling and dignity. Do not let those eyes, which are soon to see the King in His beauty, become the windows of lust. Do not let those hearts, which are before long to be filled with heaven and to overflow with ecstatic joy, be filled with pride and bitterness.

September 12

"God is jealous" (Nahum 1:2).

Your Lord is very jealous of your love, believer. Did He choose you? He cannot bear that you should choose another. Did He buy you with His own blood? He cannot endure that you should think that you are your own or that you belong to this world. He loved you with such love that He would sooner die than see you perish. He cannot endure anything standing between your heart's love and Himself. When we lean on Him, He is glad; but when we transfer our dependence to another, He is displeased and will chasten us so that He may bring us to Himself. He is also very jealous of our company. There should be no one with whom we converse so much as with Jesus. To abide in Him only, this is true love; but to commune with the world, to find sufficient solace in our carnal comforts, to prefer even the society of our fellow-Christians to fellowship with Him, this is grievous to our jealous Lord. He is happy when we abide in Him and enjoy constant fellowship with Himself. Many of the trials we experience wean our hearts from the creature and fix them more closely on Himself. Let this jealousy, which should keep us near to Christ, be a comfort to us. If He loves us so much as to care thus about our love, we may be sure that He will not allow anything to harm us and will protect us from all our enemies. Oh, that we may have grace this day to keep our hearts in sacred chastity for our Beloved alone, with sacred jealousy shutting our eyes to all the fascinations of the world!

"Who passing through the valley of Baca make it a well, the rain also filleth the pools" (Psalm 84:6).

This teaches us that the comfort obtained by one may often prove serviceable to another, just as wells would be used by the company who came after. We read a book full of consolation, which is like Jonathan's rod, dropping with honey. We think our brother has been here before us and dug this well for us as well as for himself. We notice this in the Psalms, such as that beginning, "Why art thou cast down, O my soul" (Psalm 42:5). Travelers have been delighted to see the footprint of man on a barren shore while passing through the valley of tears. We dig a well, but heaven fills it with rain. The means are connected with the end, but they do not of themselves produce it. See here the rain fills the pools so that the wells become useful as reservoirs for the water. Labor is not lost, but yet it does not supersede divine help. Grace may well be compared to rain for its purity, for its refreshing influence, for its coming from above, and for the sovereignty with which it is given or withheld. May our readers have showers of blessing, and may the wells they have dug be filled with water. They are as clouds without rain and pools without water. O God of love, open the windows of heaven and pour us out a blessing!

"There were also with him other little ships" (Mark 4:36).

Jesus was the Lord High Admiral of the sea that night, and His presence preserved the whole convoy. If we go with Jesus, we must be content to fare as He fares. When the waves are rough to Him, they will be rough to us. It is by the tempest and tossing that we will come to land, as He did before us. When the storm swept over Galilee's dark lake, all faces gathered blackness, and all hearts dreaded shipwreck. When all creature-help was useless, the slumbering Savior arose and, with a word, transformed the riot of the tempest into the deep quiet of a calm. Jesus is the star of the sea; and although there is sorrow on the sea, when Jesus is on it there is joy also. May our hearts make Jesus their anchor, their rudder, their lighthouse, their lifeboat, and their harbor. His Church is the Admiral's flagship. He Himself is the great attraction. Let us follow in His wake, mark His signals, steer by His chart, and never fear while He is within hail. Not one ship in the convoy will suffer wreck; the great Commodore will steer each one safely to the desired haven. Winds and waves will not spare us, but they all obey Him; and, therefore, whatever squalls may occur without, faith will feel a blessed calm within. His vessel has reached the haven, and so will ours.

September 15

"He shall not be afraid of evil tidings" (Psalm 112:7).

Christian, you should not dread the arrival of evil tidings. If you are distressed by them, how are you different from other men? Other men do not have your God to go to. They have never proved His faithfulness as you have done. It is no wonder if they are bowed down with fear. But you profess to be of another spirit. You have been begotten again unto a lively hope, and your heart lives in heaven and not on earthly things. Now, if you are seen to be distracted as other men, what is the value of that grace which you profess to have received? Where is the dignity of that new nature which you claim to possess? If you should be filled with alarm as others are, you would, doubtless, be led into the sins common to others under trying circumstances. The ungodly, when they are overtaken by evil tidings, rebel against God. They murmur and think that God deals harshly with them. Will you fall into that same sin? Unconverted men often run to wrong means in order to escape from difficulties, and you will be sure to do the same if your mind yields to the present pressure. Trust in the Lord, and wait patiently for Him. Your wisest course is to do as Moses did at the Red Sea—"stand still, and see the salvation of God" (Exodus 14:13). If you give way to fear when you hear of evil tidings, you will be unable to meet the trouble with that calm composure which sustains under adversity. Saints have often sung God's high praises in the fires. But if you doubt, will it magnify the Most High? Then take courage, and "let not your heart be troubled, neither let it be afraid" (John 14:27).

"Partakers of the divine nature" (2 Peter 1:4).

To be a partaker of the divine nature is not, of course, to become God. That cannot be. The essence of Deity is not to be participated in by the creature. Between the creature and the Creator there must be a gulf fixed in respect of essence. But as the first man Adam was made in the image of God, so we, by the renewal of the Holy Spirit, are in a diviner sense made in the image of the Most High and are partakers of the divine nature. We are, by grace, made like God. "God is love" (1 John 4:16). "He that loveth is born of God" (1 John 4:7). God is good, and He makes us good by His grace, so that we become the pure in heart who will see God. Do we not become members of the Body of Christ? Yes, the same blood which flows in the head flows in the hand; and the same life which quickens Christ quickens His people, for, "Ye are dead, and your life is hid with Christ in God" (Colossians 3:3). As if this were not enough, we are married to Christ. He has betrothed us unto Himself in righteousness and in faithfulness, and he who is joined to the Lord is one spirit. Oh, marvelous mystery! We look into it, but who can understand it? One with Jesus—so one with Him that the branch is not more one with the vine than we are a part of the Lord, our Savior and our Redeemer! While we rejoice in this, let us remember that those who are made partakers of the divine nature will manifest their high and holy relationship in their fellowship with others. It will be evident, by their daily walk and conversation, that they have escaped the corruption that is in the world through lust.

"Bring him unto me" (Mark 9:19).

The disappointed father turned away from the disciples to their Master in despair. His son was in the worst possible condition, and all means had failed. The child was soon delivered from the evil one when the parent, in faith, obeyed the Lord Jesus' word, "Bring thy son hither" (Luke 9:41). Children are a precious gift from God, but much anxiety comes with them. They may be a great joy or a great bitterness to their parents. They may be filled with the Spirit of God or possessed with the spirit of evil. We must spend time in more prayer on their behalf, while they are still babes. Sin is there, so let our prayers begin to attack it. Our cries for our offspring should precede those cries which accompany their actual advent into a world of sin. When they are grown up, they may wallow in sin and display enmity against God. Then, when our hearts are breaking, we should remember the great Physician's words, "Bring them unto me." We must not cease to pray until they cease to breathe. No case is hopeless while Jesus lives. Ungodly children, when they show us our own powerlessness against the depravity of their hearts, drive us to flee to the Strong One for strength. This is a great blessing to us. Whatever our morning's need may be, let it, like a strong current, bear us to the ocean of divine love. Jesus can soon remove our sorrow. He delights to comfort us. Let us hasten to Him while He waits to meet us.

"If we live in the Spirit, let us also walk in the Spirit" (Galatians 5:25).

The two most important things in our holy religion are the *life of faith* and the *walk of faith*. You will never find true faith unattended by true godliness. On the other hand, you will never discover a truly holy life which is not rooted in living faith on the righteousness of Christ. There are some who cultivate faith and forget holiness. There are others who have strained after holiness of life but have denied the faith. We must have faith, for this is the foundation; we must have holiness of life, for this is the superstructure. Of what service is the mere foundation of a building to a man in the day of tempest? Can he hide himself there? He wants a house to cover him, as well as a foundation for that house. Even so we need the superstructure of spiritual life if we would have comfort in the day of doubt. But seek not a holy life without faith, for that would be to erect a house which can afford no permanent shelter, because it has no foundation on a rock. Let faith and life be put together; and, like the two abutments of an arch, they will make our piety enduring. Like light and heat streaming from the same sun, they are alike full of blessing. O Lord, give us this day life within, and it will reveal itself without to Your glory.

"The liberty wherewith Christ hath made us free" (Galatians 5:1).

This liberty makes us *free* to heaven's charter—*the Bible*. Here is a choice passage, believer: "When thou passest through the rivers I will be with thee" (Isaiah 43:2). You are free to that. Here is another: "The mountains shall depart, and the hills be removed, but my kindness shall not depart from thee" (Isaiah 54:10). You are a welcome guest at the table of the promises. Scripture is a never-failing treasury filled with boundless stores of grace. It is the bank of heaven. You may draw from it as much as you please. Come in faith, and you are welcome to all covenant blessings. There is not a promise in the Word which will be withheld. In the depths of tribulations, let this freedom comfort you. Amid waves of distress, let it cheer you. When sorrow surrounds you, let it be your solace. This is your Father's love-token. You are free to it at all times. It is the believer's privilege to have access at all times to his heavenly Father. Whatever our desires, our difficulties, our needs, we are at liberty to spread all before Him. No matter how much we may have sinned, we may ask and expect pardon. And remember, we may plead His promise that He will provide for all our needs. This does not depend on *our* wealth. You are free to all that is treasured up *in Christ*—wisdom, righteousness, sanctification, and redemption. Your inheritance includes freedom from condemnation, freedom to the promises, freedom to the throne of grace, and freedom to enter heaven!

"The sword of the Lord and of Gideon" (Judges 7:20).

Gideon ordered his men to do two things. Covering up a torch in an earthen pitcher, he told them, at an appointed signal, to break the pitcher and let the light shine. Then, they were to the trumpet, crying, "The sword of the Lord and of Gideon! the sword of the Lord and of Gideon!" This is precisely what all Christians must do. First, *you must shine;* break the pitcher which conceals your light. Throw aside the bushel that has been hiding your candle and shine. Let your light shine before men. Let your good works be such, that, when men look at you, they will know that you have been with Jesus. Then, *there must be the sound,* the blowing of the trumpet. Take the gospel to sinners. Carry it to their door. Put it in their way. Do not allow them to escape it. Remember, that the true war-cry of the Church is Gideon's watchword, "The sword of the Lord and of Gideon!" God must do it. It is His own work. But we are not to be idle. We can do nothing of ourselves, but we can do everything by the help of our God. Let us, therefore, in His name determine to go out personally, and God will be with us. They will be put to confusion, and the Lord of hosts will reign forever and ever.

"I will rejoice over them to do them good" (Jeremiah 32:41).

The delight which God has in His saints is cause for jubilation in the believer. We cannot see any reason in ourselves why the Lord should take pleasure in us. We cannot take delight in ourselves, for we often have to groan, being burdened and conscious of our sinfulness. We feel that God's people cannot take much delight in us, for they must perceive so much of our imperfections and lament our infirmities rather than admire our graces. But we love to dwell on this transcendent truth, this glorious mystery. As the bridegroom rejoices over the bride, so does the Lord rejoice over us. We do not read anywhere that God delights in the cloud-capped mountains or the sparkling stars. But we do read that He delights in the sons of men. We do not find it written that even angels give His soul delight, yet He expresses His delight in His people in strong language. Who could have conceived of the eternal One as bursting forth into a song? Yet it is written, "He will rejoice over thee with joy; he will rest in his love; he will joy over thee with singing" (Zephaniah 3:17). As He looked on the world He had made, He said, "It is very good." But when He beheld those who are the purchase of Jesus' blood, His own chosen ones, it seemed as if the great heart of the Infinite could restrain itself no longer, and overflowed in divine exclamation of joy. Our grateful response should be, "I will rejoice in the Lord, I will joy in the God of my salvation."

"Let Israel rejoice in him" (Psalm 149:2).

Be glad of heart, believer, but take care that your gladness springs from the Lord. You have much cause for gladness in your God. Be glad that the Lord reigns, that Jehovah is King! Rejoice that He sits on the throne and rules all things! Every attribute of God should become a fresh ray in the sunlight of our gladness. Knowing that He is *wise* should make us glad, as we look at our own foolishness. Knowing that He is *mighty* should cause us to rejoice, as we tremble at our own weakness. Knowing that He is *everlasting* should always be a theme of joy when we know that we wither as the grass. Knowing that He is *unchanging* should perpetually yield us a song, since we change every hour. This gladness in God is as a deep river. We have only as yet touched its brink. We know a little of its clear, sweet, heavenly streams. But onward, the depth is greater, and the current more impetuous in its joy. The Christian feels that he may delight himself not only in what God is, but also in all that God has done in the past. Let God's people tell of His mighty acts and "sing unto the Lord, for He hath triumphed gloriously" (Exodus 15:1). They should never cease to sing, for as new mercies flow to them day by day, so should their gladness in the Lord's loving acts in providence and in grace show itself in continued thanksgiving. Be glad children of Zion and rejoice in the Lord your God.

"Accepted in the beloved" (Ephesians 1:6).

What a privilege! It includes our justification before God; but the term "acceptance," in the Greek, means more than that. It signifies that we are the objects of *divine delight.* How marvelous that we should be the objects of divine love! But it is only *"in the beloved."* Some Christians seem to be accepted in their own experience; at least, that is their apprehension. When their spirit is lively and their hopes bright, they think God accepts them, for they feel so high, so heavenly-minded, so drawn above the earth! But when their souls cleave to the dust, they are the victims of the fear that they are no longer accepted. They must see that all their high joys do not exalt them and all their low despondencies do not really depress them in their Father's sight. They stand accepted in One who never alters, in One who is always the beloved of God, always perfect, and always without spot or wrinkle. How much more they would honor the Savior if they realized this truth! Believer, rejoice! You look within and say, "There is nothing acceptable *here!*" But look at Christ and see there is everything acceptable *there.* If your sins trouble you, God will cast your sins behind His back and accept you in the Righteous One. If the devil tempts you, be of good cheer. You are accepted in Him who has broken Satan's head, and he cannot destroy you. Even glorified souls are not more accepted than you are. They are only accepted in heaven "in the beloved," and you are even now accepted in Christ after the same manner.

"For I was ashamed to require of the king a band of soldiers and horsemen to help us against the enemy in the way; because we had spoken unto the king, saying, The hand of our God is upon all them for good that seek him; but his power and his wrath is against all them that forsake him" (Ezra 8:22).

An armed regiment would have been desirable, but Ezra feared that the heathen king would think his professions of faith in God to be mere hypocrisy or imagine that the God of Israel was not able to preserve His own worshippers. He could not bring his mind to lean on an arm of flesh in a matter so evidently of the Lord. Therefore, the caravan set out with no visible protection, guarded by Him who is the sword and shield of His people. Few believers feel this holy jealousy for God. Even those who walk by faith occasionally mar the luster of their life by craving aid from man. It is a most blessed thing to stand upright on the Rock of Ages, upheld by the Lord alone. Would any believer seek state endowments for their Church if they remembered that the Lord is dishonored by their asking government aid? Cannot the Lord supply the needs of His own cause? Would we run hastily to friends and relations for assistance if we remembered that the Lord is magnified by our implicit reliance on His solitary arm? My soul, wait only on God. "But," says one, "are we not to make use of any other sources?" Assuredly, but our fault seldom lies in their neglect. Far more frequently it springs out of foolishly believing in them instead of believing in God.

"Just, and the justifier of him which believeth"
(Romans 3:26).

We have peace with God because we are justified by faith. Conscience no longer accuses. Judgment now decides *for* the sinner instead of *against* him. Memory looks back on past sins with deep sorrow for the sin, but yet with no dread of any penalty to come. Christ paid the debt of His people to the last jot and tittle and received the divine receipt. Unless God can be so unjust as to demand double payment for one debt, no soul for whom Jesus died as a substitute can ever be sent into hell. It seems to be one of the very principles of our enlightened nature to believe that God is just. This very same belief that God is just becomes the pillar of our confidence and peace! If God is just, I, a sinner must be punished. But Jesus stands in my stead and is punished for me. Now, if God is just, I, a sinner, standing in Christ, can never be punished. God must change His nature before one soul for whom Jesus was a substitute can ever by any possibility suffer the lash of the law. My hope lives, not because I am not a sinner, but because I am a sinner for whom Christ died. My trust is not that I am holy, but that He is my righteousness. My faith does not rest on what *I* am or will be or feel or know, but in what *Christ* is, in what He has done, and in what He is now doing for me.

September 26

"The myrtle trees that were in the bottom" (Zechariah 1:8).

The vision in this chapter describes the condition of Israel in Zechariah's day. Being interpreted in its aspect toward *us,* it describes the Church of God as we find it now in the world. The Church is compared to a myrtle grove flourishing in a valley. It is hidden, unobserved, secreted. It courts no honor and attracts no observation from the careless gazer. The Church, like her Head, has a glory, but it is concealed from carnal eyes. The time of her breaking forth in all her splendor is not here yet. The idea of *tranquil security* is also suggested to us. The myrtle grove in the valley is still and calm, while the storm sweeps over the mountain summits. How great is the inward tranquility of God's Church! Even when opposed and persecuted, she has a peace which the world cannot give, and which, therefore, it cannot take away. The peace of God which passes all understanding keeps the hearts and minds of God's people. The metaphor forcibly pictures the peaceful, perpetual growth of the saints. The myrtle does not shed its leaves; it is always green. The Church, in her worst time, still has a blessed strength about her. She has sometimes exhibited this strength most when her winter has been sharpest. She has prospered most when her adversities have been most severe. The myrtle is the emblem of peace and a significant token of triumph. The brows of conquerors were bound with myrtle and with laurel. Yet the Church is always victorious, and every Christian is more than a conqueror through Him that loved him. Living in peace, the saints fall asleep in the arms of victory.

September 27

"Happy art thou, O Israel; who is like unto thee, O people saved by the Lord?" (Deuteronomy 33:29).

The person who feels Christianity makes men miserable is himself an utter stranger to it. It would be strange, indeed, if it made us wretched, for see *to what a position it exalts us!* It makes us sons of God. Do you suppose that God will give all the happiness to His enemies and reserve all the mourning for His own family? Will His foes have joy and His children inherit sorrow and wretchedness? No, we will rejoice in the Lord always and glory in our inheritance, for we "have not received the Spirit of bondage again to fear; but we have received the Spirit of adoption, whereby we cry, Abba, Father" (Romans 8:15.) The rod of chastisement must rest on us in measure, but it works fruits of righteousness; and therefore, by the aid of the divine Comforter, we, the people saved of the Lord will joy in the God of our salvation. We are married to Christ. Would our great Bridegroom permit His spouse to linger in constant grief? For a while we may suffer as our Head once suffered, yet we are even now blessed with heavenly blessings in Him. We have the earnest of our inheritance in the comforts of the Spirit, which are neither few nor small. Inheritors of joy forever, we have foretastes of our portion. It is true, "Happy art thou, O Israel; who is like unto thee, O people saved by the Lord!"

September 28

"The Lord looketh from heaven; he beholdeth all the sons of men" (Psalm 33:13).

Perhaps no figure of speech represents God in a more gracious light than when He is spoken of as stooping from His throne and coming down from heaven to attend to the wants and to behold the problems of mankind. We love Him, who, when Sodom and Gomorrah were full of iniquity, would not destroy those cities until He had made a personal visitation of them. We cannot help pouring out our heart in affection for our Lord, who inclines His ear from the highest glory and puts it to the lip of the dying sinner. His heart longs after reconciliation. How can we but love Him, when we know that He numbers the very hairs of our heads, marks our path, and orders our ways? This great truth is brought near to our heart when we recollect how attentive He is, not merely to the temporal interests of His creatures but to their spiritual concerns. Though a long distance separates the finite creatures and the infinite Creator, there are links uniting both. When you weep, God is very aware of it. "Like as a father pitieth his children, so the Lord pitieth them that fear him" (Psalm 103:13). Your sigh is able to move the heart of Jehovah. Your whisper can incline His ear to you. Your prayer can stay His hand, and your faith can move His arm. Do not think that God sits on high taking no account of you. For the eyes of the Lord run to and fro throughout the whole earth, to show Himself strong on behalf of them whose heart is perfect toward Him (2 Chronicles 16:9).

"Behold, if the leprosy have covered all his flesh, he shall pronounce him clean that hath the plague" (Leviticus 13:13).

This regulation appears strange. Yet, there was wisdom in it, for the throwing out of the disease proved that the constitution was sound. We, too, are lepers and may read the law of lepers as applicable to ourselves. When a man sees himself to be altogether lost and ruined and pleads guilty before the Lord, then he is made clean through the blood of Jesus and the grace of God. When sin is seen and felt, it has received its death-blow, and the Lord looks with eyes of mercy on the soul afflicted with it. Nothing is more deadly than self-righteousness or more hopeful than contrition. We must confess that we are nothing else but sin, for no confession short of this will be the whole truth. If the Holy Spirit is at work within us, convincing us of sin, there will be no difficulty about making such an acknowledgment. It will spring spontaneously from our lips. What comfort this scripture provides. Sin that is mourned and confessed, however black and foul, will never shut a man out from the Lord Jesus. Whosoever comes to Him, He will in no wise cast out. Though dishonest as the thief, though unchaste as the woman who was a sinner, though fierce as Saul of Tarsus, though rebellious as the prodigal, the great heart of love will look on the man who feels he has no righteousness in himself and will pronounce him clean when he trusts in Jesus crucified. Come to Him, then, poor, heavy-laden sinner.

"Sing forth the honor of his name, make his praise glorious" (Psalm 66:2).

Whether we will praise God or not is not an option for us. Praise is God's due; and every Christian, as the recipient of His grace, is bound to praise God from day to day. It is true we have no commandment prescribing certain hours of song and thanksgiving, but the law written on the heart teaches us that it is right to praise God. The unwritten mandate comes to us with as much force as if it had been recorded on tables of stone or handed to us from the top of thundering Sinai. Yes, it is the Christian's *duty* to praise God. It is not only a pleasurable exercise, but it is the absolute obligation of his life. Do not think that you are guiltless in this respect or imagine that you can discharge your duty to your God without songs of praise. You are bound by the bonds of His love to bless His name so long as you live, and His praise should continually be in your mouth. "This people have I formed for myself; they shall show forth my praise" (Isaiah 43:21). If you do not praise God, you are not bringing forth the fruit which He, as the divine Husbandman, has a right to expect at your hands. Arise and sing His praise. With every morning's dawn, lift up your notes of thanksgiving and let every setting sun be followed with your songs. Cover the earth with your praises. Surround it with an atmosphere of melody, and God Himself will hearken from heaven and accept your music.

"Pleasant fruits, new and old, which I have laid up for thee, O my beloved" (Song of Solomon 7:13).

The spouse desires to give all that she produces to Jesus. Our heart has all manner of pleasant fruits, both new and old, and they are laid up for our Beloved. At this rich autumn season, let us survey our harvest. We have *new* fruits. We desire to feel new life, new joy, and new gratitude. We wish to make new resolves and carry them out by new labors. But we have some *old* fruits, too. There is our first love—a choice fruit! There is our first faith. It is the simple faith by which, having nothing, we became possessors of all things. There is our joy when first we knew the Lord; let us revive it. We have our old remembrances of the promises. How faithful God has been! Old sins we must regret. But we have repented and wept our way to the cross, and we have learned of the merit of His blood. We have fruits this morning, both new and old. But here is the point—*they are all laid up for Jesus*. Let our many fruits be laid up only for our Beloved. Let us display them when He is with us and not hold them up before the gaze of men. Jesus, none will enter to rob You of one good fruit from the soil which You have watered. All we have is Yours!

"The hope which is laid up for you in heaven" (Colossians 1:5).

Our hope in Christ for the future is the mainstay of our joy here. This hope will animate our hearts to think often of heaven for all that we can desire is promised there. Here we are weary and toilworn, but heaven is the land of *rest*. Fatigue will be forever banished. Now, we are always in the field of battle. We are so tempted within and so molested by foes without that we have little time to rest. We have suffered bereavement after bereavement, but we are going to the land of the *immortal,* where graves are unknown things. Here sin is a constant grief to us, but there we will be perfectly holy. Nothing that defiles will enter into that Kingdom. What a joy that you are not to dwell eternally in this wilderness but will soon inherit Canaan. Nevertheless, let it never be said of us that we are dreaming about the *future* and forgetting the *present.* Let the future sanctify the present to highest uses. Through the Spirit of God, the hope of heaven is the most potent force for the product of virtue. It is a fountain of joyous effort. It is the cornerstone of cheerful holiness. The man who has this hope in him goes about his work with vigor, for the joy of the Lord is his strength! He fights against temptation with ardor, for the hope of the next world repels the fiery darts of the adversary. He can labor without present reward, for he looks for a reward in the world to come.

October 3

"Are they not all ministering spirits, sent forth to minister for them who shall be heirs of salvation?" (Hebrews 1:14).

Angels are the unseen attendants of the saints of God. They bear us up in their hands lest we dash our foot against a stone. Loyalty to their Lord leads them to take a deep interest in the children of His love. They rejoice over the return of the prodigal to his father's house below, and they welcome the advent of the believer to the King's palace above. In olden times, the sons of God were favored with their visible appearance, and at this day, although unseen by us, heaven is still opened. The angels of God ascend and descend from the Son of man that they may visit the heirs of salvation. If our eyes could be opened, we would see horses and chariots of fire about the servants of the Lord. We have come to an innumerable company of angels, who are all watchers and protectors of the royal seed. To what dignity are the chosen elevated when the brilliant courtiers of heaven become their willing servants! We are defended since all twenty thousand chariots of God are armed for our deliverance! To whom do we owe all this? Let the Lord Jesus Christ be forever endeared to us, for through Him we are made to sit in heavenly places far above principalities and powers. He it is whose camp is round about them that fear Him. He is the true Michael whose foot is on the dragon. All hail, Jesus!

October 4

"At evening time it shall be light" (Zechariah 14:7).

We often look forward with forebodings to the time of old age. To many saints, old age is the choicest season in their lives. A balmier air fans the mariner's cheek as he nears the shore of immortality. Fewer waves ruffle his sea, and quiet reigns deep, still, and solemn. The pilgrims have reached the Beulah land, that happy country whose days are as the days of heaven on earth. Angels visit it, celestial gales blow over it, flowers of paradise grow in it, and the air is filled with seraphic music. Some dwell here for years, and others come to it but a few hours before their departure. But it is an Eden on earth. The setting sun seems larger than when high in the sky, and a splendor of glory tinges all the clouds which surround his going down. Ripe fruits of choice experience are gathered as the rare repast of life's evening, and the soul prepares itself for rest. The Lord's people will also enjoy light in the hour of death. Unbelief laments, the shadows fall, the night is coming, and existence is ending. No, cries faith, the night is far spent, and the true day is at hand. Light is come—the light of immortality, the light of a Father's countenance. Gather your feet into the bed, and see the waiting bands of spirits! Angels carry you away. Farewell, beloved one. Now it is light. The pearly gates are open, the golden streets shine in the jasper light. You now behold the unseen. Adieu, brother; you have light at eventide, such as we have not yet known.

"He arose, and did eat and drink, and went in the strength of that meat forty days and forty nights" (1 Kings 19:8).

All the strength supplied to us by our gracious God is meant for service, not for wantonness. When the prophet Elijah found the cake baked on the coals and the jug of water placed at his head as he lay under the juniper tree, he was commissioned to go forty days and forty nights in the strength of it. The Master invited the disciples to come and dine with Him, and after the feast was concluded, He said to Peter, "Feed my sheep." He further added, "Follow me." This is true with us also. We eat the bread of heaven that we may expend our strength in the Master's service. Some Christians are for living *on* Christ, but are not so anxious to live *for* Christ. Earth should be a preparation for heaven, and heaven is the place where saints feast and work most. They sit down at the table of our Lord and serve Him day and night in His temple. They eat of heavenly food and render perfect service. Believer, labor for Christ in the strength you gain from Him daily. We are not to retain the precious grains of truth. We must sow it and water it. Why does the Lord send down the rain on the thirsty earth and give the genial sunshine? It is to help the fruits of the earth yield food for man. Even so the Lord feeds and refreshes our souls that we may afterward use our renewed strength in the promotion of His glory.

October 6

"Whosoever drinketh of the water that I shall give him shall never thirst" (John 4:14).

He who is a believer in Jesus finds enough in his Lord to satisfy him now and keep him content forevermore. The believer is not the man whose days are weary for comfort and whose nights are long from absence of heart-cheering thought. He finds in Christ such a spring of joy, such a foundation of consolation, that he is content and happy. Put him in a dungeon, and he will find good company. Place him in a barren wilderness, and he will eat the bread of heaven. Drive him away from friendship, and he will meet the friend that sticketh closer than a brother. Sap the foundation of his earthly hopes, and his heart will still be fixed, trusting in the Lord. The heart is as insatiable as the grave until Jesus enters it, and then it is a cup full to overflowing. There is such a fullness in Christ. The true saint is completely satisfied with the all-sufficiency of Jesus. Is this the feeling in your heart? Do you feel that all your desires are satisfied in Jesus, and that you have no want now but to know more of Him and to have closer fellowship with Him? Then come continually to the fountain, and take of the water of life freely. Jesus will never think you take too much, but will always welcome you, saying, "Drink, yea, drink abundantly, O beloved."

"Wherefore hast thou afflicted thy servant?" (Numbers 11:11).

If our faith is worth anything, it will stand the test when trials come. The true jewel fears no test. It is a weak faith which can only trust God when friends are true, the body full of health, and the business profitable. True faith holds by the Lord's faithfulness when friends are gone, when the body is sick, when spirits are depressed, and the light of our Father's countenance is hidden. A faith which can say in the direst trouble, "Though he slay me, yet will I trust in him" (Job 13:15) is heaven-born faith. The Lord is greatly glorified in the graces of His people. When "tribulation worketh patience; and patience, experience; and experience, hope" (Romans 5:3-4), the Lord is honored by these growing virtues. We would never know the music of the harp if the strings were left untouched or enjoy the juice of the grape if it were not trodden in the wine-press. We would never discover the sweet perfume of cinnamon if it were not pressed and beaten or feel the warmth of fire if the coals were not utterly consumed. The wisdom and power of the great Workman are discovered by the trials through which His vessels of mercy are permitted to pass. There must be shades in the picture to bring out the beauty of the lights. Could we be so supremely blessed in heaven if we had not known the curse of sin and the sorrow of earth? Peace will be sweeter after conflict and rest more welcome after toil. The recollection of past sufferings will enhance the bliss of the glorified.

"Launch out into the deep, and let down your nets for a draught" (Luke 5:4).

We learn from this narrative the necessity of human involvement. The draught of fishes was miraculous, yet neither the fisherman nor his boat nor his fishing tackle were ignored. All were used to take the fishes. In the saving of souls, God uses many different instruments. He has selected this plan as being that by which He is most magnified in the earth. "Master, we have toiled all the night and have taken nothing" (Luke 5:5). What was the reason for this? They understood the work. Had they gone about the toil unskillfully? No. Had they lacked industry? No. They had *toiled.* Had they lacked perseverance? No. They had toiled *all the night.* Was there a deficiency of fish in the sea? Certainly not, for as soon as the Master came, they swam to the net in schools. What, then, is the reason? It is because there is no power in themselves apart from the presence of Jesus! Without Christ we can do nothing, but with Him we can do all things. *Christ's presence confers success.* Jesus sat in Peter's boat, and His will drew the fish to the net. When Jesus is lifted up in His Church, His presence is the Church's power—the shout of a King is in the midst of her. "I, if I be lifted up, will draw all men unto me" (John 12:32). Let us go out this morning on our work of soul-fishing, looking up in faith and around us in solemn anxiety. Let us toil until night comes, and we will not labor in vain. He who bids us let down the net will also fill it with fishes.

October 9

"Able to keep you from falling" (Jude 24).

In one sense the path to heaven is very safe. In other respects there is no road so dangerous. It is surrounded with difficulties. One false step—and how easy it is to take that, if grace is absent—and down we go. How many times have we exclaimed as the psalmist, "My feet were almost gone; my steps had well nigh slipped" (Psalm 73:2). If we were strong, sure-footed mountaineers, this would not matter so much; but in ourselves, how weak we are! A straw may throw us, and a pebble can wound us. We are mere children tremblingly taking our first steps in the walk of faith. Our heavenly Father holds us by the arms, or we would soon be down. Oh, if we are kept from falling, how must we bless the patient power which watches over us day by day! Think how prone we are to sin, how apt to choose danger, and how strong our tendency to cast ourselves down. These reflections will make us sing more sweetly than we have ever done, "Glory be to him who is able to keep you from falling" (Jude 24). We have many foes who try to push us down. The road is rough, and we are weak. In addition to this, enemies lurk in ambush who rush out when we least expect them. They labor to trip us up or hurl us down the nearest cliff. Only an Almighty arm can preserve us from these unseen foes who are seeking to destroy us. Such an arm is engaged for our defense. He is faithful and able to keep us from falling. With a deep sense of our utter weakness, we cherish a firm belief in our perfect safety.

October 10

"Faultless before the presence of his glory" (Jude 24).

In your mind examine that wondrous word *"faultless."* We are far from it now; but as our Lord never stops short of perfection in His work of love, we will reach it one day. The Savior who will keep His people to the end will also present them at last to Himself as a glorious Church, not having spot, wrinkle, or any such thing. They will be holy and without blemish. All the jewels in the Savior's crown are without a single flaw. But how will Jesus make us faultless? He will wash us from our sins in His own blood until we are white and fair as God's purest angel. We will be clothed in His righteousness. We will be innocent and uncondemned even in His eyes. His law will not only have no charge against us, but it will be magnified in us. Moreover, the work of the Holy Spirit within us will be altogether complete. He will make us so perfectly holy that we will have no lingering tendency to sin. We will dwell in His presence forever. The beauty of the saints will be as great as that of the place prepared for them. Oh, the joy of that hour when the everlasting doors will be lifted up, and we, being made meet for the inheritance, will dwell with the saints in light. Sin gone, Satan shut out, temptation past forever, and ourselves *"faultless"* before God—this will be heaven indeed!

October 11

"Let us lift up our heart with our hands unto God in the heavens" (Lamentations 3:41).

The act of prayer teaches us our unworthiness, which is a very beneficial lesson for such proud beings as we are. If God gave us favors without constraining us to pray for them, we would never know how poor we are. A true prayer is an inventory of wants, a catalogue of necessities, and a revelation of hidden poverty. The most healthy state of a Christian is to be constantly depending on the Lord for supplies, rich in Jesus, and mighty through God to do great exploits. Hence, the use of prayer because it lays the creature where he should be—in the very dust. Prayer is in itself, apart from the answer which it brings, a great benefit to the Christian. As the runner gains strength for the race by daily exercise, so for the great race of life we acquire energy by the hallowed labor of prayer. Prayer plumes the wings of God's young eaglets that they may learn to mount above the clouds. Prayer girds the loins of God's warriors and sends them forth to combat with their muscles firm. An earnest pleader comes out of his prayer closet rejoicing like a strong man to run his race. Prayer is that uplifted hand of Moses which routs the Amalekites more than the sword of Joshua. Prayer girds human weakness with divine strength, turns human folly into heavenly wisdom, and gives to troubled mortals the peace of God. We cannot think of anything prayer cannot do! We thank You, God, for the mercy-seat, a choice proof of Your marvelous lovingkindness. Help us to use it aright throughout this day!

October 12

"I will meditate in thy precepts" (Psalm 119:15).

There are times when solitude is better than society and silence is wiser than speech. We would be better Christians if we spent more time waiting on God and gathering, through meditation on His Word, spiritual strength for labor in His service. We ought to meditate on the things of God, because we thus get the real nutrition out of them. Truth is something like the cluster of the vine. If we would have wine from it, we must bruise it. We must press and squeeze it many times. So we must, by meditation, tread the clusters of truth if we would get the wine of consolation from it. Our bodies are not supported by merely taking food into the mouth. The process which really supplies the muscle, nerve, sinew, and the bone is the process of digestion. It is by digestion that the outward food becomes assimilated with the inner life. Our souls are not nourished merely by listening awhile to this and then to that and then to the other part of divine truth. Hearing, reading, marking, and learning all require inward digesting to complete their usefulness. The inward digesting of the truth lies for the most part in meditating on it. Why is it that some Christians, although they hear many sermons, make slow advances in the divine life? Because they do not thoughtfully meditate on God's Word. They love the wheat, but they do not grind it. They want the corn, but they will not go forth into the fields to gather it. The fruit hangs on the tree, but they will not pluck it. The water flows at their feet, but they will not stoop to drink it. Lord, deliver us from such folly as we resolve to meditate on Your Word this morning.

October 13

"Godly sorrow worketh repentance" (2 Corinthians 7:10).

Genuine repentance is the work of the Spirit of God. Repentance is too choice a flower to grow in nature's garden. Pearls grow naturally in oysters, but penitence never shows itself in sinners unless divine grace works it in them. If you have one particle of real hatred for sin, God must have given it to you. That which is born of flesh is flesh. True repentance has a distinct reference to the Savior. When we repent of sin, we must have one eye on sin and another on the cross. It will be better still if we fix both our eyes on Christ and see our transgressions only in the light of His love. True sorrow for sin is eminently practical. No man may say he hates sin if he lives in it. Repentance makes us see the evil of sin, not merely as a theory, but experimentally—as a burnt child dreads fire. True mourning for sin will make us very jealous over our tongues lest we say a wrong word. We are very watchful over our daily actions lest in anything we offend, and each night we will close the day with painful confessions of shortcomings. Each morning we will awaken with prayers that this day God would hold us up that we may not sin against Him. Sincere repentance is continual. Believers repent until their dying day. Every other sorrow yields to time, but this dear sorrow grows with our growth. We thank God we are permitted to enjoy and to suffer it until we enter our eternal rest.

October 14

"I count all things but loss for the excellency of the knowledge of Christ Jesus my Lord" (Philippians 3:8).

Spiritual knowledge of Christ will be a *personal* knowledge. I cannot know Jesus through another person's acquaintance with Him. No, I must know Him *myself*. It will be an *intelligent* knowledge. I must know Him as the Word reveals Him. I must know His natures, both the divine and the human. I must know His offices, His attributes, His works, His shame, and His glory. I must meditate on Him until I comprehend with all saints what is the breadth, length, depth, and height of His love. It will be an *affectionate* knowledge of Him. Indeed, if I know Him at all, I must love Him. An ounce of heart-knowledge is worth a ton of head-knowledge. Our knowledge of Him will be a *satisfying* knowledge. When I know my Savior, my mind will be full to the brim. I will feel that I have that which my spirit longed for. At the same time, it will be an *exciting* knowledge. The more I know of my Beloved, the more I want to know. Like the miser's treasure, my gold will make me covet more. In conclusion, this knowledge of Christ Jesus will be a most happy one. In fact, sometimes it will completely bear me up above all trials, doubts, and sorrows. Come, sit at Jesus' feet, and learn of Him all this day.

"But who may abide the day of his coming?" (Malachi 3:2).

His first coming was without external pomp or show of power. Yet, in truth, there were few who could abide its testing might. Herod and all Jerusalem were stirred at the news of the wondrous birth. Those who supposed themselves to be waiting for Him showed the fallacy of their professions by rejecting Him when He came. But what will His second advent be? What sinner can endure to think of it? "He shall smite the earth with the rod of his mouth, and with the breath of his lips shall he slay the wicked" (Isaiah 11:4). When, in His humiliation, His only words to the soldiers were, "I am He," they fell backward. What will be the terror of His enemies when He more fully reveals Himself as the "I Am"? His death shook earth and darkened heaven. What will be the dreadful splendor of that day in which, as the living Savior, He summons the living and dead before Him? Oh, that the terrors of the Lord would persuade men to forsake their sins! Though a Lamb, He is still the Lion of the tribe of Judah, rending the prey in pieces. Although He does not break the bruised reed, yet will He break His enemies with a rod of iron and dash them in pieces like a potter's vessel. But His beloved blood-washed people look for His appearing with joy and hope to witness it without fear. Let us search ourselves this morning and make our calling and election sure, so that the coming of the Lord may cause no dark forebodings in our mind. Oh, for grace to cast away all hypocrisy and to be found sincere without rebuke in the day of His appearing!

October 16

"Jesus saith unto them, Come and dine" (John 21:12).

In these words, the believer is invited to a holy nearness to Jesus. "Come and dine," implies the same table and the same meat. Sometimes it means to sit side by side and lean our head on the Savior's bosom. "Come and dine" gives us a vision of union with Jesus. Oh, what union this is! It is a depth which reason cannot fathom. "He that eateth my flesh, and drinketh my blood, dwelleth in me, and I in him" (John 6:56). It is also an invitation to enjoy fellowship with the saints. Christians may differ on a variety of points, but they have all one spiritual appetite. If we cannot all feel alike, we can all feed alike on the bread of life sent down from heaven. At the table of fellowship with Jesus, we are one bread and one cup. Get nearer to Jesus, and you will find yourself linked more and more in spirit to all who are, like yourself, supported by the same heavenly manna. If we were closer to Jesus, we would be closer to one another. We likewise see in these words the source of strength for every Christian. To look at Christ is to live, but for strength to serve Him you must "come and dine." We labor under much unnecessary weakness on account of neglecting this precept of the Master. We should feed on the marrow and fatness of the Word that we may accumulate strength therein and urge every power to its full tension in the Master's service. Thus, then, if you desire nearness to Jesus, union with Jesus, love for His people, and strength from Jesus, "come and dine" with Him by faith.

"And David said in his heart, I shall now perish one day by the hand of Saul" (1 Samuel 27:1).

The thought of David's heart at this time was a false thought. He certainly had no ground for thinking that God's anointing him was intended to be left as an empty, meaningless act. On no occasion had the Lord deserted His servant. He had been placed in perilous positions very often, but not one instance had occurred in which divine intervention had not delivered him. The trials to which he had been exposed had been varied. Yet, in every case, God graciously ordained a way of escape. David should have realized from what God had done for him that God would be his defender still. Do we doubt God's help in this same way? Is it not mistrust without a cause? Have we ever had the shadow of a reason to doubt our Father's goodness? Has He once failed to justify our trust? Our God has not left us at any time. We have gone through many trials. They have never been to our detriment but always to our advantage. The conclusion from our past experience is that He who has been with us in six troubles will not forsake us in the seventh. What we have known of our faithful God proves that He will keep us to the end. Let us not, then, reason contrary to evidence. How can we ever be so ungenerous as to doubt our God? Lord, throw down the Jezebel of our unbelief and let the dogs devour it.

"Thy paths drop fatness" (Psalm 65:11).

Many are "the paths of the Lord" which "drop fatness," but a special one is the path of prayer. No believer who is much in the prayer closet will need to cry, "My leanness, my leanness; woe unto me" (Isaiah 24:16). Starving souls live at a distance from the mercy-seat and become like the parched fields in times of drought. Prevalence with God in wrestling prayer is sure to make the believer strong. The nearest place to the gate of heaven is the throne of heavenly grace. Spend much time alone with Jesus, and you will have much assurance. Spend little time alone with Jesus, and your faith will be shallow, polluted with many doubts and fears, and lacking in the joy of the Lord. The soul-enriching path of prayer is open to the very weakest saint and no high attainments are required. See to it, dear reader, that you are often in private devotion and fellowship with Jesus. Earth has no words which can set forth the holy calm of a soul leaning on Jesus' bosom. Few Christians understand it. They live in the lowlands and seldom climb to the top. They live in the outer court. They do not enter the holy place. At a distance they see the sacrifice, but they do not sit down with the priest to eat and enjoy the fat of the burnt offering. But, reader, sit under the shadow of Jesus. Let your Beloved be as the apple tree among the trees of the woods, and you will be satisfied as with marrow and fatness. O Jesus, visit us with Your salvation.

October 19

"Babes in Christ" (1 Corinthians 3:1).

Are you mourning because you are so weak in the divine life? Because your faith is so little, and your love so feeble? Cheer up, for you have cause for gratitude. Remember that in some things you are equal to the greatest and most full-grown Christian. You are as much bought with blood as he is. You are as much an adopted child of God as any other believer. An infant is as truly a child of its parents as is the full-grown man. You are completely justified, for your justification is not a thing of degrees. Your little faith has made you completely clean. You have as much right to the precious things of the covenant as the most advanced believers, for your right to covenant mercies lies not in your growth but in the covenant itself. Your faith in Jesus is not the measure but the token of your inheritance in Him. The smallest star that gleams is set in heaven. The faintest ray of light has affinity with the great orb of day. In the family register of glory, the small and the great are written with the same pen. You are as dear to your Father's heart as the greatest in the family. Jesus is very tender over you. You are like a bruised reed. He will never break the bruised reed. Instead of being downcast by reason of what you are, you should triumph in Christ. In Christ I am made to sit in heavenly places. Am I poor in faith? Still in Jesus I am heir of all things. I will rejoice in the Lord and glory in the God of my salvation.

"Grow up into him in all things" (Ephesians 4:15).

Many Christians remain stunted and dwarfed in spiritual things. They exist but do not "grow up into him in all things." But should we rest content with being in the green blade when we might advance to the ear and eventually ripen into the full corn in the ear? Should we be satisfied to believe in Christ and to say, "I am safe," without wishing to know in our own experience more of the fullness which is to be found in Him? It should not be so. We should, as good traders in heaven's market, covet to be enriched in the knowledge of Jesus. It is all very well to keep other men's vineyards, but we must not neglect our own spiritual growth and ripening. Why should it always be winter time in our hearts? We must have our seed-time, it is true; but, Oh, for a springtime and a summer season which will give promise of an early harvest! If we would ripen in grace, we must live near to Jesus. We must hold sweet communion with Him. We must come near, as John did, and pillow our head on His breast. Then we will find ourselves advancing in holiness, love, faith, and hope—in every precious gift. As the sun rises first on mountaintops and gilds them with its light, it is one of the most delightful contemplations in the world to notice the glow of the Spirit's light on the head of a saint who has risen up in spiritual stature.

October 21

"The love of Christ constraineth us" (Matthew 5:47).

How much do you owe my Lord? Has He ever done anything for you? Has He forgiven your sins? Has He covered you with a robe of righteousness? Has He set your feet on a rock? Has He established your goings? Has He prepared heaven for you? Has He prepared you for heaven? Has He written your name in His book of life? Has He given you countless blessings? Has He laid up for you a store of mercies, which eye has not seen or ear heard? Then do something for Jesus worthy of His love. How will you feel when your Master comes if you have to confess that you did nothing for Him but kept your love shut up, like a stagnant pool, neither flowing forth to His poor or to His work. What do men think of a love which never shows itself in action? Why, they say, "Open rebuke is better than secret love" (Proverbs 27:5). Who will accept a love so weak that it does not move you to a single deed of self-denial, generosity, heroism, or zeal? Think how He has loved you and given Himself for you! Do you know the power of that love? Then let it be like a rushing, mighty wind to your soul to sweep out the clouds of your worldliness and clear away the mists of sin. The divine Spirit will make you bold as lions and swift as eagles in your Lord's service. Love should give wings to the feet of service and strength to the arms of labor. Fixed on God with a constancy that is not to be shaken, let us manifest the constraints of our love for Jesus.

"I will love them freely" (Hosea 13:4).

He who understands the meaning of this sentence is a theologian, and he who can dive into its fullness is a true master in Israel. It is a condensation of the glorious message of salvation which was delivered to us in Christ Jesus our Redeemer. The sense hinges on the word "freely." This is the glorious, suitable, divine way by which love streams from heaven to earth. It is a spontaneous love flowing forth to those who neither deserved it, purchased it, or sought after it. It is, indeed, the only way in which God can love us. "I will love them *freely.*" Now, if there were any fitness necessary in us then He would not love us freely. But it stands, "I will love you *freely.*" We complain, "Lord, my heart is so hard, and I do not feel my need of Christ. I do not feel that softening of spirit which I should desire." Remember, there are no conditions. The covenant of grace has no conditionality whatever. We, without any worthiness, may venture on the promise of God which was made to us in Christ Jesus when He said, "He that believeth on him is not condemned" (John 3:18). It is blessed to know that the grace of God is free to us at all times, without preparation, fitness, money, or price! "I will love them freely." These words invite backsliders to return. Indeed, the text was especially written for such—"I will heal their backsliding; I will love them freely" (Hosea 14:4). Backslider, surely the generosity of the promise will at once break your heart, and you will return and seek your Father's face.

"Will ye also go away?" (John 6:67).

Many have forsaken Christ. Yet, has Jesus not proved Himself all-sufficient? He appeals to you this morning. "Have I been a wilderness unto you?" (Jeremiah 2:31). When your soul has simply trusted Jesus, have you ever been confounded? Have you not up until now found your Lord to be a compassionate and generous friend to you? Has not simple faith in Him given you all the peace your spirit could desire? Can you so much as dream of a better friend than He has been to you? What can compel you to leave Christ? When we are troubled by this world or with the severer trials within the Church, we find it a blessed thing to pillow our head on the bosom of our Savior. This is the joy we have today, that we are saved in Him. If this joy is satisfying, why would we think of changing? We will not reject the sun until we find a better light or leave our Lord until a brighter lover appears. Since this can never be, we will hold Him with an immortal grasp and bind His name as a seal on our arm. As for the future, can you suggest anything which can arise that will render it necessary for you to forsake Him? If we are poor, what is better than to have Christ, who can make us rich? When we die, is it not written that "neither death, nor life, nor things present, nor things to come, shall be able to separate us from the love of God, which is in Christ Jesus our Lord" (Romans 8:38-39)? We say with Peter, "Lord, to whom will we go?"

October 24

"The trees of the Lord are full of sap" (Psalm 104:16).

Without sap the tree cannot flourish or even exist. *Vitality* is essential to a Christian. There must be *life*—a vital principle infused into us by God the Holy Spirit—or we cannot be trees of the Lord. The mere name of being a Christian is but a dead thing. We must be filled with the Spirit of divine life. This life is *mysterious*. Regeneration is wrought by the Holy Spirit entering into man and becoming man's life. This divine life in a believer afterward feeds on the flesh and blood of Christ and is thus sustained by divine food. But where it comes from and where it goes, who can explain to us? What a secret thing the sap is! The roots go searching through the soil, but we cannot see them suck out the various gases or transform the mineral into the vegetable. This work is done down in the dark. Our root is Christ Jesus, and our life is hid in Him. This is the secret of the Lord. In the Christian, the divine life is always full of energy. The believer's graces are not all in constant motion, but his life never ceases to palpitate within. He is not always working for God, but his heart is always living on Him. As the sap manifests itself in producing the foliage and fruit of the tree, so it must be with a truly healthy Christian. His grace is externally manifested in his walk and conversation. If you talk with him, he cannot help speaking about Jesus. If you notice his actions, you will see that he has been with Jesus. He has so much sap within that it must fill his conduct and conversation with life.

"For the truth's sake which dwelleth in us, and shall be with us forever" (2 John 2).

Let the truth of God obtain an entrance into the human heart where no power, human or infernal, can dislodge it. We entertain it not as a guest, but as the master of the house—this is a Christian necessity. Those who feel the vital power of the gospel and know the might of the Holy Spirit would sooner be torn to pieces than be rent away from the gospel of their salvation. What a thousand mercies are wrapped up in the assurance that the truth will be with us forever. Some truths we outgrow and leave behind, for they are but rudiments and lessons for beginners. But we cannot deal this way with divine truth. Although it is sweet food for babes, it is in the highest sense strong meat for men. The truth that we are sinners is painfully with us to humble us and make us watchful. The more blessed truth, that whosoever believes on the Lord Jesus will be saved, abides with us as our hope and joy. Our grounds and motives for believing are now stronger and more numerous than ever, and we have reason to expect that it will be so until in death we clasp the Savior in our arms. Wherever this abiding love of truth can be discovered, we are bound to exercise our love. Much error may be mingled with truth received. Let us war against the error but still love the brother for the measure of truth which we see in him. Above all, let us love and spread the truth ourselves!

"Ye looked for much, and, lo, it came to little; and when ye brought it home, I did blow upon it. Why? saith the Lord of hosts. Because of mine house that is waste, and ye run every man unto his own house" (Haggai 1:9).

Many people limit their contributions to the ministry and missionary endeavors and call such saving good economy. Little do they dream that they are impoverishing themselves. Their excuse is that they must care for their own families, and they forget that to neglect the house of God is the sure way to bring ruin on their own houses. Our God has a method in providence by which He can bless our endeavors beyond our expectations or defeat our plans to our confusion and dismay. Scripture teaches that the Lord enriches the liberal and leaves the miserly to find out that withholding tends to poverty. In a very wide sphere of observation, I have noticed that the most generous Christians have always been the most happy and almost invariably the most prosperous. I have seen the liberal giver rise to wealth of which he never dreamed. I have as often seen the stingy, ungenerous person descend to poverty by the very thriftiness by which he thought to rise. Men trust good stewards with larger and larger sums and so does the Lord. He gives by cartloads to those who give by bushels. Selfishness looks first at home, but godliness seeks first the Kingdom of God and His righteousness. Yet, in the long run, selfishness is loss, and godliness is great gain. It takes faith to act toward our God with an open hand, but surely He deserves it of us.

October 27

"It is a faithful saying" (2 Timothy 2:11).

Paul has four of these *"faithful sayings."* The first occurs in 1 Timothy 1:15: "This is a faithful saying, and worthy of all acceptance, that Christ Jesus came into the world to save sinners." The next is in 1 Timothy 4:8-9: "Godliness is profitable unto all things, having promise of the life that now is, and of that which is to come." The third is in 2 Timothy 2:12: "If we suffer, we shall also reign with him." The fourth is in Titus 3:8: "This is a faithful saying. . . .that they which have believed in God might be careful to maintain good works." We may trace a connection between these faithful sayings. The first one lays the foundation of our eternal salvation in the free grace of God as shown to us in the mission of the great Redeemer. The next affirms the double blessedness which we obtain through this salvation—the blessings of time and eternity. The third shows one of the duties to which the chosen people are called. We are ordained to suffer for Christ with the promise that "if we suffer, we shall also reign with him." The last sets forth the active form of Christian service, bidding us diligently to maintain good works. Treasure these faithful sayings. Let them be the guides of your life, comfort, and instruction. The apostle of the Gentiles proved them to be faithful, and they are faithful still. Not one word will fall to the ground. They are all worthy of acceptance. Let us accept them now and prove their faithfulness. Let these four sayings be written on the four corners of your house.

October 28

"I have chosen you out of the world" (John 15:19).

Here is distinguishing grace and discriminating regard, for some are made the special objects of divine affection. Do not be afraid to dwell on this high doctrine of election. When your mind is most heavy and depressed, you will find this scripture to be soothing. Those who doubt the doctrines of grace or cast them into the shade miss one of our richest blessings. There is no balm comparable to it. If the honey Jonathan ate enlightened his eyes, this is honey which will enlighten your heart to love and learn the mysteries of the Kingdom of God. Live on this choice dainty without fear. Meat from the King's table will not hurt His courtiers. Desire to have your mind enlarged so that you may comprehend more and more the eternal, everlasting, discriminating love of God. When you have mounted as high as election, tarry on its sister mount, the covenant of grace. Covenant engagements are the ramparts of stupendous rock which we lie behind. Covenant engagements with the Surety, Christ Jesus, are the quiet resting places of trembling spirits. The Father promised that He would give me to the Son to be a part of the infinite reward of the travail of His soul. Then, until God Himself is unfaithful or until Jesus ceases to be the truth, my soul is safe. When David danced before the ark, he told Michal that election made him do so. Come, my soul, exalt before the God of grace and leap for joy of heart.

October 29

"After this manner therefore pray ye: Our Father, which art in heaven" (Matthew 6:9).

This prayer begins where all true prayer must commence—with the spirit of adoption, "Our Father." There is no acceptable prayer until we can say, "I will arise and go to my Father." This childlike spirit soon perceives the grandeur of the Father in heaven and ascends to devout adoration—"Hallowed be thy name. Thy kingdom come. Thy will be done on earth, as it is in heaven." Next follows the heartfelt expression of dependence on God—"Give us this day our daily bread." Being further illuminated by the Spirit, he discovers that he is not only dependent, but sinful; hence he entreats for mercy—"Forgive us our debts as we forgive our debtors." Being pardoned, having the righteousness of Christ imputed, and knowing his acceptance with God, he humbly supplicates for holy perseverance—"Lead us not into temptation." The man who is really forgiven is anxious not to offend again. The possession of justification leads to an anxious desire for sanctification. "Forgive us our debts"—that is justification. "Lead us not into temptation, but deliver us from evil—that is sanctification in its negative and positive forms. As the result of all this, there follows a triumphant praise—"Thine is the kingdom, the power, and the glory, forever. Amen." We rejoice that our King reigns in providence and will reign in grace, and there will be no end of His dominion. Thus, this short model of prayer conducts the soul from a sense of adoption up to fellowship with our reigning Lord.

October 30

"I will praise thee, O Lord" (Psalm 9:1).

Praise should always follow answered prayer as the mist of earth's gratitude rises when the sun of heaven's love warms the ground. Has the Lord been gracious to you and inclined His ear to the voice of your supplication? Then praise Him as long as you live. Do not deny a song to Him who has answered your prayer and given you the desire of your heart. To be silent over God's mercies is to incur the guilt of ingratitude. It is to act as basely as the nine lepers, who, after they had been cured of their leprosy, did not return to give thanks to the healing Lord. To forget to praise God is to refuse to benefit ourselves. Praise, like prayer, is one great means of promoting the growth of the spiritual life. It helps to remove our burdens, to excite our hope, and to increase our faith. It is a healthful and invigorating exercise which quickens the pulse of the believer and prepares him for fresh enterprises in his Master's service. To bless God for mercies received is also the way to benefit our fellowmen; "the humble shall hear thereof and be glad" (Psalm 34:2). Others, who have been in like circumstances, will take comfort if we can say, "Oh! magnify the Lord with me, and let us exalt His name together. . . .this poor man cried, and the Lord heard him" (Psalm 34:3-6). Weak hearts will be strengthened and drooping saints will be revived as they listen to our songs of deliverance.

October 31

"Renew a right spirit within me" (Psalm 51:10).

A backslider, if there is a spark of life left in him, will groan after restoration. The same exercise of grace is required in this renewal as at our conversion. We needed repentance then, and we certainly need it now. At first, we needed faith to come to Christ. Now, only the same grace can bring us to Jesus. We wanted a word from the Most High to end our fears then, and we will soon discover, when under a sense of present sin, that we need it now. No man can be renewed without as real and true a manifestation of the Holy Spirit's power as he felt at first, because the work is as great. Let your personal weakness, Christian, be an argument to make you pray earnestly to your God for help. Remember, David, when he felt himself to be powerless, hastened to the mercy-seat with, "Renew a right spirit within me" (Psalm 51:10). Let this scripture be a goad in your side to drive you with an awful earnestness to Israel's strong Helper. Plead with God as though you pleaded for your very life—"Lord, renew a right spirit within me." He who sincerely prays to God to do this will prove his honesty by using the means through which God works. Be much in prayer. Live on the Word of God. Kill the lusts which have driven your Lord from you. Be careful to watch over the future uprisings of sin. Sit by the wayside and be ready when He passes by. Continue in all those blessed ordinances which will foster and nourish your dying graces. Know that all power must proceed from Him, cease not to cry, "Renew a right spirit within me."

November 1

"The church in thy house" (Philemon 2). Is there a church in your house? Are parents, children, friends, and servants all members of it? Or are some still unconverted? How a father's heart would leap for joy and a mother's eyes fill with holy tears if all were saved from the oldest to the youngest! Let us pray for this great mercy until the Lord grants it to us. Probably it had been the dearest of Philemon's desires to have all his household saved, but it was not at first granted him in its fullness. He had a wicked servant, Onesimus, who, having wronged him, ran away from his service. But his master's prayers followed him, and as God would have it, Onesimus was led to hear Paul preach. His heart was touched, and he returned to Philemon, not only to be a faithful servant, but a beloved brother. Is there an unconverted child absent this morning? Make special supplication that such may, on their return to their home, gladden all hearts with good news of what grace has done! Is there one present? Let him partake in the same earnest plea. If there is such a church in your house, order it well. Let all act as in the sight of God. Move in the common affairs of life with holiness, diligence, kindness, and integrity. More is expected of a church than of an ordinary household. Family worship must, in such a case, be more devout and hearty. Internal love must be more warm and unbroken, and external conduct must be more sanctified and Christlike. As a church let us draw near to the great Head of the one Church universal, and let us beseech Him to give us grace to shine before men to the glory of His name.

November 2

"I am the Lord, I change not" (Malachi 3:6).

It is well for us that, amidst all the variableness of life, there is One whom change cannot affect; One whose heart can never alter and on whose brow mutability can make no furrows. Everything else has changed. The sun itself grows dim with age. The world is growing old. The folding up of the wornout vesture has commenced. The heavens and earth must soon pass away. They will perish; but there is One who has immortality, and in whose person there is no change. The mariner feels delight when, after having been tossed about for many days, he steps again on the solid shore. This is like the satisfaction of a Christian, when, amidst all the changes of this troublesome life, he rests his foot on this truth—*"I am the Lord, I change not."* With God "is no variableness, neither shadow of turning" (James 1:17). Whatever His attributes were of old, they are now. His power, wisdom, justice, and truth are all unchanged. He has always been the refuge of His people and their stronghold in the day of trouble. He is their sure helper still. He is unchanged in His love. He has loved His people with an everlasting love, and He loves them now as much as He ever did. Precious is the assurance that He changes not!

"Behold, he prayeth" (Acts 9:11).

Prayers are instantly noticed in heaven. The moment Saul began to pray, the Lord heard him. Here is comfort for the distressed but praying soul. Often a poor, brokenhearted one bends his knee but can only utter his wailing in the language of sighs and tears. Yet, that groan has made all the harps of heaven thrill with music. That tear has been caught by God and treasured in heaven. The suppliant whose fears prevent his words will be well understood by the Most High. He may only look up with misty eyes. Tears are the diamonds of heaven, and sighs are part of the music of Jehovah's court. They are numbered with the sublimest strains that reach the Majesty on high. Do not think that your prayer, however weak or trembling, will be unregarded. Jacob's ladder is lofty, but our prayer will climb its starry rounds. Our God not only hears prayer but also loves to hear it. "He forgetteth not the cry of the humble" (Psalm 9:12). True, He does not regard high looks and lofty words. He does not care for the pomp and pagentry of kings. He does not listen to the swell of martial music. He does not regard the triumph and pride of man; but wherever there is a heart big with sorrow, a lip quivering with agony, a deep groan or a penitential sigh, the heart of Jehovah is open. He marks it down in the registry of His memory. He puts our prayers, like rose leaves, between the pages of His book of remembrance, and when the volume is opened at last, there will be a precious fragrance springing up from it.

November 4

"For my strength is made perfect in weakness"
(2 Corinthians 12:9).

A primary qualification for serving God with any amount of success is a sense of our own weakness. When God's warrior marches forth to battle boasting, "I know that I will conquer; my own right arm and my conquering sword will get me the victory," then defeat is not far away. God will not go forth with that man. He who reckons on victory in this way has reckoned wrongly, for "it is not by might, nor by power, but by my Spirit, saith the Lord of hosts" (Zechariah 4:6). They who go forth to fight, boasting of their prowess will return with their banners trailing in the dust and their armor stained with disgrace. Those who serve God must serve Him in His way and in His strength, or He will never accept their service. He casts away the mere fruits of the earth. He will only reap that seed sown from heaven, watered by grace, and ripened by the sun of divine love. God will empty out all that you have before He will put His own into you. The river of God is full of water, but not one drop of it flows from earthly springs. God will have no strength used in His battles but the strength which He Himself imparts. Are you mourning over your own weakness? Take courage, for there must be a consciousness of weakness before the Lord will give you victory. Your emptiness is but the preparation for your being filled, and your casting down is but the making ready for your lifting up.

November 5

"No weapon that is formed against thee shall prosper" (Isaiah 54:17).

Today is notable in English history for three great deliverances wrought by God for us. The first, in 1588, was the total destruction of the Spanish Armada by the breath of the Almighty. In 1605, on this day, the plot to destroy the House of Parliament was discovered. Today is also the anniversary of the landing of King William III at Torbay. Religious liberty was secured in 1688. This day ought to be celebrated by the songs of saints. Our Puritan forefathers most devoutly made it a special time of thanksgiving. There is a record of the annual sermons preached by Matthew Henry on this day. Our love of liberty should make us regard its anniversary with holy gratitude. Let our hearts and lips exclaim, "We have heard with our ears, and our fathers have told us, the wondrous things which You did in their day and in the old time before them." You have made this nation the home of the gospel. When the foe has risen against her, You have shielded her. Grant us more and more a hatred of evil and hasten the day of its entire extinction. We will stand on Your promise, "No weapon that is formed against thee shall prosper."

November 6

"I will pour water upon him that is thirsty" (Isaiah 44:3).

When a believer has fallen into a low, sad state of feeling, he often tries to lift himself out of it by chastening himself with dark and doleful fears. This is not the way to rise from the dust but to continue in it. It is not the law but the gospel which saves the seeking soul at first, and it is not a legal bondage but gospel liberty which can restore the fainting believer afterward. It is not fear that brings the backslider back to God but the sweet wooings of love allure him to Jesus' bosom. Are you thirsting for the living God this morning and unhappy because you cannot find Him to be the delight of your heart? Have you lost the joy of faith and is this your prayer, "Restore to me the joy of my salvation"? Are you conscious, also, that you are barren like the dry ground and that you are not bringing forth the fruit to God which He has a right to expect of you? Are you aware that you are not as useful in the Church or in the world as your heart desires to be? Then here is exactly the promise which you need: "I will pour water upon him that is thirsty." You will receive the grace you so much require, and you will have it to the utmost reach of your needs. Water refreshes the thirsty and quickens the sleeping plant life. Your life will be quickened and refreshed by fresh grace. Water swells the buds and makes the fruits ripen, and you will be made fruitful in the ways of God. Whatever good quality there is in divine grace, you will enjoy it to the full. All the riches of divine grace will be yours in plenty.

Behold, I have graven thee upon the palms of my hand" (Isaiah 49:16).

Zion said, "The Lord hath forsaken me, and my Lord hath forgotten me" (Isaiah 49:14). How amazed the divine mind seems to be at this wicked unbelief! What can be more astounding than the unfounded doubts and fears of God's favored people? The Lord's loving word of rebuke should make us blush. He cries, "How can I have forgotten thee, when I have graven thee upon the palms of My hands?" Unbelief is a strange marvel! God keeps His promise a thousand times, but the trial makes us doubt Him. He never fails. He is never a dry well. Yet, we are as continually vexed with anxieties, molested with suspicions, and disturbed with fears as if our God were the mirage of the desert. "Behold" is a word intended to excite admiration. Heaven and earth may well be astonished that rebels should obtain so great a nearness to the heart of infinite love as to be written on the palms of His hands. "I have graven *thee.*" It does not say, "thy name." The name is there, but that is not all: "I have graven *thee.*" Absorb the fullness of this! Everything about you and all that concerns you have I put there. Will you ever say again that your God has forsaken you, since He has graven *thee* on His own palms?

November 8

"As ye have received Christ Jesus the Lord"
(Colossians 2:6).

The life of faith is represented as *receiving*. It is simply the acceptance of a gift. As the earth drinks in the rain, as the sea receives the streams, as night accepts light from the stars, so we, giving nothing, partake freely of the grace of God. The saints are not, by nature, wells or streams. They are but cisterns into which the living water flows. They are empty vessels into which God pours His salvation. One cannot very well receive a shadow. We receive that which is substantial. In the life of faith, Christ becomes real to us. While we are without faith, Jesus is a mere name to us—a person who lived a long while ago, so long ago that His life is only history to us now! By an act of faith, Jesus becomes a real person in the consciousness of our heart. But receiving also means getting possession of. The thing which I receive becomes my own. When I receive Jesus, He becomes *my* Savior, so much mine that neither life nor death will be able to rob me of Him. Salvation may be described as the blind receiving sight, the deaf receiving hearing, the dead receiving life; but we have not only received these blessings, we have received Christ Jesus Himself. It is true that He gave us life from the dead. He gave us pardon of sin; He gave us imputed righteousness. These are all precious things, but we are not content with them; we have received Christ Himself. The Son of God has been poured into us, and we have received Him. How full we must be, for heaven itself cannot contain Him!

November 9

"So walk ye in him" (Colossians 2:6).

If we have received Christ Himself in our heart, our new life will manifest its intimate acquaintance with Him by a walk of faith in Him. Walking implies action. Our faith is not to be confined to our prayer closet. We must carry out into daily life that which we believe. If a man walks in Christ, he acts as Christ would act. Men will say of that man, "He is like his Master; he lives like Jesus Christ." Walking signifies progress. "So walk ye in him." Proceed from grace to grace, and run forward until you reach the uttermost degree of knowledge that a man can attain concerning our Beloved. There must be a perpetual abiding in Christ. Many Christians think that in the morning and evening they ought to come into the company of Jesus, but they give their heart to the world all day! This is poor living. We should always be with Him, treading in His steps and doing His will. Walking also implies habit. When we speak of a man's walk and conversation, we mean his habit. If we sometimes enjoy Christ and then later forget Him, sometimes call Him ours and later lose our hold, that is not a habit. We do not *walk* in Him. We must keep close to Him, cling to Him, and never let Him go. "As ye have received Christ Jesus the Lord, so walk ye in him." In the beginning Christ Jesus was the trust of your faith, the source of your life, the principle of your action, and the joy of your spirit. Let Him be the same until life's end.

November 10

"The eternal God is thy refuge" (Deuteronomy 33:27).

The word refuge may be translated "mansion" or "abiding-place." This gives the thought that God is our abode, our home. There is a fullness and sweetness in the metaphor, for dear to our heart is our home, although it may be the humblest cottage. Dearer still is our blessed God, in whom we live, move, and have our being. It is at home that we feel safe. We shut the world out and dwell in quiet security. So when we are with our God, we fear no evil. He is our shelter, our retreat, and our abiding refuge. It is at home we find rest after the fatigue and toil of the day. And so our hearts find rest in God, when, wearied with life's conflict, we turn to Him and our soul dwells at ease. So when we are with God, we can commune freely with Him, laying open all our hidden desires. If the secret of the Lord is with them that fear Him, the secrets of them that fear Him ought to be with their Lord. Home, too, is the place of our truest and purest happiness; and it is in God that our hearts find their deepest delight. We have joy in Him which far surpasses all other joy. It is also for home that we work and labor. The thought of it gives strength to bear the daily burden. We think of Him in the person of His dear Son, and a glimpse of the suffering face of the Redeemer constrains us to labor in His cause. We feel that we must work for we have brethren yet to be saved, and we have our Father's heart to make glad by bringing home His wandering sons. Happy are those who have the God of Jacob for their refuge!

November 11

"Underneath are the everlasting arms" (Deuteronomy 33:27).

God—the eternal God—is our support at all times and especially when we are sinking in deep trouble. There are seasons when the Christian sinks very low in humiliation. Under a deep sense of his great sinfulness, he is humbled before God until he scarcely knows how to pray. He appears, in his own sight, so worthless. Child of God, remember that when you are at your lowest point, underneath you are the everlasting arms of the Lord. Sin may drag you low, but Christ's great atonement is still under all. You may have descended into deep distress, but you cannot have fallen so low that He cannot save you. If every earthly prop is cut away, what then? Still underneath you are the everlasting arms. You cannot fall so deep in distress and affliction but what the covenant of grace of an ever-faithful God will still encircle you. The Christian may be sinking under trouble from within through fierce conflict, but even then he cannot be brought so low as to be beyond the reach of the everlasting arms—they are underneath him. While thus sustained, all Satan's efforts to harm avail nothing. This assurance of support is a comfort to any weary but earnest worker in the service of God. It implies a promise of strength for each day, grace for each need, and power for each duty. And, further, when death comes, the promise will still hold good. When we stand in the midst of Jordan, we will be able to say with David, "I will fear no evil, for You are with me."

November 12

"The trial of your faith" (1 Peter 1:7).

Faith untried may be true faith, but it is sure to be little faith. It is likely to remain stunted as long as it is without trials. Faith never prospers as well as when all things are against her. Tempests are her trainers, and lightnings are her illuminators. When calm reigns on the sea, spread the sails as you will, the ship will not move to its harbor. But let the howling winds rush forth and rock the vessel until her deck is washed with waves and her mast sways under the pressure of the full and swelling sail. It is then that she makes headway toward her desired haven. No faith is so precious as that which lives and triumphs in adversity. You could not have believed your own weakness had you not been compelled to pass through the rivers. You would never have known God's strength had you not been supported amid the flood waters. Faith increases in solidity, assurance, and intensity the more it is exercised with tribulation. Faith is precious, and its trial is precious too. Do not let this discourage those who are young in faith. You will have trials enough without seeking them. The full portion will be measured out to you in due season. Meanwhile, if you cannot yet claim the result of long experience, thank God for what grace you have. Praise Him for that degree of holy confidence that you have attained. Walk according to that rule, and you will have more and more of the blessing of God until your faith will remove mountains and conquer impossibilities.

"The branch cannot bear fruit of itself" (John 15:4).

How did you begin to bear fruit? It was when you came to Jesus and cast yourself on His great atonement and rested on His finished righteousness. Do you remember those early days? Have you declined since then? If you have, we charge you to remember that time of love. Repent and do your first works. Be involved in those activities which draw you nearest to Christ, because it is from Him that all your fruits proceed. Any holy exercise which will bring you to Him will help you to bear fruit. The sun is, no doubt, a great worker in creating fruit among the trees of the orchard; and Jesus is still more so among the trees of His garden of grace. When have you been the most fruitless? Has it not been when you lived farthest from the Lord Jesus Christ, when you slackened in prayer, when you departed from the simplicity of your faith, or when your graces engrossed your attention instead of your Lord? Have you forgotten where your strength dwells? We are taught, by past experience, that the more simply we depend on the grace of God in Christ and wait on the Holy Spirit, the more we will bring forth fruit. Trust Jesus for fruit as well as for life!

November 14

"I will cut off them that worship and that swear by the Lord, and that swear by Malcham" (Zephaniah 1:5).

Such persons thought themselves safe because they were with both parties. They went with the followers of Jehovah and bowed at the same time to Malcham. But duplicity is abominable with God. In the common matters of daily life, a double-minded man is despised, but in Christianity he is loathsome to the last degree. The penalty pronounced in the verse before us is terrible, but it is well-deserved. How could divine justice spare the sinner, who knows the right, approves it, professes to follow it, and all the while loves evil and gives it dominion in his heart? My soul, search yourself this morning and see whether you are guilty of double-dealing. You profess to be a follower of Jesus—do you truly love Him? Is your heart right with God? To have one foot on the land of truth and another on the sea of falsehood will involve a terrible fall and a total ruin. Christ will be all or nothing. God fills the whole universe; therefore, there is no room for another god. If He reigns in your heart, there will be no space for another reigning power. Do you rest alone on Jesus and live for Him alone? Is it your desire to do so? If so, blessed be the mighty grace which has led you to salvation. If not so, O Lord, pardon this sad offense.

November 15

"The Lord's portion is his people" (Deuteronomy 32:9).

How are they His? By His own sovereign choice. He chose them and set His love on them. He did this altogether apart from any goodness in them at the time or any goodness which He foresaw in them. He had mercy on whom He would have mercy and ordained a chosen company unto eternal life; thus, they are His by His unconstrained election. They are not only His by choice but by purchase. He has bought and paid for them to the last cent. There can be no dispute about His title. The Lord's portion has been fully redeemed, not with corruptible things, as with silver and gold, but with the precious blood of the Lord Jesus Christ. There is no mortgage on His estate. There are no suits that can be raised by opposing claimants. The price was paid in open court, and the Church is the Lord's forever. See the blood-mark on all the chosen. It is invisible to the human eye but known to Christ, for the Lord knows them that are His. He forgets none of those whom He has redeemed from among men. He counts the sheep for whom He laid down His life and remembers well the Church for which He gave Himself. They are also His by conquest. What a battle He had in us before we were won! How long He laid siege to our hearts! We had barred our gates and fenced our walls against Him. But we have become the conquered captives of His omnipotent love. Thus chosen, purchased, and subdued, the rights of our divine Possessor are inalienable. We rejoice that we never can be our own. We desire, day by day, to do His will and to show forth His glory.

November 16

"The Lord is my portion, saith my soul" (Lamentations 3:24).

It is not, "The Lord is *partly* my portion" or "The Lord is *in* my portion;" but He Himself makes up the sum total of my soul's inheritance. Within the circumference of that circle lies all that we possess or desire. The Lord is my portion, not His grace or His love or His covenant, but Jehovah Himself. He has chosen us for His portion, and we have chosen Him for ours. It is true that the Lord must first choose us, or else we would never choose Him for ourselves. The Lord is our all-sufficient portion. It is not easy to satisfy man's desires. But all that we can wish for is to be found in our divine portion, so that we ask, "Whom have I in heaven but thee? and there is none upon earth that I desire beside thee" (Psalm 73:25). Well may we delight ourselves in the Lord who makes us drink of the river of His pleasures. Our faith stretches its wings and mounts like an eagle into the heaven of divine love as its proper dwelling place. "The lines are fallen unto me in pleasant places; yea, I have a goodly heritage" (Psalm 16:6). Let us rejoice in the Lord always. Let us show to the world that we are a happy and blessed people, and thus induce them to exclaim, "We will go with you: for we have heard that God is with you" (Zechariah 8:23).

November 17

"To whom be glory forever. Amen" (Romans 11:36).

This should be the single desire of the Christian. All other wishes must be subservient to this one. The Christian may wish for prosperity in his business but only so far as it may help him to promote this—"To Him be glory forever." He may desire to attain more gifts and more graces, but it should only be for His glory. You are not acting as you should if you are moved by any other motive than a single eye to your Lord's glory. As a Christian, let this ambition fire your soul. Make God your only object. Depend on it. Where self begins, sorrow also begins. Let your desire for God's glory be a growing desire. You blessed Him in your youth, but do not be content with such praises as you gave Him then. Has God prospered you in business? Give Him more because He has given you more. Has God given you experience? Praise Him by stronger faith than you exercised at first. Is your knowledge growing? Then sing more sweetly. Do you enjoy happier times than you once had? Have you been restored from sickness, and has your sorrow been turned into peace and joy? Then give Him more music. Give honor to your great and gracious Lord by your own individual service and increasing holiness.

November 18

"A spring shut up, a fountain sealed" (Song of Solomon 4:12).

In this metaphor, which has reference to the inner life of a believer, the idea of *secrecy* is very plain. It is a spring shut up. There were springs in the Middle East over which an edifice was built so that none could reach them except those who knew the secret entrance. Such is the heart of a believer when it is renewed by grace. There is a mysterious life within which no human skill can touch. The Scripture includes not only secrecy but *separation*. It is not the common spring of which every passerby may drink. It is one kept and preserved from all others. It is a fountain bearing a particular mark—a king's royal seal—so that all can perceive that it is not a common fountain but a fountain owned by a proprietor. So it is with the spiritual life. The chosen of God were separated by God in the day of redemption to possess a life which others do not have. It is impossible for the redeemed to feel at home with the world or to delight in its pleasures. There is also the idea of *sacredness*. The spring shut up is preserved for the use of some special person. The Christian's heart is a spring kept for Jesus. Every Christian should feel that he has God's seal on him. He should be able to say like Paul, "From henceforth let no man trouble me, for I bear in my body the marks of the Lord Jesus" (Galatians 6:17).

November 19

"Avoid foolish questions" (Titus 3:9).

Our days are few and are far better spent in doing good than in disputing over matters which are of minor importance. Our churches suffer from petty wars over absurd points and unimportant questions. After everything has been said that can be said, neither party is any wiser. Therefore, the discussion no more promotes knowledge than love. Questions on points wherein Scripture is silent, on mysteries which belong to God alone, on prophecies of doubtful interpretation, and on mere modes of observing human ceremonies are all foolish; and wise men avoid them. Our business is neither to ask nor answer foolish questions, but to avoid them altogether. There are, however, some questions, which we must not avoid but fairly and honestly answer such as these: Do I believe in the Lord Jesus Christ? Am I renewed in the spirit of my mind? Am I walking, not after the flesh, but after the Spirit? Am I growing in grace? Does my conversation adorn the doctrine of God my Savior? Am I looking for the coming of the Lord and watching as a servant should do who expects his master? What more can I do for Jesus? Such inquiries as these urgently demand our attention. Let us be peacemakers and endeavor to lead others, both by our precept and example, to "avoid foolish questions."

"O Lord, thou hast pleaded the causes of my soul" (Lamentations 3:58).

Observe how positively the prophet speaks. He does not say, "I hope that God has pleaded the causes of my soul." He speaks of it as a matter of fact not to be disputed. Let us, by the aid of the gracious Comforter, shake off those doubts and fears which so often mar our peace and comfort. Notice how gratefully the prophet speaks, ascribing all the glory to God alone! There is not a word concerning himself or his own pleadings. He does not ascribe his deliverance in any measure to any man, much less to his own merit. But he says, "O Lord, *thou* hast pleaded the causes of my soul; *thou* hast redeemed my life." A grateful spirit should be cultivated by the Christian. Earth should be a temple filled with the songs of grateful saints, and every day should be a smoking censer filled with the sweet incense of thanksgiving. How joyful Jeremiah seems to be while he records the Lord's mercy! How triumphantly he lifts up the strain! He has been in the low dungeon and is the weeping prophet. We hear the voice of Jeremiah going up to heaven, "Thou hast pleaded the causes of my soul; thou hast redeemed my life." Children of God, seek after a vital experience of the Lord's lovingkindness. When you have it, speak positively of it, sing gratefully, and shout triumphantly.

November 21

"Grieve not the Holy Spirit" (Ephesians 4:30).

All that the believer has comes from Christ. Moreover, as all the blessings flow to you through the Holy Spirit, so also no good thing can come out of you apart from the sanctifying operation of the same Spirit. Even if the good seed is sown in you, it lies dormant until He works in you. Do you desire to speak for Jesus? How can you unless the Holy Spirit touches your tongue? Do you desire to pray? Alas! What dull work it is unless the Spirit makes intercession for you! Do you desire to subdue sin? Would you be holy? Would you imitate your Master? Do you desire to rise to superlative heights of spirituality? Are you wanting to be made, like the angels of God, full of zeal and ardor for the Master's cause? You cannot without the Spirit—"Without me ye can do nothing" (John 15:5). Branch of the vine, you can have no fruit without the sap! Child of God, you have no life within you apart from the life which God gives you through His Spirit! Then let us not grieve Him or provoke Him to anger by our sin. Let us not quench Him in one of His faintest motions in our soul. Be ready to obey every prompting of the Holy Spirit. Let us attempt nothing without Him. Let us depend on Him alone. May this be our prayer, "Open my heart and my whole being to Your incoming, and uphold me with Your free Spirit when I have received that Spirit in my inward parts."

"Israel served for a wife, and for a wife he kept sheep" (Hosea 12:12).

Jacob, while reasoning with Laban, describes his own toil: "This twenty years have I been with you. That which was torn of beasts I brought not unto you: I bare the loss of it; of my hand you did require it, whether stolen by day, or stolen by night. Thus I was: in the day the drought consumed me, and the frost by night; and my sleep departed from mine eyes" (Genesis 31:38). Even more toilsome than this was the life of our Savior here below. He watched over all His sheep until He gave as His last account, "Those that thou gavest me, I have kept, and none of them is lost" (John 17:12). His hair was wet with dew, and sleep departed from his eyes. He was in prayer all night, wrestling for His people. No shepherd sitting beneath the cold skies could ever utter such complaints as Jesus Christ might have, if He had chosen to do so, because of the sternness of His service in order to procure His spouse. It is sweet to dwell on the spiritual parallel of Laban having required all the sheep at Jacob's hand. If they were torn of beasts, Jacob must make it good. If any of them died, he must stand as surety for the whole. Was not the toil of Jesus for His Church the toil of one who was under suretyship obligations to bring every believing one safe to the hand of Him who had committed them to His charge? Look on toiling Jacob, and you see a representation of Him of whom we read, "He shall feed his flock like a shepherd" (Isaiah 40:11).

"Fellowship with him" (1 John 1:6).

When we were united by faith to Christ, we were brought into such complete fellowship with Him that we were made one with Him. His interests and our interests became mutual and identical. We have fellowship with Christ in His *love*. What He loves, we love. He loves the saints—so do we. He loves sinners—so do we. We have fellowship with Him in His *desires*. He desires the glory of God—we also labor for the same. He desires that the saints may be with Him where He is—we desire to be with Him there too. He desires to drive out sin—behold, we fight under His banner. He desires that His Father's name may be loved and adored by all His creatures—we pray daily, "Let Thy kingdom come, and Thy will be done on earth, even as it is in heaven." We have fellowship with Christ in His *sufferings*. We are not nailed to His cross to die a cruel death; but when He is reproached, we are reproached. We have fellowship with Him in His *labors*. We are to minister to men the Word of truth. Our meat and drink, like His, is to do the will of Him who has sent us and to finish His work. We also have fellowship with Christ in His *joys*. We are happy in His happiness, we rejoice in His exaltation. Have you ever tasted that joy, believer? There is no purer or more thrilling delight to be known this side of heaven than that of having Christ's joy fulfilled in us.

"The glorious Lord will be unto us a place of broad rivers and streams" (Isaiah 33:21).

Broad rivers and streams produce fertility and abundance in the land. Places near broad rivers are remarkable for the variety of their plants and their plentiful harvests. God is all this to His Church. Having God she has abundance. What can she ask for that He will not supply? "In the mountain shall the Lord of Hosts make unto all people a feast of fat things" (Isaiah 25:6). If you suffer any lack, it is your own fault. Broad rivers and streams also point to commerce. Our glorious Lord is to us a place of heavenly merchandise. Through our Redeemer we have commerce with the past. The wealth of Calvary, the treasures of the covenant, the riches of the ancient days of election, and the stores of eternity all come to us down the broad stream of our gracious Lord. We have commerce, too, with the future. What bounties and blessings come to us from the millennium! What visions we have of the days of heaven on earth! Through our glorious Lord we have commerce with angels. Better still, we have fellowship with the Infinite One. Broad rivers and streams are especially intended to set forth the idea of security. Rivers were a defense in the past. Oh, beloved, what a defense is God to His Church! The devil cannot cross this broad river of God. How he wishes he could turn the current. But fear not, for God abides immutably the same, and Satan cannot destroy us.

November 25

"To preach deliverance to the captives" (Luke 4:18).

None but Jesus can give deliverance to the captives. Real liberty comes from Him only. It is a liberty righteously bestowed for the Son, who is Heir of all things, has a right to make men free. It is a liberty which has been dearly purchased by His blood. He makes you free, but it is by His own bonds. You go clear, because He bore your burden for you. You are set at liberty, because He has suffered freely in your place. Jesus asks nothing of us as a preparation for this liberty. He finds us sitting in sackcloth and ashes and bids us put on the beautiful array of freedom. He saves us just as we are and without our help or merit. Satan may plot to enslave us, but if the Lord is on our side, whom will we fear? The world, with its temptations, may seek to ensnare us, but mightier is He who is for us than all they who are against us. Our own deceitful hearts may harass and annoy us, but He who has begun the good work in us will carry it on and perfect it to the end. If we are no more under the law, but free from its curse, let our liberty be practically exhibited in our serving God with gratitude and delight. "I am thy servant, and the son of thine handmaid: thou hast loosed my bonds" (Psalm 116:16). Lord, what will You have me to do?

"Whatosever thy hand findeth to do, do it with thy might" (Ecclesiastes 9:10).

Whatsoever thy hand findeth to do refers to works that are *possible*. There are many things which our *heart* finds to do which we will never do. We must not be content with forming schemes in our heart and talking about them. We must carry out "whatsoever our hand findeth to do." One good deed is worth more than a thousand brilliant theories. Let us not wait for large opportunities but do just the things we "find to do" day by day. We have no other time in which to live. The past is gone, and the future has not arrived. We never have any time but the *present*. Then do not wait until your experience has ripened into maturity before you attempt to serve God. Endeavor now to bring forth fruit. Do it *promptly*. Do not fritter away your life in thinking of what you intend to do tomorrow. No man ever served God by doing things tomorrow. We honor Christ by the things we do today. Whatever you do for Christ, do it with heart, soul, and strength. Where is the might of a Christian? It is not in himself, for he is perfect weakness. His might lies in the Lord of Hosts. Then let us seek His help. Let us proceed with prayer and faith. When we have done what our "hand findeth to do," let us wait on the Lord for His blessing.

"Joshua, the high priest, standing before the angel of the Lord" (Zechariah 3:1).

In Joshua, the high priest, we see a picture of each and every child of God who has been drawn near by the blood of Christ and has been taught to minister in holy things. Jesus has made us priests and kings to God, and even here on earth we exercise the priesthood of consecrated living and hallowed service. But this high priest is said to be *"standing* before the angel of the Lord," that is, standing to minister. This should be the perpetual position of every true believer. Every place is now God's temple, and His people can as truly serve Him in their daily employments as in His house. They are to be always ministering, offering the spiritual sacrifice of prayer and praise and presenting themselves as a living sacrifice. Notice where Joshua stands to minister—it is before the angel of Jehovah. It is only through a mediator that we poor, defiled ones can ever become priests to God. I present what I have before the messenger, the angel of the covenant, the Lord Jesus; and through Him my prayers find acceptance wrapped up in His prayers. If I can bring Him nothing but my tears, He will put them with His own tears, for He once wept. If I can bring Him nothing but my groans and sighs, He will accept these as an acceptable sacrifice, for He once was broken in heart and sighed heavily in spirit. When I am standing in Him, I am accepted in the Beloved. See, then, the position of the Christian—"a priest—standing—before the angel of the Lord."

"For I rejoiced greatly when the brethren came and testified of the truth that is in thee, even as thou walkest in the truth." (3 John 3).

The truth was in Gaius, and Gaius walked in the truth. Truth must enter into the soul, penetrate and saturate it, or else it is of no value. Doctrines held as a matter of creed are like bread in the hand, which ministers no nourishment to the frame. But doctrine accepted by the heart is as food digested, which, by assimilation, sustains and builds up the body. In us truth must be a living force, an active energy, and an indwelling reality. If it is in us, we cannot part with it. A man may lose his garments or his limbs, but his inward parts are vital and cannot be torn away without absolute loss of life. A Christian can die, but he cannot deny the truth. Now, it is a rule of nature, that the inward affects the outward. When the truth is kindled within, its brightness soon beams forth in the outward life and conversation. It is said that the food of certain worms colors the cocoons of silk which they spin. The nutriment on which a man's inward nature lives colors every word and deed proceeding from him. To walk in the truth imports a life of integrity, holiness, faithfulness, and simplicity—the natural product of those principles of truth which the gospel teaches and the Spirit of God enables us to receive. Be it ours today, O gracious Spirit, to be ruled and governed by Your divine authority. May nothing false or sinful reign in our hearts, lest it extend its malignant influence to our daily walk among men.

"Thou shalt not go up and down as a tale-bearer among thy people. . . .thou shalt in any wise rebuke thy neighbor, and not suffer sin upon him" (Leviticus 19:16-17).

Tale bearing emits a threefold poison. It injures the teller, the hearer, and the person concerning whom the tale is told. Whether the report is true or false, we are by this precept of God's Word forbidden to spread it. The reputations of the Lord's people should be very precious in our sight, and we should be ashamed to help the devil dishonor the Church and the name of the Lord. Some tongues need a bridle rather than a spur. Many glory in pulling down their brethren, as if thereby they raised themselves. We ourselves may one day need forbearance and silence from our brethren, so let us render it cheerfully to those who require it now. Speak evil of no man. The Holy Spirit, however, permits us to censure sin and prescribes the way in which we are to do it. It must be done by rebuking our brother to his face, not by railing behind his back. This course is manly, brotherly, Christlike, and under God's blessing. Remember, hundreds have been saved from gross sin by the timely, wise, affectionate warnings of faithful ministers and brethren.

November 30

"And Amaziah said to the man of God, But what shall we do for the hundred talents which I have given to the army of Israel? And the man of God answered, The Lord is able to give thee much more than this" (2 Chronicles 25:9).

This seemed to be a very important question to the king of Judah, and possibly it is of even more weight with the tried and tempted Christian. To lose money is at no time pleasant. "Why lose that which may be so useful to us? What will we do without it? Remember the children and our small income." All these things and a thousand more would tempt the Christian to put forth his hand to unrighteous gain or keep himself from carrying out his conscientious convictions when they involve serious loss. All men cannot view these matters in the light of faith; and even with the followers of Jesus, the doctrine of "we must live" has quite sufficient weight. *The Lord is able to give thee much more than this* is a very satisfactory answer to the anxious question. Our Father holds the purse strings; and what we lose for His sake, He can repay a thousandfold. If we obey His will, we may rest assured that He will provide for us. Saints know that a grain of heart's-ease is of more value than a ton of gold. God's smile in a dungeon is enough for a true heart, but His frown in a palace would be hell to a gracious spirit. Our treasure is above, where Christ sits at the right hand of God. Meanwhile, even now, the Lord makes the meek to inherit the earth, and no good thing does He withhold from them that walk uprightly.

December 1

"Thou hast made summer and winter" (Psalm 74:17).

My soul, begin this wintry month with your God. The cold snows and the piercing winds all remind you that He keeps His covenant with day and night. You can be assured that He will also keep that glorious covenant which He has made with you in the person of Jesus Christ. He who is true to His Word in the revolutions of the seasons of this poor, sin-polluted world will not prove unfaithful in His dealings with His own well-beloved Son. Winter in the soul is by no means a comfortable season. If it is on you just now, it will be very painful to you. But there is this comfort, namely, that the Lord allows it. He is the great Winter King and rules in the realms of frost. Our circumstances come to us with wise design. Frosts kill noxious insects and put a stop to raging diseases. They break up the clods and sweeten the soil. Oh, that such good results would always follow our winters of affliction! How we prize the fire just now! How pleasant is its cheerful glow! Let us prize our Lord in the same manner, who is the constant source of warmth and comfort in every time of trouble. Let us draw near to Him and find joy and peace in believing. Let us wrap ourselves in the warm garments of His promises and go forth to labors which fit the season.

December 2

"Thou art all fair, my love" (Song of Solomon 4:7).

The Lord's admiration of His Church is wonderful, and His description of her beauty is glowing. She is not merely fair, but *"all* fair." He views her in Himself, washed in His sin-atoning blood and clothed in His righteousness. He considers her to be full of comeliness and beauty. No wonder that such is the case, since it is but His own perfect excellency that He admires. The holiness, glory, and perfection of His Church are His own glorious garments on the back of His own well-beloved spouse. She is positively lovely and fair! She has actual merit! Her deformities of sin are removed. In addition, she has, through her Lord, obtained a meritorious righteousness. Believers have a positive righteousness given to them when they become "accepted in the Beloved" (Ephesians 1:6). The Church has a real worth and excellence which cannot be rivaled by all the nobility and royalty of the world. If Jesus could exchange His elect bride for all the queens and empresses of earth or even for the angels in heaven, He would not, for He puts her first and foremost—"fairest among women." One day, from the throne of His glory, He will avow the truth of this statement before the assembled universe. "Come, ye blessed of my Father" (Matthew 25:34) will be His solemn affirmation of the loveliness of His elect.

"There is no spot in thee" (Song of Solomon 4:7).

Having pronounced His Church positively full of beauty, our Lord confirms His praise by a precious negative: "There is no spot in thee." It is as if the thought occurred to the Bridegroom that the world would insinuate that He had only mentioned her comely parts and had purposely omitted those features which were deformed or defiled. He sums up all by declaring her universally and entirely fair and utterly devoid of stain. If He had said there is no hideous scar, no horrible deformity, or no deadly ulcer, we might have marveled. But He testifies that she is free from the slightest spot. If He had but promised to remove all spots sooner or later, we would have had eternal reason for joy. But He speaks of it as already done. Oh, my soul, here is marrow and fatness for you. Eat your fill and be satisfied with royal dainties. Christ Jesus has no quarrel with His spouse. She often wanders from Him and grieves His Holy Spirit, but He does not allow her faults to affect His love. He sometimes chides, but it is always in the tenderest manner and with the kindest intentions. There is no remembrance of our follies. He does not cherish ill thoughts of us, but He pardons and loves us just as much after the offense as before it. Our precious Husband knows our silly hearts too well to take any offense at our ill manners.

December 4

"I have much people in this city" (Acts 18:10).

This should be a great encouragement to try to do good, since God has among the vilest of the vile those people who *must* be saved. When you take the Word to them, you do so because God has ordained you to be the messenger of life to their soul. They are as much redeemed by blood as the saints before the eternal throne. They are Christ's property; and yet, perhaps, they are still lovers of the tavern and haters of holiness. If Jesus Christ purchased them, He will have them. God is not unfaithful to forget the price which His Son has paid. He will not suffer His substitution to be in any case an ineffectual, dead thing. Tens of thousands of redeemed ones are not regenerated yet, but regenerated they must be. This is our comfort when we go forth to them with the quickening Word of God. "Neither pray I for these alone," said the great Intercessor, "but for them also which shall believe on me through their word" (John 17:20). Poor, ignorant souls, who know nothing about prayer for themselves, but Jesus prays for them. Their names are on His breastplate; and before long, they must bow their stubborn knee, breathing the penitential sigh before the throne of grace. When their moment comes, *they will obey,* for God will have His own. They must obey, for the Spirit is not to be withstood when He comes forth with fullness of power. "He shall see of the travail of his soul" (Isaiah 53:11).

December 5

"Ask, and it shall be given you" (Matthew 7:7).

I know of a place in England where a ration of bread was served to every passerby who chose to ask for it. Whoever the traveler was, he only had to knock at the door of St. Cross Hospital, and there was a ration of bread for him. Jesus Christ so loves sinners that He has built the hospital of the cross. Whenever a sinner is hungry he has only to knock and have his needs supplied. Whenever a soul is black and filthy, he has but to go there and be washed. The fountain is always full, always effective. No sinner ever went into it and found that it could not wash away his stains. Sins which were scarlet and crimson have all disappeared, and the sinner has been made whiter than snow. Nothing that is good for him will be denied him. He will have all he needs as long as he lives; and he will have an eternal heritage of glorious treasure when he enters into the joy of his Lord. If all these things are to be had by merely knocking at mercy's door, O my soul, knock hard this morning, and ask large things of your generous Lord. Do not leave the throne of grace until all your needs have been spread before the Lord and by faith you have a comfortable prospect that they will all be supplied. No unbelief should hinder when Jesus promises.

December 6

"As is the heavenly, such are they also that are heavenly" (1 Corinthians 15:48).

The head and members of the Body of Christ are of one nature. They are not like that monstrous image which Nebuchadnezzar saw in his dream. The head was of fine gold, but the belly and thighs were of brass, the legs were of iron, and the feet were part iron and part clay. Christ's mystical body is no absurd combination of opposites. The members were mortal, and therefore Jesus died. The glorified Head is immortal, and therefore the body is immortal too. The record stands: "Because I live, ye shall live also" (John 14:19). As is our loving Head, such is the body, and every member in particular. A chosen Head and chosen members; an accepted Head and accepted members; a living Head and living members. If the Head is pure gold, all the parts of the body are of pure gold also. Pause here, devout reader, and see if you can contemplate the infinite condescension of the Son of God in thus exalting your wretchedness into blessed union with His glory. In remembrance of mortality, you may say to corruption, "You are my father," and to the worm, "You are my sister." Yet, in Christ you are so honored that you can say to the Almighty, "Abba, Father," and to the Incarnate God, "You are my brother and my husband." Surely if relationships to ancient and noble families make men think highly of themselves, we have much more reason to glory above them all.

"Base things of the world hath God chosen" (1 Corinthians 1:28).

Walk the streets by moonlight, and you will see sinners. Watch when the night is dark and the wind howling, and you will see sinners. Go to the jail and walk through the wards, and see men whom you would not like to meet at night. There are sinners there. Go where you will, you need not ransack the earth to find sinners, for they are common enough. You may find them in every street of every city, town, and village. It is for such that Jesus died. If you would find the grossest specimen of humanity, I would have hope for him yet, because Jesus Christ is come to seek and to save sinners. Electing love has selected some of the worst to be made the best. Worthless dross He transforms into pure gold. Redeeming love has set apart many of the worst of mankind to be the reward of the Savior's passion. Effectual grace calls forth many of the vilest of the vile to sit at the table of mercy. Therefore, let none despair. Reader, there is love looking out of Jesus' tearful eyes and love streaming from those bleeding wounds. By that faithful love, that strong love, that pure and abiding love, by the heart of the Savior's compassion, we urge you, do not turn away as though it were nothing to you. Believe on Him, and you will be saved. Trust your soul with Him, and He will bring you to His Father's right hand in glory everlasting.

"Thou hast a few names even in Sardis which have not defiled their garments; and they shall walk with me in white, for they are worthy" (Revelation 3:4).

We may understand this to refer to *justification*. That is, they will enjoy a constant sense of their own justification by faith. They will understand that the righteousness of Christ is imputed to them, and that they have all been washed and made whiter than the newly-fallen snow. Again, it refers to joy and gladness, for white robes were holiday attire among the Jews. They who have not defiled their garments will have their faces always bright. They will understand what Solomon meant when he said, "Go thy way, eat thy bread with joy, and drink thy wine with a merry heart; for God hath accepted thy works" (Ecclesiastes 9:7). He who is accepted of God will wear white garments of joy and gladness while he walks in sweet communion with the Lord Jesus. Why are there so many doubts, and so much misery and mourning? Is it because so many believers defile their garments with sin and lose the joy of their salvation and the comfortable fellowship of the Lord Jesus? Those who have not defiled their garments here will most certainly possess joys inconceivable, happiness beyond a dream, bliss which imagination knows not, and a blessedness which even the stretch of desire has not reached. In His sweet company they will drink of the living fountains of waters.

December 9

"Therefore will the Lord wait, that he may be gracious unto you" (Isaiah 30:18).

God often delays in answering prayer. We have several instances of this in sacred Scripture. Jacob did not get the blessing from the angel until near the dawn of day—he had to wrestle all night for it. The poor woman of Syrophenicia was answered not a word for a long while. Paul sought the Lord three times that "the thorn in the flesh" might be taken from him. He received no assurance that it would be taken away, but instead received a promise that God's grace would be sufficient for him. If you have been knocking at the gate of mercy and have received no answer, I will tell you why the mighty Maker has not opened the door and let you in. Our Father has reasons peculiar to Himself for keeping us waiting. Sometimes it is to show His power and His sovereignty so that men may know that Jehovah has a right to give or to withhold. More frequently the delay is for our profit. Perhaps you are kept waiting in order that your desires may be more fervent. You will prize the gift all the more because of its long tarrying. There may also be something in you that needs to be removed before the joy of the Lord is given. If your prayers are not immediately answered, they are certainly not forgotten. Your prayers are all filed in heaven. In a little while your prayers will be fulfilled to your satisfaction. Do not let despair make you silent. Continue in earnest supplication.

"So shall we ever be with the Lord" (1 Thessalonians 4:17). Even the sweetest visits from Christ are brief and transitory. One moment our eyes see Him, and we rejoice with unspeakable joy, but in a little while our Beloved withdraws Himself from us. Oh, how sweet to think of the time when we will not behold Him at a distance but see Him face to face! He will no longer be as a wayfaring man tarrying but for a night, but He will eternally enfold us in the bosom of His glory! In heaven there will be no interruptions from care or sin; no weeping will dim our eyes. No earthly business will distract our happy thoughts. We will have nothing to hinder us from gazing forever on the Sun of Righteousness with unwearied eyes. Oh, if it is so sweet to see Him now and then, how sweet to gaze on that blessed face forever and never have a cloud rolling between and never have to turn one's eyes away to look on a world of weariness and woe! Blest day, when will you dawn? The joys of sense will leave us soon. If to die is to enter into uninterrupted communion with Jesus, then death is indeed gain, and the black drop is swallowed up in a sea of victory.

December 11

"Faithful is he that calleth you, who also will do it" (1 Thessalonians 5:24).

Heaven is a place where we will never sin and where we will cease our constant watch against an indefatigable enemy. There will be no tempter to ensnare our feet. There the weary are at rest. Heaven is the "undefiled inheritance." It is the land of perfect holiness and complete security. But do not the saints even on earth sometimes taste the joys of blissful security? The doctrine of God's Word is that all who are in union with the Lamb are safe. Those who have committed their souls to the keeping of Christ will find Him a faithful and immutable preserver. Sustained by such a doctrine, we can enjoy security even on earth. Believer, let us often reflect with joy on the doctrine of the perseverance of the saints and honor the faithfulness of our God by a holy confidence in Him. May our God bring home to you a sense of your safety in Christ Jesus. May He assure you that your name is graven on His hand and whisper in your ear the promise, "Fear not, I am with thee." Look on Him, the great Surety of the covenant, as faithful and true, and, therefore, bound and engaged to present you, the weakest of the family, with all the chosen race before the throne of God. "Faithful is he that calleth you, who also will do it."

December 12

"His ways are everlasting" (Habakkuk 3:5).

What He has done at one time, He will do yet again. Man's ways are variable, but God's ways are everlasting and the result of wise deliberation. He orders all things according to the counsel of His own will. Human action is frequently the hasty result of passion or fear and is followed by regret and alteration. But nothing can take the Almighty by surprise. His ways are the outgrowth of an immutable character, and in them the fixed and settled attributes of God are clearly to be seen. Unless the Eternal One Himself can undergo change, His ways must remain forever the same. He is eternally just, gracious, faithful, wise, and tender. Humans act according to their nature. When their nature changes, their conduct varies also. But God's ways will remain everlastingly the same. The sun and moon stand still when Jehovah marches forth for the salvation of His people. Who can stay His hand or say to Him, "What are you doing?" But it is not might alone which gives stability. God's ways are the manifestations of the eternal principles of right and, therefore, can never pass away. Wrong breeds decay and involves ruin, but the true and good have about them a vitality which age cannot diminish. This morning let us go to our heavenly Father with confidence, remembering that Jesus Christ is the same yesterday, today, and forever.

"Salt, without prescribing how much" (Ezra 7:22).

Salt was used in every offering made by fire to the Lord. From its preserving and purifying properties, it was the grateful emblem of divine grace in the soul. When Artaxerxes gave salt to Ezra the priest, he set no limit to the quantity. We may be quite certain that when the King of kings distributes grace among His royal priesthood, the supply is not cut short by Him. Often we are restricted in ourselves but never in the Lord. He who chooses to gather much manna will find that he may have as much as he desires. There is no such famine in Jerusalem that the citizens should eat their bread by weight and drink their water by measure. "Ask what thou wilt, and it shall be given unto thee" (Mark 6:22). Parents need to lock up the candy jars, but there is no need to keep the salt shaker under lock and key, for few children will eat too greedily from that. A man may have too much money or too much honor, but he cannot have too much grace. More wealth brings more care, but more grace brings more joy. Abundance of the Spirit is fullness of joy. Believer, go to the throne for a large supply of heavenly salt.

December 14

"They go from strength to strength" (Psalm 84:7).

There are various renderings of these words, but all of them contain the idea of progress. They grow stronger and stronger. Usually, if we are walking, we go from strength to weakness. We start fresh but before long the road becomes rough and the sun becomes hot. We must sit down to rest. But the Christian pilgrim, having obtained fresh supplies of grace, is as vigorous after years of toilsome travel and struggle as when he first set out. He may not be quite so elated and bouyant as he once was, but he is much stronger in all that constitutes real power. He may move slowly, but he moves more surely. Some gray-haired veterans have remained as firm and zealous in their grasp of truth as they were in their younger days; however, it must be confessed it is often otherwise. The love of many waxes cold, and iniquity abounds. But this is their own sin and not the fault of the promise: "The youths shall faint and be weary, and the young men shall utterly fall; but they that wait upon the Lord shall renew their strength; they shall mount up with wings as eagles; they shall run, and not be weary; and they shall walk, and not faint" (Isaiah 40:30-31). Fretful spirits sit down and trouble themselves about the future. "Alas," say they, "We go from affliction to affliction." Very true, you of little faith, but then you go from strength to strength also! You will never find a bundle of affliction which does not have sufficient grace bound up in the midst of it.

"Orpah kissed her mother-in-law; but Ruth clave unto her" (Ruth 1:14).

Both of them had an affection for Naomi and, therefore, set out with her on her return to the land of Judah. But the hour of testing came. Naomi unselfishly set before each of them the trials which awaited them. If they cared for ease and comfort, she urged them to return to their Moabitish friends. At first both of them declared that they would cast in their lot with the Lord's people. But on further consideration, Orpah, with much grief and a respectful kiss, left her mother-in-law and went back to her idolatrous friends. Ruth, however, with all her heart, gave herself up to the God of her mother-in-law. It is one thing to love the ways of the Lord when all is fair and quite another to cleave to them under all discouragements and difficulties. Where do you stand? Is your heart fixed on Jesus? Have you counted the cost, and are you solemnly ready to suffer all worldly loss for the Master's sake? Worldly treasures are not to be compared with the glory to be revealed. Orpah is heard of no more. In glorious ease and idolatrous pleasure her life melts into the gloom of death. Ruth lives in history and in heaven, for grace has placed her in the noble line from which came the King of kings. Blessed among women will those be who for Christ's sake can renounce all.

December 16

"Come unto me" (Matthew 11:28).

The cry of the Christian religion is the gentle word, "Come." The Jewish law harshly said, "Go, take heed to your steps as to the path in which you will walk. Break the commandments, and you will perish; keep them, and you will live." The law was a dispensation of terror which drove men before it like a whip. The gospel draws with bands of love. Jesus is the Good Shepherd going before His sheep, bidding them follow Him. He is always leading them onward with the sweet word, "Come." The law repels; the gospel attracts. The law shows the distance which there is between God and man; the gospel bridges that awful chasm and brings the sinner across it. From the first moment of your spiritual life until you are ushered into glory, the language of Christ to you will be "Come, come unto Me." As a mother puts out her finger to her little child and coaxes him to walk by saying, "Come," even so does Jesus. He will always be ahead of you, bidding you follow Him as the soldier follows his captain. He will always go before you to pave your way and clear your path, and you will hear His animating voice calling you after Him all through life. In the solemn hour of death His sweet words with which He ushers you into the heavenly world will be— "Come, ye blessed of my Father" (Matthew 25:34).

December 17

"I remember thee" (Jeremiah 2:2).

Let us note that Christ delights to think on His Church and to look on her beauty. As the bird returns often to its nest and the wayfarer hastens to his home, so does the mind continually pursue the object of its choice. We cannot look too often on the face of our Lord Jesus. From all eternity, "His delights were with the sons of men" (Proverbs 8:31). His thoughts rolled to the time when His elect should be born into the world. He viewed them in His foreknowledge. David wrote, "In thy book all my members were written, which in continuance were fashioned, when as yet there was none of them" (Psalm 139:16). When the world was set on its pillars, He was there. On the plains of Mamre, by the brook of Jabbok, beneath the walls of Jericho, and in the fiery furnace of Babylon the Son of man visited His people. Because His soul delighted in them, He could not rest away from them. He had written their names on His hands and graven them on His side. As the breastplate containing the names of the tribes of Israel was the most brilliant ornament worn by the high priest, so the names of Christ's elect were His most precious jewels and glittered on His heart. He never ceases to remember us.

December 18

"Rend your heart, and not your garments" (Joel 2:13).

Garment-rending and other outward signs of religious emotion are easily manifested and are frequently hypocritical. But to feel true repentance is far more difficult and far less common. Men will attend to the most multiplied and minute ceremonial regulations that are pleasing to the flesh. But true faith is too humbling, too heart-searching, and too thorough for the tastes of carnal men. They prefer something more ostentatious, flimsy, and worldly. Eye and ear are pleased, self-conceit is fed, and self-righteousness is puffed up. But they are ultimately deceived, for in death and at the day of judgment, the soul needs something more substantial than ceremonies and rituals to lean on. Apart from vital godliness, all religion is utterly vain. Offered without a sincere heart, every form of worship is a sham and an impudent mockery of the majesty of heaven. Heart-rending is divinely wrought and solemnly felt. It is a secret grief which is personally experienced, not in mere form, but as a deep, soul-moving work of the Holy Spirit on the heart of each believer. The text commands us to rend our hearts, but they are naturally hard as marble. How, then, can this be done? We must take them to Calvary. A dying Savior's voice rent the rocks once, and it is as powerful now. O blessed Spirit, let us hear the death-cries of Jesus, and our hearts will be rent even as men rend their vestures in the day of lamentation.

December 19

"The lot is cast into the lap, but the whole disposing thereof is of the Lord" (Proverbs 16:33).

If the disposal of the lot is the Lord's, whose is the arrangement of our whole life? If the simple casting of a lot is guided by Him, how much more the events of our entire life—especially when we are told by our blessed Savior, "The very hairs of your head are all numbered" (Matthew 10:30). It would bring a holy calm over your mind, dear friend, if you were always to remember this. It would so relieve your mind from anxiety that you would be better able to walk in patience, quiet, and cheerfulness as a Christian should. When a man is anxious, he cannot pray with faith. When he is troubled about the world, he cannot serve his Master. His thoughts are of serving himself. "Seek ye first the kingdom of God, and his righteousness; and all these things shall be added unto you (Matthew 6:33). You are meddling with Christ's business and neglecting your own when you fret about your circumstances. Be wise, attend to obeying, and let Christ manage the providing. Come and survey your Father's storehouse, and ask whether He will let you starve while He has laid up so great an abundance in His garner. If He remembers even sparrows, will He forget one of the least of His poor children? "Cast thy burden upon the Lord, and he will sustain thee. He will never suffer the righteous to be moved" (Psalm 55:22).

December 20

"Yea, I have loved thee with an everlasting love" (Jeremiah 31:3).

The Holy Spirit is often pleased to witness with our spirits of the love of Jesus. He takes of the things of Christ and reveals them to us. No voice is heard from the clouds, and no vision is seen in the night; but we have a testimony more sure than either of these. If an angel should fly from heaven and inform the saint personally of the Savior's love to him, the evidence would not be one bit more satisfactory than that which is borne in the heart by the Holy Spirit. Ask those of the Lord's people who have lived the nearest to the gates of heaven, and they will tell you that they have had seasons when the love of Christ toward them has been a fact so clear and sure that they could no more doubt it than they could question their own existence. Yes, beloved believer, you and I have had times of refreshing from the presence of the Lord, and then our faith has mounted to the height of assurance. We have had confidence to lean our heads on the bosom of our Lord, and we have no more questioned our Master's affection to us than John did when he rested there. Jesus has killed our doubts by the closeness of His embrace. His love has been sweeter than wine to our souls.

"Yet he hath made with me an everlasting covenant" (2 Samuel 23:5).

This covenant is divine in its origin. Oh, that great word—He! God, the everlasting Father, has positively made a covenant with you. Yes, God spoke the world into existence by a word. He, stooping from His majesty, takes hold of your hand and makes a covenant with you. The Prince of the kings of the earth, Shaddai, the Lord All-sufficient, the Jehovah of all ages, the everlasting Elohim— "He hath made with me an everlasting covenant." But notice, it is particular in its application. "Yet hath he made with *me* an everlasting covenant." Here lies the sweetness of it to each believer. It is nothing to me that He has made peace for the world; I want to know whether He has made peace for me! It is little that He has made a covenant; I want to know whether He has made a covenant with me. If God the Holy Spirit gives me this assurance, then His salvation is mine, His heart is mine, and He Himself is mine. An everlasting covenant means a covenant which had no beginning and which will never, never end. How sweet, amid all the uncertainties of life, to know that "the foundation of God standeth sure" (2 Timothy 2:19). How blessed to have God's own promise, "My covenant will I not break, nor alter the thing that is gone out of my lips" (Psalm 89:34).

December 22

"I will strengthen thee" (Isaiah 41:10).

God is able to do all things! Believer, until you can drain dry the ocean of omnipotence or break the towering mountains of almighty strength into pieces, you never need to fear. The strength of man will never be able to overcome the power of God. The same God who directs the earth in its orbit has promised to supply you with daily strength. While He is able to uphold the universe, do not think that He will prove unable to fulfill His own promises. Remember what He did in the former generations. Remember how He spoke, and it was done; how He commanded, and it stood fast. Will He that created the world grow weary? He hangs the world on nothing. Will He who does this be unable to support His children? Doesn't He hold the ocean in the hollow of His hand? How can He fail you? When He has put such a faithful promise as this on record, will you for a moment indulge the thought that He has outpromised Himself and gone beyond His power to fulfill? No! You must doubt no longer. O my God and my strength, I can believe that this promise will be fulfilled, for the boundless reservoir of Your grace can never be exhausted. The overflowing storehouse of Your strength can never be emptied by Your friends or pilfered by Your enemies.

December 23

"Friend, go up higher" (Luke 14:10).

When the life of grace first begins in the soul, we do indeed draw near to God; but it is with fear and trembling. The soul, conscious of guilt and humbled thereby, is in awe over the solemnity of its position. It is cast to the earth by a sense of the grandeur of Jehovah, in whose presence it stands. But as the Christian grows in grace, his fear has all its terror taken out of it. He will never forget the solemnity of his position and will never lose that holy awe which must encompass a gracious man when he is in the presence of the God who can create or destroy. It becomes a holy reverence and no more an overshadowing dread. He is called up higher, to greater access to God in Christ Jesus. Then the man of God, walking amid the splendors of deity and veiling his face, will approach the throne reverently and bowed in spirit. Seeing there a God of love, of goodness, and of mercy he will realize the character of God rather than His absolute deity. He will see in God His goodness rather than His greatness. While prostrate before the glory of the Infinite God, the soul will be sustained by the refreshing consciousness of being in the presence of boundless mercy and infinite love and by the realization of acceptance in the Beloved. Thus the believer is bidden to come up higher and is enabled to exercise the privilege of rejoicing in God and drawing near to Him in holy confidence, saying, "Abba, Father."

"For your sakes he became poor" (2 Corinthians 8:9).

The Lord Jesus Christ was eternally rich, glorious, and exalted; but "though he was rich, yet for your sakes He became poor." The rich saint cannot be true in his communion with his poor brethren unless he gives his substance to minister to their necessities. Likewise, it is impossible that our divine Lord could have had fellowship with us unless He had imparted to us of His own abounding wealth and had become poor to make us rich. Had He remained on His throne of glory, and had we continued in the ruins of the fall without receiving His salvation, communion would have been impossible on both sides. Our position by the fall, apart from the covenant of grace, made it as impossible for fallen man to communicate with God as it is for Belial to be in agreement with Christ. It was necessary that the righteous Savior give to His sinning brethren of His own perfection and that we, the poor guilty, should receive of His fullness grace for grace. Thus in giving and receiving, the one might descend from the heights, and the others ascend from the depths, and so be able to embrace each other in true and hearty fellowship. Jesus must clothe His people in His own garments, or He cannot admit them into His palace of glory. He must wash them in His own blood, or else they will be too defiled for the embrace of His fellowship. Believer, here is love! For *your sake* the Lord Jesus became poor, that He might lift you up into communion with Himself.

December 25

"Behold, a virgin shall conceive, and bear a son, and shall call his name Immanuel" (Isaiah 7:14).

Jesus is Jehovah incarnate, our Lord and our God, and yet our brother and friend. Let us adore and admire Him. His miraculous conception was a thing unheard of before and unparalleled since. "The Lord hath created a new thing in the earth, A woman shall compass a man" (Jeremiah 31:22). The first promise ran thus: *"The seed of the woman,"* not the offspring of the man. Our Savior, although truly man, was, as to His human nature, the Holy One of God. By the power of the Holy Spirit, He was born of the virgin without the taint of original sin which pertains to all those who are born of the flesh. Every believer is a portrait of Christ. Let us joyfully remember our dear Redeemer's glorious birth. When did angels indulge in midnight songs, or did God ever hang a new star in the sky before? To whose cradle did rich and poor make so willing a pilgrimage and offer such hearty and unsought obligations? Earth may rejoice and men may cease their labor to celebrate "the great birthday" of Jesus. The golden name, Immanuel, is inexpressibly delightful. God with us in our nature, our sorrow, our lifework, our grave; and now we with Him, in resurrection, ascension, triumph, and second advent splendor. The babe of Bethlehem appears to be manifestly with us in weakness. Oh, for true spiritual fellowship with Immanuel all this day!

December 26

"The last Adam" (1 Corinthians 15:45).

Jesus is the head of His elect. In Adam every heir of flesh and blood has a personal interest because Adam is the covenant head and representative of the race. Every redeemed soul is one with the Lord since He is the Second Adam, the sponsor and substitute of the elect in the new covenant of love. The apostle Paul declares that Levi was in the loins of Abraham when Melchizedek met him. It is a certain truth that the believer was in Jesus Christ, the mediator, when in eternity the covenant settlements of grace were decreed, ratified, and made sure forever. Thus, whatever Christ has done, He has done for the whole body of His Church. We were crucified in Him and buried with Him. (See Colossians 2:10-13.) To make it still more wonderful, we are risen with Him and even ascended with Him to the seats on high. (See Ephesians 2:6.) It is thus that the Church has fulfilled the law and is accepted in the Beloved. It is thus that she is regarded with complacency by the just Jehovah, for He views her in Jesus and does not look on her as separate from her covenant head. As the anointed Redeemer of Israel, Christ Jesus has nothing distinct from His Church; but all that He has, He holds for her. All that the Second Adam is or does is ours as well as His, seeing that He is our representative. Here is the foundation of the covenant of grace.

"Can the rush grow up without mire?" (Job 8:11).

The rush plant is spongy and hollow and so is a hypocrite. There is no substance or stability in him. The rush plant is shaken to and fro in every wind, just as formalists yield to every influence. For this reason the rush is not broken by the tempest, neither are hypocrites troubled with persecution. Perhaps the text for this day may help me to try myself, whether I am a hypocrite or not. The rush by nature lives in water and owes its very existence to the mire and moisture wherein it has taken root. Let the mire become dry, and the rush withers very quickly. Its greenness is absolutely dependent on circumstances. Is this my case? Do I only serve God when I am in good company or when religion is profitable and respectable? Do I love the Lord only when temporal comforts are received from His hands? If so, I am a base hypocrite. Like the withering rush, I will perish when death deprives me of outward joys. But can I honestly assert that when bodily comforts have been few and my surroundings have been rather adverse to grace than helpful to it, I have still held fast my integrity? Then I have hope that there is genuine, vital godliness in me. A goodly man often grows best when his worldly circumstances decay. He who follows Christ for gain is a Judas. They who attend Him out of love are His own beloved ones. Lord, let me find my life in You and not in the mire of this world's favor or gain.

December 28

"The life which I now live in the flesh, I live by the faith of the Son of God" (Galatians 2:20).

When the Lord in mercy passed by and saw us in our blood, He first of all said, "Live," because life is one of the absolutely essential things in spiritual matters. Until it is given, we are incapable of partaking in the things of the Kingdom. The life which grace confers on the saints at the moment of their quickening is none other than the life of Christ. Like the sap from the stem, faith runs into us, the branches, and establishes a living connection between our souls and Jesus. Faith is the grace which perceives this union, having proceeded from it as its firstfruit. Faith knows His excellence and worth, and no temptation can induce it to place its trust elsewhere. Christ Jesus is so delighted with this heavenly grace that He never ceases to strengthen and sustain faith by the loving embrace and all-sufficient support of His eternal arms. Here, then, is established a living, sensible, and delightful union which casts forth streams of love, confidence, sympathy, complacency, and joy, whereof both the bride and bridegroom love to drink. When the soul can evidently perceive this oneness between itself and Christ, the pulse may be felt as beating for both and the one blood as flowing through the veins of each. Then the heart is as near heaven as it can be while on earth and is prepared for the enjoyment of the most sublime and spiritual kind of fellowship.

December 29

"Hitherto hath the Lord helped us" (1 Samuel 7:12).

The word "hitherto" seems like a hand pointing in the direction of the *past*. Twenty years or seventy years and hitherto the Lord has helped us! Through poverty or wealth, sickness or health, at home or abroad, and in trials or triumphs the Lord has helped us! We delight to look down a long avenue of trees. It is pleasing to gaze from end to end of the long vista. Even so look down the long aisles of your years, at the green boughs of mercy overhead and the strong pillars of lovingkindness and faithfulness which bear up your joys. But the word also points *forward*. For when a man gets up to a certain mark and writes "hitherto," he is not yet at the end. There is still a distance to be traveled. There are more trials, more joys; more temptations, more triumphs; more prayers, more answers; more toils, more strength; and more fights, more victories. Is it over now? No! There is more yet—awakening in Jesus' likeness, thrones, harps, songs, psalms, white raiment, the face of Jesus, the society of saints, the glory of God, the fullness of eternity, and he infinity of bliss. Be of good courage, believer. He who has helped you "hitherto" will help you on your journey all the way through.

December 30

"Better is the end of a thing than the beginning thereof" (Ecclesiastes 7:8).

Look at our Lord and Master. In His beginning, He was despised and rejected of men; a man of sorrows and acquainted with grief. Do you see the end? He sits at His Father's right hand knowing His enemies will be made His footstool. "As he is, so are we also in this world" (1 John 4:17). You must bear the cross, or you will never wear the crown; you must wade through the mire, or you will never walk the golden pavement. Cheer up, then, poor Christian. "Better is the end of a thing than the beginning thereof." How contemptible is the appearance of a caterpillar. It is the beginning of a thing. Yet, later notice that insect with gorgeous wings and full of happiness and life; that is the end thereof. That caterpillar is like yourself, until you are wrapped up in the chrysalis of death. But when Christ appears you will be like Him, for you will see Him as He is. That rough-looking diamond is put on the wheel of the lapidary. He cuts it on all sides. It loses much—much that seemed costly to itself. That very diamond which was severely cut by the lapidary, now glitters in the king's crown. You may venture to compare yourself to such a diamond, for you are one of God's people; and this is the time of the cutting process. Let faith and patience have their perfect work, for in the day when the crown will be set on the head of the King Eternal, Immortal, Invisible, one ray of glory will stream from you. "They shall be mine," saith the Lord, "in the day when I make up my jewels" (Malachi 3:17).

December 31

"In the last day, that great day of the feast, Jesus stood and cried, saying, If any man thirst, let him come unto me and drink" (John 7:37).

Patience had her perfect work in the Lord Jesus. Until the last day of the feast, He pleaded with the Jews. On this last day of the year, He pleads with us and waits to be gracious to us. Admirable is the long-suffering of the Savior in bearing with some of us year after year, notwithstanding our provocations, rebellions, and resistance of His Holy Spirit. Wonder of wonders that we are still in the land of mercy. He entreats us to be reconciled. How deep must be the love which makes the Lord weep over sinners. Surely at the call of such a cry our willing hearts will come. All that man needs to quench his soul's thirst is provided. Though the soul is utterly famished, Jesus can restore it. Proclamation is made, most freely, that every thirsty one is welcome. He bore our sins in His own body on the tree. Come now and drink, before the sun sets on the year's last day! A fool, a thief, a harlot can drink. Sinfulness of character is no bar to the invitation to believe in Jesus. The mouth of poverty is welcome to stoop down and take a deep drink of the flowing flood. Blistered, leprous, filthy lips may touch the stream of divine love. They cannot pollute it, but will themselves be purified. Jesus is the source of hope. Dear reader, hear the Redeemer's loving voice as He cries to each of us, "If any man thirst, let him come unto me and drink."